ADVANCE PRAISE

"I can't thank Dr. Jackman enough for writing this book and for being an inspiration in my own entrepreneurial journey. This book encourages a mindset shift around what it means to be Black, a therapist, and an entrepreneur all in one. Anyone who reads this book will find both the encouragement and the practical tools needed to be successful as a Black therapist."
—**Marshaun Glover, PhD, MBA**, founder and owner of New Life Therapy and cofounder and owner of Match Medical Practice Solutions LLC

"*The Black Therapist's Guide to Private Practice and Entrepreneurship* is a must-read for Black mental health professionals. This expertly crafted guide provides a comprehensive roadmap to building thriving private practices. From shifting your money mindset and behaviors to branding strategies and financial planning, this book empowers you to expand your reach and create generational wealth while honoring the cultural nuances of Black mental health."
—**Candice Nicole Hargons, PhD,** associate professor, Rollins School of Public Health and author of *Good Sex: Stories, Science, and Strategies for Sexual Liberation*

"Dr. Jackman's *The Black Therapist's Guide to Private Practice and Entrepreneurship* is packed with concrete, empowering strategies to help Black therapists thrive. From branding to soul care, she covers it all. I recommend this book to those who are just emerging in the mental health field as well as those who are ready to take their business to the next level."
—**Thema Bryant, PhD,** bestselling author of *Homecoming: Overcome Fear and Trauma to Reclaim Your Whole, Authentic Self*

"This book arrives at a critical moment when Black mental health professionals are in high demand to address the diverse and complex needs of the Black community. It not only equips readers with practical strategies for launching an entrepreneurial journey, but also thoughtfully addresses the unique structural and interpersonal challenges Black therapists face when navigating an often-uncharted path."
—**Kathy Lopes, LICSW,** vice president of the National Association of Black Social Workers

The Black Therapist's Guide to Private Practice and Entrepreneurship

The Black Therapist's Guide to Private Practice and Entrepreneurship

Charmain F. Jackman, PhD

Norton Professional Books

An Imprint of W. W. Norton & Company
Independent Publishers Since 1923

Note to Readers: This book is intended as a general information resource for professionals practicing in the field of psychotherapy, social work, and mental health. It is not a substitute for appropriate training or clinical supervision. Standards of clinical practice and protocol vary in different practice settings and change over time. No technique or recommendation is guaranteed to be safe or effective in all circumstances, and neither the publisher nor the author(s) can guarantee the complete accuracy, efficacy, or appropriateness of any particular recommendation in every respect or in all settings or circumstances. Consult with a qualified health-care professional before embarking on any new health-care practices. Also, readers should not regard this as a substitute for legal, tax, or other professional advice and, if professional advice or other expert assistance is required, the services of a competent professional should be sought.

Any URLs displayed in this book link or refer to websites that existed as of press time. The publisher is not responsible for, and should not be deemed to endorse or recommend, any website other than its own or any content that it did not create. The author, also, is not responsible for any third-party material.

For information about permission to reproduce selections from this book, write to Permissions, W. W. Norton & Company, Inc., 500 Fifth Avenue, New York, NY 10110

For information about special discounts for bulk purchases, please contact W. W. Norton Special Sales at specialsales@wwnorton.com or 800-233-4830

Manufacturing by Versa Press
Production manager: Ramona Wilkes and Gwen Cullen

ISBN: 978-1-324-05359-0

W. W. Norton & Company, Inc., 500 Fifth Avenue, New York, NY 10110
www.wwnorton.com

W. W. Norton & Company Ltd., 15 Carlisle Street, London W1D 3BS

1 2 3 4 5 6 7 8 9 0

This is dedicated to my entrepreneurial ancestors, especially my grandmother Eurita and my grandfather Clifford; to my early models of entrepreneurship: my parents, Frances Parquet and Dalton Jackman; to my Uncle Al and late Aunty Kay; to my confidantes on this journey: my husband, Jeff, and my sister, Cherine; and to my children, Sydney and Simone, who I hope will be inspired to carry on the legacy of entrepreneurship in our family.

CONTENTS

APPENDICES

ACKNOWLEDGMENTS

My entrepreneurship journey has not been a solo one. I could never have accomplished any of my successes as a business owner without the support, advice, and cheerleading from friends, mentors, and fellow entrepreneurs. There are so many people that have helped me along this path—whether it's answering a question, sending me an opportunity, purchasing a product or service, modeling good business practices, introducing me to people in their network, reading my newsletters and sharing them with others, reviewing a document, or teaching me a new skill—all of these have helped me to get to this point today. With that, I extend my sincere and utmost gratitude to them.

A huge thank you to my parents, Dalton and Frances, for showing me the path of entrepreneurship. The life lessons you taught me are invaluable. You modeled how to work hard and pursue your dreams. Thank you for all the sacrifices you made, which made it possible for me to follow my dream.

To the loves of my life: Jeff Lahens, you are the epitome of what it means to be a spouse and partner. Your unconditional support and love assures me that you have my back. Sydney and Simone, my beautiful children, I am so proud of you. Thank you for listening as I practice my talks and for joining me at events. My sister, thanks for listening, editing, and offering your brilliance to support my business. My cousins: Michael and Derick, and my late Uncle Leonard, you have been the big brothers I never had, and you have supported my journey.

Dr. Susan Shoobe and Dr. Bill DeFranc, I thank you for generously sharing how you started your private practices. Your stories rekindled my desire to own a business. Thanks also to Dr. Maria Hiraldo and Dr. Monica Campbell, who shared their journey in starting courses focused on private practice and entrepreneurship and inspired me to start mine.

To my mentor, Dr. Jessica Henderson Daniel: without knowing it, asking me to lead a workshop for the Harvard Medical School ALANA interns and fellows sparked a journey that I could not have imagined. You always encouraged your mentees to dream big and your path exemplified what it means to unwaveringly pursue a dream.

My business coach, Kim Olds. You know how to keep it real. Thanks immensely for all the support you have given to me.

I have been blessed to be surrounded by communities who uplift me: the Boston Women of Color in Psychology group, a community I cofounded with Dr. Robyn Glover. A special nod to Dr. Carita Anderson, you are the best cheerleader there is—thanks for being an amazing accountability partner. My vision board group: Cherine, Beverly, Clementine, Edwine, Yawa, Thato, Jeanette, Keeana, U-Meleni, Lavinia, Vivian, Gorata, and Melanee, we have supported each other's dreams and held each other to the fire. I am still amazed at our collective success. A special shout-out to Jeanette and Clementine who offered to read a very rough draft of this book. My Goldman Sachs Black in Business growth group: Jasmine, DJ, Esperanza, Krystal, Nalaija, Patience, Raven, and Rhonda, thanks for holding space and allowing me to be vulnerable with you all. Drs. Natalie Cort and Gemima St. Louis, your sponsorship has been immeasurable. You helped me to take the Personal Branding workshop to a whole new level. I appreciate you.

I have been blessed to participate in a number of accelerator programs that have bolstered my knowledge and skills. To the staff, mentors, and cohort members from the following programs: Roxbury Innovation Center, Babson Women Innovating Now Growth Lab (Fall 2020), The Capital Network (Spring 2021), EForAll (Winter 2022), MassChallenge Health Tech (2022), All Raise Black and Latinx Media Mastery, and Goldman Sachs Black in Business (Fall 2023).

To the American Psychological Association (APA) Leadership Institute for Women in Psychology (LIWP) Cohort 10, who held space as I wept on our final day after I shared my goal of full-time entrepreneurship, knowing the moves I would need to make for this dream to come true. A special shout-out to Dr. Maysa Akbar, who unabashedly introduced herself as owning a business with over $1M in revenue. You got my attention because these are words that I had never heard from a psychologist before.

To my colleagues at Boston Children's hospital, my colleagues at Boston Arts Academy, and students from 2015–2021, you made it hard to leave.

The Boston Public Schools Women Educators of Color (WEOC) program that helped me recognize that I had so much more to offer. To my advisory board members: Edwine Alphonse, Jill Borelli, Yawa Degboe, Leslie Forde, Andy Reimer, Rachel Spekman, and Will Tomlinson. Thank you for your sage advice that keeps me grounded on my entrepreneurial journey.

Last, but certainly not least, the InnoPsych Team: Denisse, Jennae, Christine, Kavontae, Sueann, and all the contractors and consultants who help us to amplify our impact worldwide. I am immensely grateful for your trust.

My Entrepreneurship Journey

∙∙

The Black Therapist's Guide to Private Practice and Entrepreneurship is the book *I* needed in graduate school and as an early career psychologist when my dream of owning a private practice was slowly dying. You see, I knew from an early age that I wanted to become a psychologist *and* that I wanted to own a private practice—it was very clear to me. However, by the time I completed graduate school with a doctoral degree in hand, I had convinced myself that private practice was not for me. I had gained top-notch clinical training at the University of Southern Mississippi–Hattiesburg through coursework, practica, and internships that landed me a position at one of the top pediatric hospitals in the world, Boston Children's Hospital, a training hospital for Harvard Medical School (PR Newswire, 2000). My childhood dream of becoming a psychologist had taken me from Barbados to Iowa, Mississippi, and then to Boston, Massachusetts, and it was now a reality . . . except, I no longer wanted to be an entrepreneur. I had achieved a huge part of my childhood dream—I was a psychologist after all— and that was quite enough. But as Paulo Coelho (1996) states in his book *The Alchemist: A Fable About Following Your Dreams*, "When you want something, all the universe conspires in helping you to achieve it."

So, by destiny, around 2004 I met two wonderful colleagues, Susan and Bill, both early-career psychologists like me who had started their private practices. We met as members of a steering committee for an early-career psychologists group and hit it off. I was so impressed that they had successfully launched their private practices and I needed to know how they did it. They made time to talk to me about how they had started their practices. I was astounded that they had started businesses so quickly, but I also learned that psychology was a second career for both of them. Susan in particular was like a business coach, long before I had ever heard of business coaching. She guided me through the process of starting a private practice, shared resources, and answered my many questions. We had the idea to host an event about starting a private practice for other early-career psychologists, which was a huge success. However, I was on a student visa at the time and could not start a business . . . but I was not deterred. These conversations with Susan and Bill sparked something in me: they had reawakened my entrepreneurial desires and helped me make a significant shift in my mindset: *I* could launch a private practice, *and* now I knew how to do it. Since we will talk quite a bit about our mindsets throughout this book, here is how I define it: our deep-rooted beliefs that shape how we see ourselves and the world, which then guides how we tackle obstacles and seize opportunities.

Then in 2005, I took the steps to start my solo private practice, InPsych, providing therapy, forensic psychological evaluations, and consulting. I operated my private practice while working two part-time positions (one in the juvenile courts and one at a high school), which together was my full-time work. It was a very successful business. Without any marketing, I always had clients and got referrals from colleagues and clients alike. Then in 2009, one of my former supervisors, Dr. Jessica Henderson Daniel, asked me to lead a workshop (a paid opportunity) for the Harvard Medical School psychology predoctoral interns and postdoctoral fellows. I had gone through this program and all the speakers were impressive. This was a huge honor. Reflecting about what I would have wanted at that stage of my training, I decided to focus on personal branding. The workshop was a hit! The trainees resonated with the content, and I was invited back for 10 years straight. I also kept hearing questions about starting a private practice, which led me to create my first private practice course, *Launch a Private Practice in Seven Days!*, which evolved into the *Thriving Therapreneur Masterclass* and the *Thriving Therapreneur Coaching Program*. All of these programs have served as the foundation for this book you are reading now.

A number of books have been written about how to start private practices for mental health providers, but none of them center on the specific experiences of Black therapists and the challenges (and opportunities) we encounter when it comes to entrepreneurship. The entrepreneurial journey is different for us, and sometimes people are oblivious or insensitive to the historical and structural barriers that we face when starting businesses.

This is why I wrote *The Black Therapist's Guide to Private Practice and Entrepreneurship*. I wanted to create a resource that speaks to the unique needs of Black therapists, one that not only names the barriers we face at every step of the entrepreneurial journey, but also offers specific strategies and a realistic road map for us to confidently launch, operate, and grow thriving businesses. This book is for Black therapists who desire to lead mission-driven, profitable businesses: Black therapists who want to do good but not sacrifice their health and well-being on their way to building generational wealth; Black therapists who are passionate about mental health and want to design businesses that center the health and well-being of their communities. This book is for Black therapists who were directed to the front lines and never imagined themselves as business owners. This book is for Black therapists who desire to turn their passion into profit while doing good and protecting their peace. If that's you, let's get to it.

A Quick Note. While I center the experiences of Black therapists, please note that this book is relevant to all people whose ancestors have been exploited, oppressed, and othered and, frankly, who are still being exploited, oppressed, and othered. In addition to Black therapists, I will include more expansive language, such as *people of color*, *therapists of color*, *BIPOC* (Black, Indigenous, and other people of color), and the global majority. I will sometimes use specific racial and ethnic terms, such as *Latinx*, *Asian American*, and *Pacific Islander*. I recognize that our language for racial and ethnic identities is fluid and always evolving, but books are static once they have been printed. With that understanding in mind, if there is a word that you would rather use, I invite you to insert the term that describes you best.

The Black Therapist's Guide to Private Practice and Entrepreneurship is also for allies. If you are a person who is in a position of power or decision-making in the mental health field, then you need to read this book. It's for clinical supervisors, training directors, deans, department chairs, and people responsible for accrediting graduate programs: this book will help you gain insight into what you can do to disrupt the way you train Black and other students of color and provide strategies to helping these students develop an entrepreneurial mindset around their education and practice as mental health professionals. Additionally, fostering innovative thinking, seeing opportunities where others see problems, and engaging in curiosity, creativity, and experimentation to solve problems are great tools that can benefit all students, no matter where their careers lead them. My hope is that graduate programs will include innovation concepts into their training programs as it will benefit the mental health field tremendously.

I wrote *The Black Therapist's Guide to Private Practice and Entrepreneurship* with you in mind. I will take you through every stage of starting a private practice or business, from idea to execution. Throughout the book I share my personal experiences, lessons I've learned, and hacks that have helped me reach my business goals. I offer sample documents of various sorts to give you a sense of the documents you may need for your practice, knowing that you will need to tailor these to fit whatever is required for your business. Because requirements differ by state, you should consult with an attorney for legal documents and contracts. The chapters are designed specifically to address the stages of building a practice, *in a specific order*, so don't skip ahead—take each chapter as it comes. In each chapter, I share information that has helped me and my coaching clients build thriving businesses. This is an opportunity to learn from my journey, avoid mistakes I made, and benefit from lessons I learned. I try to be very real and transparent with my wins and losses as I was building my business, and I share my personal reflections and experiences throughout the book. You will see *REFLECTION TIME* prompts, which are designed to help you process the many emotions, thoughts, and actions that emerge on the entrepreneurial journey. The *MINDSET WORK* prompts will help you challenge beliefs that could interfere or sabotage your success, and the *TAKE ACTION EXERCISES* are practical actions and tasks that will help to move your business forward. Other *EXERCISES* will help you develop key mindsets and access materials you need to help your business to thrive. I've also included a few *MINDFUL MOMENTS* to help you through some of the emotionally charged exercises and points along the entrepreneurship journey. I encourage you to *trust the process* and to resist the urge to skip through these prompts or to skip chapters—your business will be better for it. You might find it helpful to use a special journal where you can respond to the prompts and activities, as we will use exercises in early chapters to build on information in later chapters. Each chapter concludes with a *MOMENTUM AND MINDSET CHECK* that summarizes the main points of each chapter and offers two reflection questions. Once you have launched your business, you may find it helpful to revisit particular chapters or sections, and to refresh your memory on how to execute a particular strategy. If that makes sense to you, you should do that.

While this book is focused on mental health businesses, the information is applicable to other types of businesses, such as coaching; to other types of therapists, such as massage rehabilitation therapists; other wellness professionals and healers, dieticians, professional tutors, and more.

Finally, if you have ever questioned whether entrepreneurship is the path for you, I hope that you will find your answer by the end of this book. Entrepreneurship can be unpredictable, exhausting, frustrating, and draining. It can often feel risky, and it requires you to do hard tasks, things that are far outside your comfort zone—but with high risk can come high rewards. Entrepreneurship can also be liberating, energizing, rewarding, and lucrative. I will show you how to tap into your skills, create a niche, and equip yourself with the tools for success. Remember that your ancestors have passed on ways to heal through the generations. It is no accident that you are in a healing profession. Entrepreneurship allows you to reach others with your gift and it is no accident that you are reading this book.

Are you ready to start your journey to financial prosperity and generational wealth? Then, let's go . . .

The Black Therapist's Guide to Private Practice and Entrepreneurship

Fact or Myth

Therapists Are Not Supposed to Be Entrepreneurs

....

Entrepreneurship is our history, our present,
and our legacy.

ARE YOU AN ENTREPRENEUR?

☐ Yes
☐ No

If you answered no, I'm glad that you are reading this book, because your answer will likely change by the end of it, and maybe even by the end of this chapter.

If you answered yes, I'm excited that you are reading this book because you are looking for ways to ensure that your private practice or wellness business continues on a path to growth and success.

I've been asking this question of therapists in workshops and coaching sessions for almost a decade. In a crowded room, there is usually one person who confidently raises their hand for yes; a few people will half-raise their hands indicating an uncertain response. But the overwhelming response is no—not many entrepreneurs in a room of therapists. There are many levels to why Black therapists don't see themselves as entrepreneurs. Let's take a deeper look at some systemically perpetuated and harmful misconceptions.

Black People Are NOT Supposed to Be Entrepreneurs

According to a Pew Research article (Leppert, 2024), only 2.8% of U.S. businesses are owned by Black people even though we represent 13% of the population. Interestingly, 28% of Black-owned businesses are in the health-care sector. Hispanic-owned businesses account for 7%, Asian-owned 11%, and businesses owned by Native Americans, Alaska Natives, Native Hawaiians, and Other Pacific Islanders together total only 1%. These entrepreneurial inequities have roots in enslavement where Black people were forced to provide unpaid labor and have systematically been maintained by laws, policies, and practices like sharecropping and redlining (i.e., discriminatory lending practices based on where people live, and specifically for people living in predominantly Black neighborhoods). The Black Wall Street massacre in Tulsa, Oklahoma, serves as an example of how the system permitted the demise of a financially thriving Black community. Even today, Black entrepreneurs have less access to capital (Goldman Sachs, 2024), are unlikely to have loans approved, especially as sole proprietors (Hollingshead, 2023), and experience more predatory lending terms (Goldman Sachs, 2024). The message? *Black people are NOT supposed to be entrepreneurs.*

Black People Are NOT Supposed to Be Therapists

Our economic and social systems also want us to believe that Black people are not supposed to be therapists. We are poorly represented in the mental health workforce. According to the American Psychological Association (2022a), Black psychologists account for only 3% of all psychologists trained to provide clinical care (i.e., health service providers), Hispanics* for 6%, Asians for 3%, and American Indian/Alaska Natives for 1%. Other mental health professionals of color have similar low representation. For example, among new social workers who earned their master's degree in social work (MSW) between 2017 and 2019, 22% identified as Black/African American and 14% identified as Hispanic/Latino (Salsberg, Quigley, Richwine, et al., 2020). Data from Zippia (2024a) shows that of licensed mental health counselors and licensed professional counselors, 11.3% identified as Black/African American and 12.2% as Hispanic/Latino; and for

---

* Language used in the data report from the American Psychological Association

licensed marriage and family therapists, 7% identified as Black/African American and 13.9% as Hispanic or Latino (Zippia, 2024b). These demographic data highlight the lack of racial diversity within the mental health workforce that has existed for decades and are a result of the systemic policies and practices that have served to keep BIPOC individuals from pursuing careers in the mental health field. These barriers include the time involved in obtaining an advanced degree, lost years of income if enrolled in college and graduate school, cost of graduate school, debt from graduate school, low availability of scholarships for graduate school, low starting salaries for therapists, plus cultural messages that deter BIPOC individuals from entering the field, such as "Mental health doesn't exist" and "Therapists don't make any money." *"Black people are not supposed to be therapists."*

Black Therapists Are NOT Supposed to Be Entrepreneurs

This subliminal message that therapists are not supposed to be entrepreneurs was communicated to me throughout my graduate school tenure, and sadly, I am not the only one: most mental health professionals that I encounter have had this same experience during their training program. We had no explicit conversations about business ownership or how to start a private practice. On the rare occasion that the topic came up, it was usually a professor sharing a clinical example from their practice, and rarely about the business side of the practice.

It gets even deeper because *Black* therapists are not supposed to be entrepreneurs. It did not help that I did not see BIPOC therapists owning mental health businesses or private practices until later in my career. Only 12% of psychologists in private practice are people of color (American Psychological Association, 2022b). Of my professors in grad school, only two had part-time practices, and I did not meet a BIPOC private practice owner until a predoctoral internship—almost 10 years into training to become a psychologist. Plus, the psychologists and therapists that I knew did not talk about their private practices or businesses, which made it even more mysterious and unattainable. I knew a fair share of Black entrepreneurs, but they were not therapists, and many of them were hustling to survive, so that was not attractive either. *For BIPOC individuals, it's a double bind:* We don't become therapists and we opt out of entrepreneurship. *Black therapists are not supposed to be entrepreneurs.*

Despite these low numbers, since grad school I have encountered so many Black therapists who are entrepreneurs and running profitable practices. We are here. Our stories matter. And I use my business, InnoPsych, as a platform to make us more visible. We are creating a thriving community for Black and BIPOC therapists because we know that representation matters. We need to see each other . . . *sawabona* (Zulu for "I see you") . . . and we need to practice *ujima* (Swahili for collective work and responsibility) and *ujamaa* (Swahili for cooperative economics). Entrepreneurship is our history, our present, and our legacy.

Even though I come from a long line of entrepreneurs—my grandparents, my parents, my Aunty Kay, and my Uncle Al—and had engaged in a number of entrepreneurial endeavors in high school and college, entrepreneurship still seemed unattainable when I had finished graduate school, as I describe in the introduction. I entered graduate school with an entrepreneurial mindset, a solid *belief in my ability to build a successful business that offers value and solves a problem for my ideal clients*, but it got buried during my training (that ain't right!). But it's OK, it came back with a fury.

CASE STUDY: ARE YOU AN ENTREPRENEUR?

I had a coaching client who had helped a colleague build a private practice. However, this client did not see all the ways they had helped to build the successful practice. I asked my usual question: "Are you an entrepreneur?" I could see them processing the question, and then they responded "No." I gave them a homework assignment to define the word *entrepreneur*. The next time we met I could see that they had a break-through. Through this exercise, they realized that the way they defined *entrepreneur* was interfering with their ability to see themselves as an entrepreneur. This simple exercise not only helped them to recognize how they were already operating as an entrepreneur but also helped them gain confidence in their ability to build a thriving business.

WHAT GRAD SCHOOL FAILED TO TEACH YOU ABOUT ENTREPRENEURSHIP . . . AND WHY

The United States was built on the unpaid labor of Black and First Nation peoples and there was no intention for our people to prosper, then or now. Systemic policies continue to maintain power structures and inequities for certain groups, mostly people of color. There has been a systematic agenda to patholo-gize our lived experiences—even escaping from enslavement was pathologized (i.e., *drapetomania*, a diagnosis given to Black freedom seekers who were enslaved when they attempted to escape the forced labor estate)—and to disconnect us from our indigenous healing practices. Unfortunately, the mental health field and professional associations have also been complicit in these practices and have contributed to decades of racist research, writings, and teachings, for which several organizations have publicly apologized in recent years (American Psycho-logical Association 2021a, 2021b, 2023; American Psychiatric Association, 2021; National Association of Social Workers [NASW], 2021).

Graduate programs for mental health professionals consist of master- and doctoral-level studies in a range of disciplines including psychology, social work, counseling, expressive arts, and marriage and family therapy. These programs are accredited by professional bodies that are tasked with adherence to high-quality standards to protect the public, ensure uniformity in training, and pro-vide guidance for practicum and internship experiences. Ultimately, graduate school programs have the primary mission of ensuring that their students have the tools to provide quality mental health care to a wide range of clients, and offering courses related to entrepreneurship is not part of the accreditation cri-teria (American Psychological Association, 2018; Commission on Accreditation for Marriage and Family Therapy, 2017; Council on Social Work Education, 2022; National Board for Certified Counselors, 2020). Graduate programs focus on the courses required to maintain the institution's accreditation and to get you licensed, so you can understand why adding more topics would not be a prior-ity: there is no incentive to do so. Plus, where would you fit business courses in an already packed course of study? It's just not practical with the current setup.

DISRUPTING THE NARRATIVE ABOUT THERAPISTS AND ENTREPRENEURSHIP

When I left Barbados for college, I was very clear that I wanted to become an entrepreneur. My dream was to own a private practice, just like Dr. Bob on the *Bob Newhart Show* (the first psychologist I ever "met"). I even double majored in psychology and business administration with that goal in mind. As you read in the introduction, when I started graduate school this was still my goal, but 5 years later, upon completing my doctoral training, I was convinced that private practice was not for me. My fire or passion had fizzled out completely. It is strange, looking back at this, because I did not notice that a part of my dream was dying along the way. I just recall at one point thinking about my career plans, and I had a strong reaction against being in private practice.

As I mentioned earlier, during my graduate school program I had a couple professors with part-time practices. However, when they discussed their private practices, it was to share case examples about their clients—nothing about the business side, except to maybe complain about how managed care was changing the practice of therapy. Still, I would hold onto these snippets of information, so it's not a surprise that by the time I completed my graduate program I had no interest in being a business owner. I believed that private practice was too hard and that there was no way I could make a living or support a family with what insurance companies were reimbursing mental health providers. I assumed that it would be more profitable to work for an organization. In many ways I had decided that entrepreneurship was not for me, and my dream went dormant.

REPRESENTATION REALLY MATTERS

It was 2000; we had survived the Y2K hysteria and things were about to change for me in a big way. I was matched to my top choice for the predoctoral internship year, which meant leaving Mississippi for Boston. Being in Boston was transformative. It was also the first time that I had a Black supervisor, and it was the first time that I saw a Black psychologist with a private practice. I also had more supervisors who had private practices, but they all had full-time or part-time jobs. These examples communicated to me the need to have a "stable" job because full-time entrepreneurship was not profitable or practical. Nevertheless, my Black supervisor would drop gems every now and then about her private practice, and I listened intently. I surmised that her private practice gave her autonomy to meet with clients that she did not get to work with during her full-time position. She was also very successful. Her house was beautiful and, like a museum, was filled with Black art. For me, she represented Black excellence in mental health and entrepreneurship.

Seeing this representation of entrepreneurship by a Black psychologist caused something to shift for me: it made me question whether I truly had given up on entrepreneurship for myself. I wanted to know more, but I did not know what questions to ask (you don't know what you don't know), and honestly, back then I was too intimidated to ask her questions about her private practice. (Incidentally, this supervisor invited me to lead a workshop about personal branding for the Harvard Medical School's African, Latino, Asian, and Native American [ALANA] fellows in 2009, a workshop that I would deliver for 10 consecutive years, and that personal branding workshop eventually evolved into a full private practice course, which then led to this book you are reading now.)

Then in 2004 my entrepreneurship dreams started to reignite. By this time I had completed my doctoral program and was now a licensed psychologist. I was looking for opportunities to connect with other psychologists and joined a local professional association. When I commit to something, I go all in, so it was not a surprise that I soon became a member of the steering committee for the early-career group. As we got to know one another, I discovered that two of my early-career psychologist colleagues had started their own private practices soon after completing their doctoral program. I was shocked—but their experiences inspired me, and I knew if they could figure it out, then I could too.

What also surprised me is that my early-career colleagues talked *positively* about their entrepreneurship experiences, and their businesses were not failing, as my professors had implied might happen. On the contrary, they were operating successful private practices. I found the courage to ask questions—and I had lots of questions, but they were open to sharing their experiences. The information they shared was practical and accessible, just what I needed to rekindle the desire for starting a private practice. As our group was planning out the calendar of events, I suggested that we host a workshop on starting a private practice for early-career mental health practitioners. I knew they were others like me who wanted this information and needed to know that private practice was possible. They agreed, and would you believe, it was one of the best-attended programs we organized. Like I had suspected, other mental health practitioners like me were yearning for information about starting a private practice but needed guidance.

Without knowing it, my colleagues showed me that starting a private practice was possible. They shifted the narrative I was telling myself that entrepreneurship was not for me. I could now see that therapists could be entrepreneurs—successful entrepreneurs. While I had convinced myself that entrepreneurship was not the way, my ancestors were working to remind me of my purpose. They were working with the universe to make sure that I remembered what I was called on this Earth to do. I hope you are starting to see that you can start and operate a successful private practice as well.

Reflection Time

Let's take a few minutes to reflect on the early messages you have received about entrepreneurship. Find a quiet space, and respond to the following journal prompts:

- Thinking back to your childhood, how did the adults around you talk about entrepreneurship?
- What messages did you receive about entrepreneurship in your family?
- Who were entrepreneurs or business owners that you knew? How were they viewed in your community?
- What messages did you receive about entrepreneurship in your graduate school program?
- How did these messages shape your decision about the job positions you took (or plan to take) after completing your graduate program?
- What are your thoughts about entrepreneurship now?

THE ENTREPRENEURSHIP JOURNEY . . . IS IT FOR YOU?

To be clear, entrepreneurship is not for everyone, and that's OK. If you do decide that working for a company or agency is your best choice, then there will be a limit to how much you earn. I am not knocking this option; I spent 17 years of my career working for different institutions that decided how much I was worth. However, it became clear to me that no matter how many hours I worked above my contracted time, the new ideas I brought to the organization, or any committees I joined and/or led, my salary would stay the same. I might be rewarded with a new title, but I would not earn more money (except for the 3–5% annual increase), and my worth to the organization would be unchanged.

I was excited to take the leap to full-time entrepreneur, but those fears about entrepreneurship were powerful. Nevertheless, when the time came, I was ready. I had prepared in many ways, especially financially, and it was time to launch. Entrepreneurship has been liberating for me. It has given me back control over my schedule, the clients I want to work with, how I carve out time for myself and my family, and most importantly, my health. Still, I was not prepared for the emotional roller-coaster that comes with full-time entrepreneurship (more about the entrepreneurial journey in Chapter 13), the number of meetings I'd have to take, or the amount of time it takes to close deals. It's a lot, but I have no interest in going back to the 9-to-5 grind. I'm committed to this journey, knowing it will be challenging, and that I will be better for it.

Reflection Time

Let's take some time to reflect on being an entrepreneur. Find a quiet space, and respond to the following journal prompts:

- How do you define an entrepreneur?
- What comes up for you when you think about entrepreneurship for yourself?
- What comes up for you when you think about 9-to-5 or hell-time employment?

The Golden Handcuffs

It became clear to me that, as much as my leaders liked me and the work I did, their loyalty would always be to the organization, not to me or the other employees. I knew that "if I drop[ped], down dead tomorrow" (a common Barbadian phrase used to emphasize a point), I would be replaced. There may be a few weeks of disruption (or maybe a few months), but they would figure it out and move on. It was sobering when I came to that realization, but it was also the motivation I needed to take the leap into full-time entrepreneurship.

Now don't get me wrong, working for an organization definitely provided a sense of security. The financial benefits of a 9-to-5 full-time position, or the *golden handcuffs*, include a regular paycheck that arrives every 2 weeks, 2–4 weeks of paid time off each year (more for those working in school settings), sick leave, a pension or retirement plan, and, dare I say, health insurance. Given the skyrocketing costs of health care in the United States, staying in a 9-to-5 job for health benefits is a legit advantage, especially if you or a family member has a chronic health concern. These benefits can keep you locked into a job (it did for me) and make it really hard to leave for the perceived uncertainty of entrepreneurship.

The reality is that entrepreneurship is tough. Think about it: as an entrepreneur you have to put in a whole lot of effort to find clients, nurture relationships with clients, and secure contracts. You are responsible for generating revenue, paying the expenses, and covering the full costs of health care and paid time off for yourself and employees. Plus, if you don't work, you don't get paid (unless you have a passive income stream—more about that later). Starting my private practice and eventually transitioning to full-time entrepreneurship was not an easy decision to make.

Even though full-time entrepreneurship was definitely the path I wanted to take, it took many years for me to take the leap. During that gap, I had convinced myself that entrepreneurship was not for me. You may be having these exact thoughts too, but you are reading this book, so I know you have a desire to challenge these thoughts. We often say *knowledge is power*, and it is absolutely true in this situation. I realized that I lacked the knowledge, tools, and skills to operate a profitable and thriving private practice. Once I had those skills and tools, my mindset started to change, and it became easier to start my entrepreneurial journey.

Working for an organization is extremely attractive, especially for Black and BIPOC mental health practitioners. The insurmountable debt from graduate school leaves very few career options for BIPOC therapists. That steady paycheck is a necessity. However, my 9-to-5 dictated my caseload, and there was little autonomy on the types of clients I met with. My caseload was huge, and no one was turned away—the clients had to be seen. I was "working like a horse" (another common Barbadian idiom). My vacation had to be approved by someone else, and I would often feel guilty if I needed a mental health day. Often, if I were sick I would still go to work because I felt I was needed, or because I wanted to save my sick time rather than take the day to recuperate and rest (in introspect, this makes no sense). I did not consider the toll the stress was taking on my body. In most capitalist societies, the priority is *the work not the worker*, and I was trapped in that thinking, too—*decolonization alert!* I would prioritize my work over my own physical or mental health. I was in a daze—brainwashed, even. When I was finally able to break free from that thinking, I could not believe the extent to which I had neglected my physical and mental health. My tank was low and I was on a fast track to burning out. Many therapists end up exiting the field at this stage—I was lucky to have stayed.

Reflection Time

Let's take a few minutes to reflect on income for mental health professionals. Find a quiet space, and respond to the journal prompts below:

- How much do you estimate therapists earn in the public sector (i.e., government, schools, hospitals)?
- How much do you estimate therapists earn in private practice?
- How much would you want (or need) to earn to feel comfortable as a full-time entrepreneur?

WHAT DO SUCCESSFUL THERAPISTS AND ENTREPRENEURS HAVE IN COMMON?

Believe it or not, therapists and entrepreneurs have quite a bit in common. For example, they both focus on helping people improve their lives and introduce novel ways to solve problems. But there's more. Below is a list of qualities of excellent clinicians and entrepreneurs:

1. *Opportunistic observers:* Therapists keep a keen eye on body language and information clients share; entrepreneurs observe the environment and look for trends and possible opportunities in the marketplace.
2. *Creative problem-solvers:* Therapists and entrepreneurs help clients/customers engage in new and creative ways to address their problems. They are flexible and willing to change when they see that something is not working.
3. *Communicators:* Therapists are trained in the language of communication, such as oral and body language, active listening, and giving and receiving feedback. Successful entrepreneurs need great interpersonal skills to communicate with customers, to network and create new business opportunities, and to close deals.
4. *Goal-setters:* Therapists create treatment plans based on clients' goals, and these goals are used to track and monitor progress. Entrepreneurs also set short- and long-term goals for their business and use metrics and key performance indicators (KPIs; more on this later) to track their progress.

5. *Risk managers:* While the type of risk is different, both therapists and entrepreneurs deal with risk management. Therapists must routinely assess clients for safety concerns, whether self-injury or threats of harm to self or others. Entrepreneurs frequently assess risk involved with investing time and money on business opportunities, creating and launching new products/services, and marketing to a new client base.

6. *Adventurers:* Entrepreneurs and therapists are willing to take on challenging situations and accept that they may experience setbacks along the way. They know that they may encounter unfamiliar situations, but they are willing to proceed. They make plans and take action to get results.

7. *Optimists:* As therapists, we have hope and remain optimistic that our work with clients will lead to positive changes and outcomes. Similarly, entrepreneurs are guided by aspirational visions and missions that are geared to solving everyday problems, making life easier for their customers, and changing the world.

As you can see from this list, therapists and entrepreneurs share many characteristics. While your graduate training did not explicitly prepare you for the role of entrepreneur, your clinical training skills can easily be transferred to entrepreneurship. Sometimes we are so intimidated by the word *entrepreneur* or have such outdated assumptions about what entrepreneurship is that we don't see the ways we are already practicing it (see case study: "Are you an entrepreneur?").

Reflection Time

- What skills do you already possess that you can transfer to entrepreneurship?
- What is one entrepreneurial quality that you want to develop?

BUILDING WEALTH WHILE DOING GOOD

One of the prevailing messages about careers in mental health is that it is a low-paying occupation. Unfortunately, this is true for some depending on position, work setting, discipline, and licensure status. People worry, rightfully so, about surviving on a typical therapist's salary. The reality is that most therapists are sitting on a gold mine of expertise, but do not receive guidance on generating revenue from their knowledge and wisdom. We are conditioned to believe that we need more experience, more professional development, or more supervision before we can stand on our own or practice independently. You can leverage your expertise to build a niche and serve clients in numerous ways (more on that when we get to Chapters 5 and 12). I will provide you with tools to generate passive income, to identify new revenue-generating products/services, and ultimately to build wealth using your expertise, all while doing good in your community.

I want to be absolutely clear with you that being a mental health professional is a noble career, with a lot of personal reward from helping people, that *can* be a financially rewarding career as well. So my invitation is for you to shed that scarcity mindset: the belief that you do not have what you need and that resources are limited, which can lead people to operate in fear and anxiety and to worry that they will lose what they have. Cultivate an *abundance mindset*, the belief that you have enough resources and will not want for anything, and get ready to bloom—get ready to thrive!

TRUTHS AND TRENDS ABOUT THE MENTAL HEALTH FIELD

There are a few more things that I want to share in case there is still any doubt in your mind about entrepreneurship. Mental health is a field and an industry that is thriving, with a growing need for inclusive mental health solutions. There is more than enough to share.

Mental Health Is a Rapidly Growing Public Health Concern

In the wake of the pandemic, mental health has become a major public health concern. In 2021, the U.S. Surgeon General, Dr. Vivek Murthy, released a report titled "Protecting Youth Mental Health" (Office of the U.S. Surgeon General, 2021), which highlighted the critical challenges facing our country related to youth mental health; in 2022, he published a report titled "Framework for Workplace Mental Health and Well-Being," which calls attention to increasing workplace stress and strategies leaders can use to support their employees (Office of the U.S. Surgeon General, 2022); in 2023, he released a another report, "Our Epidemic of Loneliness and Isolation," addressing the "loneliness" epidemic and offering community and connection as ways people can heal (Office of the U.S. Surgeon General, 2023a); and again in 2023, he released the report "Social Media and Youth Mental Health," which explores the impact of social media on youth mental health (Office of the U.S. Surgeon General, 2023b). In 2024, Dr. Murthy published yet another report, this time addressing the "Mental Health and Well-Being of Parents" (Office of the U.S. Surgeon General, 2024). While these reports highlight troubling concerns, many of us knew these issues existed long before the pandemic. Now we are seeing national, even global attention to these concerns, and that is different. The silver lining is that these are opportunities for therapists to lend their expertise and to build businesses that can help solve these problems.

We have also seen that the Health Resources and Services Administration (HRSA), a government agency within the U.S. Department of Health and Human Services that provides equitable health care to the nation's highest-need communities and offers grants to address the mental health workforce, has allocated $387 million in its budget for "Behavioral Health Workforce Development Programs to train 18,000 behavioral health providers and $37 million for SAM-HSA's Minority Fellowship Programs to almost double the number of fellows— increasing the amount of culturally competent behavioral health professionals" for fiscal year 2024 (U.S. Department of Health and Human Services, n.d., p. 2). As a result, HRSA is distributing millions of dollars to organizations addressing workforce issues in mental health. *Opportunities.*

The mental health industry is a rapidly growing field, estimated to be worth over $115 billion by 2030 (*Fortune Business Insights*, 2023). Additionally, mental health technologies such as digital mental health apps and telehealth have received large investments of venture capital funding over the past 5 years. The mental health software industry was valued at $4.5 billion in 2021 and is expected to grow to over $69 billion by 2030 (GlobeNewswire, 2022). *Opportunities.* While artificial intelligence has engaged in ways that mimic the therapy process, it will never be able to replace therapists because the human connection cannot be fully dubbed by technology. These high-growth areas present opportunities for mental health professionals to lend their wisdom and to launch businesses.

The Demand for BIPOC Mental Health Providers Is Huge

More people of color are seeking therapy, and as a result, the demand for BIPOC mental health providers has skyrocketed. More and more Black and Brown celebrities are publicly sharing their mental health journeys, and others are creating access by providing scholarships for free therapy. This is opening up new market segments that have previously been ignored and excluded by mainstream mental health institutions. For example, more Black women, and even Black men, are seeking therapy and other well-being resources. Additionally, as these new therapy seekers become more informed about mental health, they are no longer satisfied with seeing just *any* therapist—they want a therapist who comes from a similar racial and/or ethnic background (see Figure 1.1), someone who gets them. They want a choice in providers and are learning to better advocate for their needs. So, we need more mental health professionals of color, and we need them now. We need *you.*

We are seeing an influx of people of color who have shed the stigma that has long been associated with mental health. In a survey conducted by my company InnoPsych (2024), 84.6% of survey respondents, and 88.3% among respondents of color, stated that they wanted to work with a therapist from a similar racial or ethnic background. Therapists are raising attention to segments of BIPOC

I want a therapist who shares my racial and/or ethnic background.

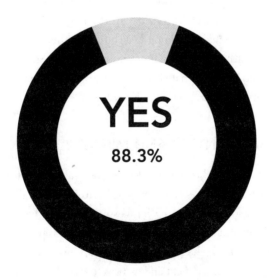

Figure 1.1 Preferences for racial and ethnic backgrounds of therapists (data from InnoPsych, 2024) *Source:* Demp Agency

populations that have historically had low engagement with mental health resources, such as BIPOC males (Jackman, 2022).

It is exciting to see that the next wave of mental health theories focuses on changing mental health to address the needs of individuals and communities who have historically been ignored or worse, pathologized, by the "founding fathers" of psychology. *Decolonizing therapy*, a term coined by social worker Jennifer Mullan (2023), addresses how the history of colonization has contributed to the development and proliferation of racist practices and policies within established mental health institutions and has contributed to harm to BIPOC groups. There has also been a call to acknowledge and change the way these institutions continue to practice. For example, the American Psychological Association (2021a, 2023), the American Psychiatric Association (2021), and the National Association of Social Workers (2021) have all published apologies for racism that led to biased research, policies, and practices. Other perspectives, such as liberation psychology (Comas-Díaz & Torres, 2020) and liberation health (Martinez & Fleck-Henderson, 2014), are amplifying voices of the oppressed and equipping therapists with culturally affirming therapeutic approaches, which in turn are leading to better therapy outcomes for BIPOC individuals and communities (Goode-Cross & Grim, 2016). For example, addressing racial stress and trauma in therapy and in workplaces is another way Black therapists are making their mark in the field (Jackman, 2023; Williams, 2023).

In sum, as you can see, the mental health field is thriving, and the need for inclusive mental health solutions will continue to grow. So congratulate yourself . . . you are in an industry that is here to stay. Black therapists can be successful business owners and entrepreneurs. *We need you.*

CHAPTER 1 MOMENTUM AND MINDSET CHECK

You are defying the odds. This chapter elevates the reality that it is by design that Black people and other people of color have been systematically excluded from the mental health field, from owning businesses, and from being owners of private practices. While our graduate programs have not prepared us for entrepreneurship, we need to refuse the narrative that we are not entrepreneurs. We need more BIPOC therapists in the field and as private practice owners and entrepreneurs for our communities and clients, and to build generational wealth, because *representation matters.* With the current trends in mental health, there is a vital need for our therapy services and our culturally affirming and inclusive businesses. You have the power to change the field and to change the entrepreneurial landscape. You are needed . . . now.

- What is one takeaway that you have as you finish this chapter?
- What is a mindset shift that you have made after reading this chapter?

Think and Act Like a "Thriving Therapreneur"

....

Cultivating the right mindset and habits is key to thriving in business.

DEAR THERAPIST, YOU DO NOT NEED TO BE TIRED, BURNED OUT, AND POOR

How often have you heard this sentiment? "Being a therapist is a noble and professionally rewarding career, but it doesn't pay." I certainly did, and I was quite alright with that because I wanted to do good.

This sentiment was pervasive over 25 years ago when I was starting out in the field, and sadly, it still exists today. I'm here to set the record straight: the idea that therapists cannot create businesses that build wealth was a lie back then and it is even more so now. The fact that we are not encouraged to think like entrepreneurs is a major disservice. I am going on record to say you can do good and make money too. It starts with shifting your mindsets about money and entrepreneurship.

Your training has equipped you with a range of skills and expertise that you can leverage into financially viable businesses. However, little attention or intention is given to how to monetize your expertise and wisdom beyond therapy services. We have to acknowledge the mental health industrial complex: the system of pharmaceutical companies, health insurance payers, police, prisons, social services, and mental health institutions that work together to put profit over patient care or provider care, and to punish and control people who come from intentionally underinvested and historically excluded groups (Mullan, 2023). And we have to acknowledge that it functions on capitalism and maintaining power: those on the front lines see patients (mostly where therapists of color are directed), and those in leadership (mostly White) make decisions for providers and clients; control funding, salaries, and reimbursement rates; and generally serve as gatekeepers to the field. So, in some ways, it is by design that you are *not* taught how to use your expertise to expand your finances, because you are needed on the front lines. Unfortunately, the mental health industrial complex can be exploitative, and BIPOC therapists end up burning out due to high case-loads, lack of resources, and inattention to professional growth, sometimes leaving clinical work behind or leaving the field altogether.

Having served as a clinical supervisor for almost 20 years and a business coach for therapists for over 10 years, I am invested in helping you map out how to leverage your wisdom to build generational wealth, to craft a career that you want, and most of all, protect your peace along your career journey. I have also experienced burnout, and I want you to build a lifelong mental health career that offers you the work-life harmony you desire, without having to leave the field prematurely.

MY CHILDHOOD MONEY MINDSET

From an early age, I knew that my calling was to help people, and money was not a motivator for me. I was satisfied with having a comfortable life. I can vividly recall having conversations with my friends about what my future life would look like. I'm sure you can relate to this. At the time, I wished for a successful career as a psychologist, a nice home, and enough money to travel the world. These seemed like radical goals back then, but as you can see, they were tiny and not very specific! I recall thinking and even vocalizing that I didn't want a lot of money.

But as I matured I have come to realize that my mindset about money and wealth was flawed and was limiting my growth. I needed to shift how I viewed money and understand that my ideas about wealth and money had changed. Now, I don't want to worship money, but I also understand that money will help me to transform my passions into purposeful products and services that can help others. And yes, I want to travel the world, and I'll need money to do that in the way that I want to—in style. (Like first class, or even a private jet! Yes, I said it.) Shifting my mindset about money has allowed me to step out of my comfort zone, dream boldly, and release my fears.

SHIFTING MINDSETS

Throughout this book, you will have the opportunity to examine how the messages you received in childhood and your life experiences shape your self-perception and views about owning a business. Entrepreneurship is a mindset game, and having a healthy mindset is key to your success in business. You may have self-defeating thoughts, harsh inner critics, and scarcity mindsets that impact how you approach the challenges and opportunities that you will encounter on the entrepreneurial journey—so we will examine them, name them, and change them.

MY EARLY STRUGGLE IN PRIVATE PRACTICE

When I started my private practice in 2005, it was a side hustle. This side hustle provided a nice supplemental income, but I did not see myself as an entrepreneur. I conducted therapy sessions, forensic evaluations, and psychological assessments, collected payments, and kept it going. I didn't have revenue or growth goals. I did not think about client retention or new business development. People found me through word of mouth—from other clients or professionals. I certainly did not think about growth metrics or key performance indicators. I was happy in my 9-to-5 and felt satisfied with operating a private practice "on the side." It gave me a sense of independence and pride.

After my first child was born in 2010, my mindset about my career and business started to shift. I had taken 3 months of maternity leave, and I went back to work part-time for another 3 months. I kept some of my therapy clients, and I did a few forensic evaluations. But motherhood was humbling and taught me quite a bit about soul-care. I could no longer pull all-nighters to get a report completed and then show up for my 9-to-5 on 3 hours of sleep and expect to function well. I was exhausted all the time, my memory was foggy, I was forgetful, and people at work expected the same prechild level of productivity. Lack of sleep was not going to work with an infant. I was not thriving, and I needed to make some drastic changes in my life if I wanted to avoid a case of full-blown burnout, or worse, a trip to the emergency room.

With very little examination, I made a decision to stop providing high-conflict custody evaluations. These evaluations offered a fair amount of flexibility, as I could schedule interviews in the evenings and on the weekends, but writing the reports were time-consuming. My reports were 55 single-spaced pages on average. Oh yes! They were a bear to write. A high level of scrutiny was involved as there was often the possibility of testifying in court. However, these evaluations were a lucrative part of my business, as no insurance was involved and the hourly rate was high. Additionally, the courts had added a new certification requirement that was geared to ensuring high-quality reports. The field was attracting people who were poorly trained, and the courts wanted to put in some guidelines to ensure clients received quality care. I had completed a 2-year postdoctoral fellowship and was highly trained, and I saw the certification process as very basic. Plus, the timing of these training sessions was inconvenient, given my full-time work: to attend the annual training sessions, I would have to take one or two personal days off work. So, I abruptly decided to stop doing these evaluations.

Here is where the entrepreneurial mindset would have been helpful. I made the decision to discontinue these evaluations based on emotions, not as a business decision. I was upset that I had to attend these trainings, for which I was overqualified, and was an instructor for at times. In addition, the custody evaluations were morally challenging because, time and time again, I saw people use their children as pawns in their divorce process. I did not have a business coach or bookkeeper at the time who could have guided me to use business metrics to make my decision. This service definitely generated the most revenue for the business, but it was also time intensive. If I had considered my key performance indicators

(discussed in Chapter 11) and if I had known my numbers, I might have
made a different decision—a decision based on financial data, not
just emotion.

THE THRIVING THERAPRENEUR DEFINED

According to the *Merriam-Webster* dictionary, *thriving* is a verb meaning "to grow
vigorously; to gain in wealth or possessions; [and] to progress toward or realize a
goal despite or because of circumstances" (Merriam-Webster, n.d.).

Therapreneur is a blended word formed by joining *thera*pist and entre*preneur*.
My signature coaching program is called the *Thriving Therapreneur*.

My belief is that mental health professionals are sitting on a wealth of knowledge that they can leverage into thriving businesses; they just need to gain the
knowledge, tools, and skills to accomplish this. In my view, a "Thriving Therapreneur" understands that creating successful businesses also means that you
have to prioritize your health and well-being. What good is business success if
you are not around to enjoy the benefits?

FROM SURVIVAL PRIVATE PRACTICES TO THRIVING
BUSINESSES

A pattern I have noticed is that when therapists get into business, it is primarily to
operate a therapy practice or private practice. Starting a private practice is relatively
easy, as there is a low barrier to entry. You can rent or sublease an office space, and
in today's market all you really need is a computer and access to high-speed internet.
It is what people in business call *low-hanging fruit*. (I know, I know, you bought this
book because starting a private practice seems very hard because you didn't learn
how to in school. I get it. But in the grand scheme of things, it is not very hard to
start a basic private practice. You will see that very soon, I promise you.)

Among psychologists, 43% operate a private (independent) practice, the larg-
est segment of employment, though only 12% are psychologists of color (American Psychological Association, 2022b). It is a model that has been repeated time
and time again, and as long as you are licensed or have a licensed supervisor, there
are very few, if any, barriers to getting started. Many mental health professionals
start their private practices while working full-time or part-time positions.

Survival Private Practices

My first entry into entrepreneurship was in the form of a private practice. In 2005 I started a sole proprietorship, and my primary services were workshops and forensic evaluations. I saw clients who were going through custody battles or high-conflict divorces and who needed a guardian ad litem (GAL) to conduct evaluations to help determine the parenting arrangements. Referrals would come from being on a GAL list, directly from attorneys, or from other GALs. I soon expanded into therapy clients and would occasionally get called on to speak or lead workshops. I did not have a marketing plan, and outside of my website and business cards, I did not do any marketing. The majority of new business was word-of-mouth referrals from past and current clients and colleagues. However, 15 years later, I realized that while my private practice provided supplemental income, I did not have a growth plan and I was not building wealth. Additionally, what became crystal clear to me was that the only way that I made money was when I was working in my business, seeing clients or writing reports. It's what I call being "on the hour for the dollar": if you don't work, there is no income coming in. I could make more money when I saw more clients, or make less money when my clients took vacation or when I reduced my hours. This is my definition of a *survival private practice*, a business where the owner only earns revenue when they themselves provide a service.

Do not get me wrong—I was very proud of my survival practice, and it provided me with a great deal of supplemental income that allowed me to travel and provide additional perks for my family. By intentionally saving money and being frugal, I was able to pay off my student loan debt from the government of Barbados and save money for an 18% down payment for my first home. My survival private practice had only active income sources (i.e., revenue generated from providing a direct service). Additionally, I had no system in place to generate *passive income* (ongoing revenue that requires little effort after an initial investment of time/money, such as book royalties, on-demand courses, or online product sales) or to build *generational wealth* (accumulation of assets that you pass down through the generations). In fact, I was not sleeping a whole lot, because I was constantly working on the business or working my job. I didn't know how to shut off—*not working meant not earning.*

I was also chasing money. I said yes to just about every opportunity that came my way because it was about the money, whether it was a fit for my business or not. For a long time I saw anyone who wanted a therapist or an evaluation. For speaking or workshops, I rarely negotiated my fees and accepted very low rates. I was clearly operating in survival mode, and eventually this led to my first bout of burnout.

Truth is, it is simply unsustainable to live by working all the time. Plus, chasing money is not a productive or effective way to run a business, and you end up with a business that has no purpose, vision, or mission. Warren Buffet's quote, "If you don't find a way to make money while you sleep, you will work until you die," was definitely what was happening to me.

In 2017, after being in private practice for over 10 years, I started to think about my business differently. I was now a mom of two and was dealing with another bout of burnout from working a full-time job, operating a private practice, and being a mom and a wife. I was getting antsy, but I was unsure of the next move. The likely next step was to pursue a higher-level position within the organization.

As part of my career advancement strategy, I applied to and was accepted into two leadership development programs, one organized by the institution I was working for at the time and one with the American Psychological Association. These leadership programs helped me rethink my professional goals and pushed me to dream bigger. By mid-2018 I completed both programs and felt ready to take on the world. As part of my 5-year goals, I had created a vision that would lead me to full-time entrepreneurship. But guess what I did? I applied for three full-time positions and got two interviews, but did not receive any offers. It hurt, but later I realized the universe had intervened. I had clearly stated that I wanted to pursue full-time entrepreneurship, and here I was applying for jobs. The universe found a way to say, "Stop it, you are not pursuing your purpose."

While these positions did not work out, I was facing another struggle in my personal life. My marriage was at a crossroads, and I desperately wanted to work with a Black woman therapist, but I had the hardest time finding one. Six months later, my husband and I finally got connected to a couples therapist . . . a White couples therapist. It was not what we wanted, but we needed therapy. My White therapist eventually helped me find a Black woman therapist for individual therapy. I couldn't believe how difficult the process was to find a therapist of color. At that moment I knew I had to do something about it. That was how the seed for InnoPsych was planted. InnoPsych is the company I started in 2019, with a mission to disrupt racial inequities in mental health.

As I started to explore what InnoPsych could be, I was very excited about growth opportunities. I dove deep into my research about entrepreneurship by listening to entrepreneur memoirs on audiobooks (e.g., Marc Ecko's memoir, *Unlabel: Selling You Without Selling Out* [2013]) and to podcasts about entrepreneurs and their journeys (e.g., *Trailblazers.FM* podcast by Stephen A. Hart [2016]; the *Worksmart* podcast by Morgan DeBaun [2021]). I learned about the ups and downs of the entrepreneurial journey and how to face failure and orchestrate comebacks. I was inspired and excited about the journey, but the best part for me was shifting my mindset from hustling to thriving, to building wealth, and to growing enterprises, not just businesses. I was fired up, and I was ready.

However, I realized that I would need to leave my full-time job. One fact that kept coming up was that my salary would be limited and determined by someone else. There would always be a ceiling on my income, no matter how hard I worked or what I contributed to the organization. The reality is that as a Black woman, little value was placed on my contributions, my talent, or my excellence. I was not a political player in the workplace, which is something that I would need to advance. While it was extremely frightening to think about leaving the security of a regular paycheck, good health insurance, paid vacation and sick time, and a team of coworkers for the uncertainty and risk that comes with entrepreneurship, I knew it would be necessary.

Thriving Businesses

As my career goals were changing and I was leaning into the idea of full-time entrepreneurship, I was learning that being a successful entrepreneur was more than the money in the bank. I was coming into a new definition of success. For me, a successful entrepreneur included the health of my body and my mind, the quality of my friendships and my spiritual practices, along with asset building skills. It was no longer about hustling. I wanted to thrive in my businesses and in my life, and that meant I would need to shake things up.

In contrast to a survival practice, a *thriving business* offers the opportunity for you to operate in abundance, giving you surplus to pour back into the business and to support other causes of interest. Thriving is also about releasing the scarcity mindset that can limit your thinking. It's about dreaming so big that your dreams scare you. It means that you have created a business that generates money while you are asleep—literally and figuratively. That's thriving!

- Thriving businesses have *multiple streams of income* from active and passive sources.
- Thriving businesses have a *solid team* in place to handle the operations of the business.
- Thriving businesses *make space for the CEO* to do CEO activities such as visioning, expansion, and high-revenue-generating activities.
- Thriving businesses have *abundant profit* that allows money to be reinvested into the business, to compensate the team generously, and to donate to causes that matter to their communities.

That's thriving!

Are you ready to shake up some things in your life?
Are you ready to build a thriving enterprise?
Are you willing to open your mind and to dream beyond your wildest dreams?
Are you willing to dream up a thriving enterprise as part of your legacy?
Let's do it!

Reflection Time

Let's take some time to reflect on the concept of thriving. Find a quiet space, and respond to the journal prompts below:

- What does thriving look like for you?
- How would you define a Thriving Therapreneur?
- Think about the success milestones that will help you to thrive (e.g., revenue, team, and locations). Give as many details as possible.

MAKING THE MENTAL SHIFT TOWARD ENTREPRENEURSHIP

People cannot change their habits without first changing their way of thinking.

—Marie Kondo, *The Life-Changing Magic of Tidying Up*

I recognize that it's not easy to all of a sudden see yourself as an entrepreneur, especially when your clinical training has not prepared you for it. Being on my own entrepreneurial journey, I've noticed that my beliefs and actions are crucial ingredients to my success as an entrepreneur. How you *think* about your skills and expertise will be a game changer and will have a direct impact on your business growth. Your mindset is a superpower and is instrumental to the type of business you intend to lead. Some people have an inner critic that creates self-doubt, which can be detrimental during challenging times. Others possess fear that can be disabling when trying something new such as starting a new business or launching a new product or service. They may end up abandoning an idea before it even reaches the light of day.

CONFRONTING FEAR

FEAR, **F**alse **E**vidence **A**ppearing **R**eal, is a common experience for people venturing into entrepreneurship. It may be fear of networking, fear of money (not having enough, or sometimes too much money comes with its own set of issues), fear of change, fear of success, and most feared of all, fear of failure. These fears can lead to *cognitive distortions*, erroneous ways people interpret information. These distortions unfortunately cause anxiety and can impact how we feel about ourselves and our abilities. Below I have outlined five cognitive distortions relevant to entrepreneurship. Truth be told, I struggled with some of these cognitive distortions myself. Finding ways to combat these cognitive distortions is key to unlocking your potential as an entrepreneur:

1. *Catastrophizing:* "If I start a business, it will fail." There is an outdated statistic that 90% of new businesses fail within the first year (Patel, 2015), portraying entrepreneurship as extremely risky and untenable. Who wants to put time, effort, and money into an activity that is more than

likely to fail? Fortunately, this is not true at all. In fact, only 20% of businesses fail in the first year and 50% of businesses fail after 5 years (McIntyre, 2020). However, these data do not apply to health-care businesses,
such as a mental health practice (especially given the growth trends
discussed in Chapter 1). If you have a dream to start a business, and you
don't do it because of fear, do you consider that a failure too?

2. *Negative focus:* "Entrepreneurship is too hard—I can't do it." Entrepreneurship is definitely challenging, but you have done hard things. You
have applied to graduate school, taken standardized tests, written many
papers, and may have even written a thesis or dissertation. Need I go on?
When you only focus on the negative aspects of entrepreneurship, you
ignore the many benefits. For example, the freedom that comes with creating your own schedule or working with the types of clients you most
enjoy. Plus, once you have the tools and skills, entrepreneurship will feel
more practical and manageable.

3. *Predicting the future:* "My business won't make enough money to cover my
lifestyle/current salary." This is another thought pattern that is connected
to failure. It is very common among the therapists I have coached to have
no idea what it costs to support their lifestyle. They have no idea what
their monthly expenses are, even when they pay their bills on time. This
cognitive distortion actually comes from a lack of knowledge or proper
management of their personal finances, which in turn feeds the fear of
entrepreneurship. Knowledge is power. When you understand your personal and business finances, you are able to set realistic goals and make
sound business decisions.

4. *All-or-nothing thinking:* "I must have all the details worked out before I
can launch my business," or "I don't have enough money (capital) to start
a business." A common mistake I hear is that entrepreneurs need to have
all the pieces in place before they can start their business. Perfection or
nothing. With a mental health business, you have more freedom to start
a business without needing "everything" (whatever that is in your mind)
completed. You will need some capital to cover your upfront costs, but
you can make a plan that won't overwhelm your budget.

5. *Negative labeling:* "I don't deserve wealth," or "I'm not an entrepreneur."
Some therapists have associated the caring profession with not deserv-
ing wealth. Another statement that I hear is that therapists are here to

help and they feel inauthentic building wealth as a therapist. I definitely had this mindset and believed that helping people somehow meant that I could not build wealth too. You absolutely deserve wealth! You have worked hard *and* you care, and you have many valuable resources and solutions to offer your clients. *You can build wealth while doing good.*

Mindset Work

- Reflect on a thinking pattern or mindset that has held you back or that gets in the way of your success.
- What function is this mindset serving? (It likely came at a time when you needed it, but you don't anymore.)
- What are some of the thoughts or beliefs that you have been carrying around that are blocking you from starting your business?

Exercise: Thought Restructuring

Thought restructuring is a cognitive behavioral therapy technique that is used to counter cognitive distortions and provide healthier ways of thinking. Take one thought at a time and answer the questions below:

1. *Name one cognitive distortion and identify what is at the root of this thought.* For example, is it due to fear of failure? Fear of success? Fear of change?
2. *What is the evidence for this thought?* For example, if you think that your business will fail, what evidence are you relying on?
3. *What if the opposite were true?* For example, instead of thinking that your business is doomed to fail, what if your business was guaranteed to succeed? What would success look like?
4. *Now, write two or three affirming statements that you can use to counter the cognitive distortion.* For example, "My business is guaranteed to succeed."

When you notice that you are having a negative thought, use this simple three-step thought-restructuring process to interrupt your cognitive distortions:

1. Name the cognitive distortion.
2. Interrupt the thought—stop and notice.
3. Replace the cognitive distortion with a productive thought
   or affirmation.

Consider the following example: "My business won't make enough money to cover my current salary or desired lifestyle."

1. *Name the cognitive distortion:*
   – Predicting the future: "I am feeling worried about being able to
     bring in enough revenue to cover my expenses."
2. *Interrupt the thought—stop and notice:*
   – Ahh . . . my worries about money are creating anxiety about the
     success of my business.
   – I am feeling nervous about making this next big step in my business.
3. *Replace the cognitive distortion with a productive thought or affirmation:*
   – Reading this book will help me get the tools to launch a
     profitable business.
   – If my business were to fail, there would be lessons that I could use
     to start my next business.
   – I have a unique service that solves my clients' issues, and this will
     bring in a steady stream of income.

FIVE MINDSETS FOR THRIVING THERAPRENEURS

Mindset theory has been around for a long time, dating back to the early 1900s according to Merriam-Webster's dictionary. However, in the 1970s Carol Dweck, author of *Mindset: A New Psychology of Success* (2006), introduced growth mindsets and fixed mindsets. According to Dweck, people with fixed mindsets believe that we are born with a prescribed amount of intelligence, which does not change, whereas people with growth mindsets believe that effort, openness to learning, and perseverance contribute to success. As a result, people with fixed mindsets tend to give up easily and avoid challenges and may feel a sense of hopelessness, while people with growth mindsets work harder and are more willing to try in the face of challenges and setbacks.

Which mindset do you have about entrepreneurship?

☐ *Fixed mindset:* You believe that successful entrepreneurs are born with all they need to start a business and that you are unable to build skills that help you grow.

☐ *Growth mindset:* You believe that entrepreneurship skills can be learned and that you can improve your skills.

☐ *Mixed mindset:* A bit of both.

The way you think about entrepreneurship is a key to your success. Entrepreneurs have mindsets that guide them through the good times and the tough times of operating a business. Without a doubt, you will encounter challenges along your entrepreneurial journey, and if your belief system or mindset is that challenges and failures are bad for business, then you will not likely go the distance to succeed. However, if you believe that challenges and failures are opportunities to learn and grow, then you will likely be successful, whether in that business or another. How you think about challenges and how you respond to them makes the difference.

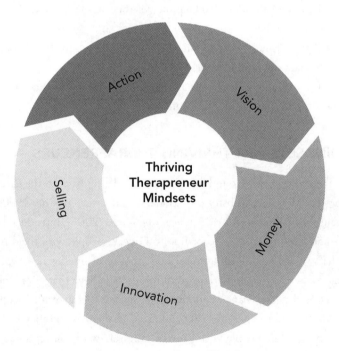

Figure 2.1 Five Thriving Therapreneur mindsets *Source:* Charmain F. Jackman and Demp Agency

Over the past 16 years, working as an entrepreneur and coaching therapists along their entrepreneurship journey, I have developed five mindsets that I think are essential to growth and success. I discuss each mindset in detail throughout the book and provide opportunities for you to connect and gain clarity about how each mindset connects to you. For now, Figure 2.1 provides a brief overview as we lay the foundation for this deeper exploration.

Mindset 1: Vision

A dream written down with a date becomes a goal. A goal broken down into steps becomes a plan. A plan backed by action makes your dreams come true.

—Greg Reid, author

I dare to say that every entrepreneurial journey has to start with a *vision*, your life's purpose put into action. A vision also captures your goals and the impact you want to make in the world. As an entrepreneur, it is important to take time to reflect on your vision: write it down, draw it, or depict in a visual format such as a vision board (more on visioning in Chapter 5) share it with others and review it frequently. These steps increase the likelihood that you will accomplish your life's goals. If you are having trouble connecting to your vision, look back at the essays you wrote for college or graduate school. You may be surprised to find the answers there. Another strategy is reflecting on the impact that you want to make on the world.

- What is your vision or life's purpose?
- What is driving you to entrepreneurship?

Mindset 2: Innovation

Being successful as an entrepreneur means you have to stay current while also planning for the future. An innovation mindset—having the ability to see opportunities where others see problems—and engaging in curiosity, creativity, and experimentation to solve problems, requires you to keep up-to-date with trends, anticipate market shifts, and even start your own trends. As Govindarajan (2016) shares in his book *The Three Box Solution: A Strategy for Leading Innovation*, business leaders have to think about the future as they are running the business and must "selectively forget the past" (p. 13). He describes his three-box strategy to innovation as a "natural tension among the values of preservation, destruction, and creation" (p. 13). To avoid stagnation in your private practice or wellness business, you will have to study our field with an eye to gaps and opportunities, observe trends in other industries, and make connections between other fields and the mental health field. Being innovative can also help you stand out from other businesses. Creating new products and services, inventing and delivering a treatment in a new way, or tapping into new market segments are all ways that you can innovate (more on *growing your business* in Chapter 11).

- What is your big idea for solving an issue in the mental health field?
- What is a new therapy approach, product, or service that you can bring to the mental health field?

Mindset 3: Money

One of the biggest shifts in your thinking as an entrepreneur will likely be your relationship with money, a relationship that will impact how you make decisions about your business and your lifestyle. Ultimately, it can impact how your business grows and succeeds. Your mindset about money guides how you think and feel when money is not coming in and when money is flowing. Getting right with your money is the most impactful change that you can make as an entrepreneur. It may involve exploring past financial traumas, looking into money areas that you have avoided, examining your spending habits, and reflecting on the messages you received about money as a child (more on money relationships in Chapter 3).

- How does money make you feel?
- As you think about building wealth, what thoughts and feelings are coming up for you?

Mindset 4: Selling

Talking about your business, informing the uninformed, is another important task of entrepreneurship. For many therapists, this can feel icky or "sales-y." You may be thinking, "I just want to help people, not sell to people." However, if people don't know what you do, you won't be able to help them (more about sales and marketing in Chapter 6). Additionally, for some people of color and immigrants who were raised with collectivist values, talking about your individual accomplishments can be hard because the family is central, not individuals.

As a result, you may have been socialized to be humble and to downplay your accomplishments. Others can highlight your wins, but not you. However, as an entrepreneur, sharing your accomplishments and your company's strengths and advantages over competitors is essential to bringing in customers (more about the *cultural dilemma of promotion* in Chapter 4). As a business owner, you will need to step out of your comfort zone to sell your products and services, to pitch your business to complete strangers, to promote your business on social media, and to network with potential clients and other entrepreneurs to increase visibility of your company. There is no way around it.

- What comes up for you as you think about promoting your personal brand?
- What is an accomplishment or win that you have achieved that would be relevant to share with your target audience?

Mindset 5: Action

Developing a mindset that is focused on action and executing your ideas will guide you to success. Without action, there is no business. Without action, your ideas stay in your head, swirling around with no real-world feedback or input. Getting a product or service out to the market even if it has flaws allows you to get feedback from users, which can help you refine and create a product that is useful to them. Making decisions with what you know in the moment helps you to move the business forward. It's the balance between making impulsive decisions and perseverating over a decision. As a mentor once said to me, "No decision is a decision." Avoid letting perfection be a guiding factor because it halts action and progress. Your actions will be guided by your goals and processes (more on growth processes in Chapter 11).

- What generally stops you from taking action?
- What helps you to take action?

ACT LIKE AN ENTREPRENEUR

You are familiar with the saying *fake it till you make it*, but what are the actions that thriving entrepreneurs do every day to drive their success? There are many entrepreneurship books on how to be a successful business owner. You can spend time reading all those books, which would be educational—but the common denominator among successful business owners and entrepreneurs is their *habits*.

Getting to Thriving by Taking Stock of Your Habits

Your habits are everyday actions you take or decisions you make often without conscious thought (e.g., brushing your teeth). Your habits, whether they are good or bad, limiting or motivating, guide how you get stuff done. Taking stock of your daily habits is an intentional exercise to bring conscious awareness to the ways that you move through your daily or weekly schedule. It's also an important exercise for your entrepreneurial journey as your habits influence how you will show up in your business. Your habits impact your success as a business owner.

The Habits That Limit You

Let's start with understanding the habits that limit you. These limiting habits may seem innocent on the surface but can eventually cause big problems. Habits such as procrastination or self-sabotage may start with poor time management (e.g., running late for meetings, turning in assignments late, overscheduling) but are rooted in perfectionism and people-pleasing behaviors (e.g., saying yes to everything). It's true that some limiting habits may feel good in the moment, but they can interfere with your goals and progress.

If you have ever heard me speak at events about self-care, I have confessed my struggle with getting sufficient sleep at night. Since I was a teenager I have been known in my family as the "night owl." Then in college and in graduate school, being able to stay up late at night was rewarded. And, it continued to be part of my story as a working professional. There was a time that I was proud to admit that I could function on only 3 hours of sleep or how late I stayed up. In retrospect, that was a lie I told myself. I was not functioning as well as I thought.

So why do we engage in activities that limit our success? The truth is that there are benefits to our limiting habits—that's why we continue to do them. When I stay up late, it is the quietest time in my house, and I love that. There are no interruptions from my family or distractions from phone calls. It's easier to get into a flow state, that fuels my productivity.

Now, I know that it is not a healthy sleep schedule, but this is a habit that has been cemented for over 30 years and is extremely hard to disrupt. I know the health concerns. My mom reminds me that going to sleep after midnight shortens your lifespan, and there is research to back that up (Johnson, Jackson, Williams, et al., 2019; Ramirez, 2024; Walker, 2024). Truth is, I also feel the difference when I go to bed before midnight and get 7 or 8 hours of sleep. I feel refreshed, energetic, and focused, which then causes me to stay up late the next night . . . that's a vicious cycle I am actively working on breaking. As I dig deeper, I realize that my late-night schedule is connected to taking on too many projects. I have a hard time saying no. It comes from people-pleasing behaviors and a scarcity mindset that are deeply ingrained. But knowledge is power, and I have developed some strategies to help me work through my limiting habits.

HABIT CHANGES FOR GETTING TO SLEEP

1. I have made getting to bed before midnight and getting at least 7 hours of sleep a goal.
2. I have drastically changed the number of hours I work per week by leaving my 9-to-5 to work full time as an entrepreneur.
3. I am changing my relationship with work by understanding my workload and saying no to opportunities when I do not have the bandwidth for them.
4. I'm practicing going to bed when I am tired.
5. I'm practicing not working after 7:00 p.m.
6. I have an amazing bedtime routine that involves sound healing and aromatherapy.
7. I have an accountability partner.
8. I recognize that perfection is not the goal.
9. I give myself grace when I fall short of my goal.
10. I remember how good I feel when I get at least 7 hours of sleep.

Reflection Time

Let's take a few minutes to reflect on your habits. Find a quiet space, and respond to the following journal prompts:

- Write down three habits that you want to change.
- For one of these limiting habits, write up to five actions that you can take to change this habit.

The Habits That Activate You

Now on to the habits that activate you. You could not have made it to the place you are now without some productive habits. These are habits that get you going in the morning. They help you keep appointments, finish projects, and persist in the face of adversity. These habits are worth elevating on your entrepreneurial journey.

Reflection Time

Now, let's reflect on the habits that activate you.

- What are the habits that help you to get going every day?
- What are the habits that help you to get in a flow state or get tasks completed?

Building Habits for Success

What are the habits that help you achieve success? Are there rituals or actions that you do in a particular order every time that help you get the results that you want? Do you have routines that you activate when you are feeling down? Information is power, and the power gained from knowing what activates or limits you can guide you in operating a profitable business. For example, know the habits that get you into a flow state or put you in a good mood.

In a poignant article, Thimble (2021) shared these 10 habits of successful entrepreneurs:

1. Read
2. Stick to a daily routine

3. Listen to uplifting music
4. Plan tomorrow, today
5. Meditate
6. Start the day with exercise
7. Stay current
8. Make time to unplug
9. Journal
10. Pace yourself

These are great habits to aspire to, but it is more important to identify habits that are specific to you and your needs. What are the practices that help you to operate at your optimal level? For example, when I worked in my 9-to-5, eating lunch was a priority because I get *hangry* if I don't eat. Because I rarely had time to go out to buy lunch, bringing lunch from home was a necessity. As a result, one of my daily success habits was eating three nutritious meals. Here are more of my daily habits for success:

1. Morning/evening prayer
2. Eat three nutritious meals
3. Incorporate aromatherapy (or scent) into my surroundings
4. Talk to a family member or friend about something funny
5. Listen to meditation music
6. Review my schedule at the start of the day
7. Read an article or listen to an audiobook
8. Walk outdoors
9. Quiet time (sit for 10 minutes in the car before entering the office or my house)
10. Recite an affirmation or smile at myself in the mirror

Take Action Exercise

- Write down 10 daily habits that you will practice on your entrepreneurial journey.

CHAPTER 2 MOMENTUM AND MINDSET CHECK

I know your mind is on fire right now, but it is worth it. This chapter was all about examining the messages that you were exposed to from childhood and exploring how they have shaped your beliefs and behaviors. You had a chance to locate whether you approach life through a scarcity or abundance mindset and to learn the differences between a survival and a thriving business. You tackled your fears and cognitive distortions and practiced strategies to overcome these faulty ways of thinking, through thought restructuring and habit change. I introduced the five mindsets of Thriving Therapreneurs (i.e., vision, innovation, money, promotion, and action) that I believe every therapist should possess. Finally, I shared how habits (the good ones and the not so good) can fuel or sabotage your business success.

- What is one takeaway that you have as you finish this chapter?
- What is a mindset shift that you have made after reading this chapter?

Cultivating a Wealth-Building Mindset

Paving the Way for Financial Freedom

••

*Unhealthy money mindsets and habits have to go
as you grow.*

EARLY MONEY MESSAGES

From very early on my parents taught me to save, save, save! I loved it. I enjoyed
going to the bank every week to deposit my money (there was no online banking then) and keeping track of my transactions in my bank book. It felt very
good seeing my money grow after making deposits. I also remember going to
the grocery stores and waiting excitedly to get the coins from any change my
parents received from their shopping (there were no credit cards back then—it
was all cash). My parents would joke that I would also get them to buy me books
with their money while always holding on to my money. I never wanted to
spend my money.

You can see clearly that the early messages I received were about *saving* money.
My parents emphasized the importance of saving and followed through with
behaviors that reinforced that message: going to the bank each week, depos-
iting money in a savings account, and reminding me of the behaviors through

storytelling. Saving was important, and I was rewarded for it. As a result, saving became a dominant behavior that I developed around money. Saving for the future, saving for a rainy day—just save your money.

In addition to saving money, I also learned about *not wasting* money or spending money frivolously. My parents were very practical when it came to money. I always had what I needed, and we definitely took vacations and traveled, but saving money was always an underlying narrative. During these vacations they shopped for bargain items and would purchase in bulk and ship these items back home for personal use and to resell. At the supermarket, we would compare prices to find the least expensive option for the various products. My mother, to this day, loves to find a good deal. The message was crystal clear: make every penny count.

I have carried these early messages about money well into my adulthood, and they have even been a source of pride. Having a bank account with funds to cover my expenses and more gives me peace of mind. Not having credit card debt or other debt (except a mortgage) feels really good. I was fortunate to pay off my college debt within 5 years of starting my first professional job. For me, it does not feel good to be in debt. I hate credit card fees and if I am ever charged a fee, I will call to have that refunded, and it works most of the time. Save money, do not waste money! That was my mantra for a long time.

In my mind, I thought that I was *good* with money: I was great at saving money; I paid my bills on time, did not live above my means, had no credit card debt—I was feeling very proud. By all accounts I should have been doing really well. My money was growing, but slowly (high interest rates for savings accounts were a thing of the past). It dawned on me that saving money in a bank as the sole financial strategy would not get me to that goal of generational wealth.

It was hard when I came to the realization that the lessons my parents so dutifully taught me about saving money were insufficient. It was *one piece* of a really intricate thousand-piece puzzle about financial freedom—a really *small* piece. If I wanted my money to grow, I was going to need to learn new lessons. And if I wanted financial freedom, there were even more lessons that I would need to learn.

ADULT RELATIONSHIPS WITH MONEY

Your socialization around money in childhood plays a major role in how you engage with money into adulthood. Many people go through life with little awareness about how their relationship with money impacts every aspect of our lives: social, work, family, and spending. I was socialized to save money, and that was something I cherished. It also contributed to me developing a scarcity mindset around money: I often looked at my financial situation as not having enough, and I worried that some financial event would wipe out what little money I had. This left me feeling anxious, avoidant, and risk averse around money. So I would hoard my coins. I know I missed out on special occasions for family and friends because I was saving my money. What good is money if you don't use it . . . wisely?

In 2017, I was enrolled in the American Psychological Association's Leadership Institute for Women in Psychology (LIWP), a leadership program for mid-career psychologists. I'm so grateful that money was on the agenda. Through discussions, I learned that I saw money as dirty and corrupt and people with money as greedy; as a result, I wanted no part of being wealthy. The faculty helped us reframe our thinking about money. They explained that our negative views about money limit women in terms of negotiating for higher salaries, going for promotions, or thinking bigger about their careers. I was blown away. I had never had any professional discussions about money like this, had never negotiated for my salary, and had always taken what was offered to me (more on that later) . . . and I had been in the field for over a decade at that point. I had some serious unlearning to do.

FINANCIAL TRAUMA

As you are a therapist, you know that trauma is the response people have when they are in a life-or-death situation (e.g., experiencing a car accident, a natural disaster, or a physical assault). When people experience a traumatic event, they may feel fear and anxiety, avoid reminders of the trauma event, experience flashbacks, be keyed up or on edge, and isolate themselves.

Similarly, financial trauma occurs when people experience a significant event or series of events that severely impact their finances, such as a sudden loss of employment, identity theft, someone stealing your money, Wall Street crash, or food and housing insecurity caused by poverty. Financial trauma can be passed down through generations and can lead to challenging relationships with money. For example, some people may overspend and live above their means, while others may develop a scarcity mindset about money and hold on tightly to their money (Noll, 2021). Chloe McKenzie (n.d.) takes this idea a step further, exploring financial trauma and its impact on Black women through the lens of systemic oppression. She defines financial trauma as the "response to the cumulative harming of a person's wealth-building capacity and relationship with money." In addition to financial trauma, she includes descriptions of *financial abuse*, resulting from structures, policies, and practices that continue to impair a "person's financial capability," such as redlining (Egede, Walker, Campbell, et al., 2023); and *financial shaming*, which includes racist cultural messages such as *welfare queens* that blame Black women for the financial harm they experience. These financial traumas can have a profound effect on how Black women engage with money and their finances.

PERSONAL REFLECTION: MY FINANCIAL TRAUMA

I loved saving money in my silver piggy bank—a souvenir from one of my vacations in New York. One day I started to notice that some money was missing. I was an only child (at the time), so there were no siblings to blame. However, I had a good friend who often came over to my home after school and on weekends. As my parents and I tried to figure out what was happening, it dawned on us that it could have been my friend. My parents came up with the plan to see if it was her. Unfortunately, the trap worked . . . and she took the money. It was painful to learn it was her.

My parents had a conversation with my friend's parents, but unfortunately, that was the end of our friendship. I just wish she had asked to borrow the money. What a hard lesson to learn at a young age, for both of us! Now I wish we would have handled things differently, for her and for me. I recognize that young children make mistakes, and having an opportunity to repair the harm would have been helpful for me and possibly for her too. A few years later, my mother had a similar experience with one of her friends. My mom was extremely sad to discover her friend's betrayal because she would have helped her friend if she had asked. Like mine, that was the end of their friendship. So many experiences of financial trauma, but we often don't speak about them.

When I started my first real job after earning one of my degrees, I needed an organization to sponsor my work visa. It was a very vulnerable position to be in. My supervisor, someone I thought I could trust, offered me a position. I was so grateful that I said yes without negotiating the salary (I had no clue that I could negotiate, and I would not have known how to anyway, at that time). A few years later that supervisor left, and a new director took over. The new supervisor called me to her office one day and told me that my salary was extremely low, and she would work to get me at an appropriate rate. I had been exploited by my prior supervisor, and I did not even know it! That really hurt both emotionally *and* financially. These experiences made me more protective of my money and distrustful of others around my money. But I learned that I needed to heal my relationship with money.

As Black therapists, it is essential that we understand the systemic barriers we are facing as entrepreneurs, so that we don't engage in self-blame or feel inadequate. The system is working very hard to disempower Black people and to keep us poor and oppressed. It is by design that financial literacy is not taught in schools, that banks charge Black people higher interest rates because we are deemed a higher risk, and that predatory lending is rampant in Black communities. Therefore, it is our responsibility to learn more about money and finances and to pass on this knowledge to others. Egede, Walker, Campbell, and colleagues (2023) outline the modern impacts of redlining and continued intentional underinvestment in Black and Brown communities that result in poor educational, economic, and health outcomes.

Reflection Time

Let's take some time to reflect on the early messages and experiences that you have had with money. Find a quiet space, and respond to the journal prompts below.

If you notice that you are having a strong emotional reaction, take a break, take some breaths, and come back to it when you are ready or use the MINDFUL MOMENT below. Uncovering this information and facing some of those early experiences will be hard, but it will help you lean in versus avoiding your personal and business finances.

- What is the first memory you have of money?
- What are two or three early messages that you received about money in childhood?

- What is a painful memory that you have about money?
- What have you done to release the emotional trauma around this issue?
- What is a positive memory you have about money?
- Notice what emotions are coming up for you as you reflect on these questions.

MINDFUL MOMENT

Let's take a moment to pause and connect back to your body. Center yourself and calm your mind.

1. Take three deep breaths. Now, bring attention to your reflections. Notice the thoughts and feelings that are emerging for you.
2. Notice what is happening in your body. Notice any tension, pain, change in body temperature.
3. Think of a word that describes how you are feeling at this moment.
4. Take three more deep breaths and then continue to the Reflection Time section below.

Four Strategies to Support Healing From Financial Trauma

1. *Feel your feelings:* You may feel angry, ashamed, guilty, exploited, betrayed, and many other emotions when we experience financial trauma. Allow yourself to feel what you feel—it is a necessary part of the healing process.
2. *Reflect on your money messages:* Create space to reflect on the messages you received about money and finances and to examine how they impact the decisions you make now. Note which messages you might want to release and which ones you want to keep.
3. *Get informed:* Learn how money works. Instead of avoiding finances, dive in. Read books or blogs and listen to podcasts to expand your knowledge, and share that knowledge with others.
4. *Get support:* Work with a mental health therapist to help you deal with the harm, and consult a financial professional to help you get your finances back on track.

SHIFTING YOUR MINDSET TO BUILD WEALTH

A wealth-building mindset captures the beliefs, attitudes,
and actions that a person has about money and wealth.

The research shows that many therapists have a natural tendency to avoid money discussions, which has created an erroneous belief that doing good means that you cannot be wealthy (Britt, Klontz, Tibbetts, et al., 2015). Yet, therapists have shared with me a desire to start businesses so that they can build generational wealth. Generational wealth refers to "assets that you own entirely, as well as the knowledge needed to properly manage them, which are passed on through generations to come" (R. Taylor, personal communication, February 23, 2022). As therapists, you have a wealth of knowledge that you can tap into to build multiple streams of profitable income. You can do good and you can build wealth. It starts with developing financial literacy so that you understand money and finances. It also means feeling empowered to ask questions and to seek out experts who can help you shift your mindset and build healthy financial habits. Financial literacy is your key to a wealth-building mindset. Let's get started.

THE KLONTZ MONEY SCRIPT INVENTORY (KMSI)

On my journey to learn more about my relationship with money, I did what most psychologists do when they don't have an answer to a problem: research it. Through my research, I discovered this concept of money scripts, "unconscious trans-generational beliefs about money [that are] developed in childhood and drive adult financial behaviors" (Klontz & Britt, 2012) that was coined by Dr. Brad Klontz, psychologist. In addition, Klontz developed an assessment tool, the *Klontz Money Script Inventory* (*KMSI*; Klontz, Britt, Mentzer, et al., 2011), which helps to identify the money scripts people have. Of course I took the inventory, and I was blown away by my findings. It was right on target!

Klontz Money Scripts

Based on research by Klontz, Britt, Mentzer, and colleagues (2011), they developed four distinct money scripts, described below:

Money avoidance: As the name suggests, people who have a money avoidance script generally hold the belief that "money is the root of all evil." They view people with money as greedy, which turns them away from wanting money, and they believe that they do not deserve money. As a result, they may give away their money or engage in behaviors that keep them in a certain socioeconomic status.

Money focus (previously money worship): People with the money focus script tend to believe that more money leads to "power and happiness" and solves all their problems. They believe that there is never enough money, which can lead them to pursue earning money at the expense of family. People with money focus tend to live above their means and may carry a high debt balance. They may also loan out money to others, even when they cannot afford it.

Money status: People with the money status script believe that their self-worth is tied to their net worth. As a result, they focus on attaining external symbols of wealth and may overspend to achieve the lavish lifestyle they think they deserve, even if that means living above their means. They may be prone to excessive gambling and may be financially dependent on others.

Money vigilance: People with the money vigilance script tend to keep a close watch on what they spend and what they save. They are less likely to use credit cards and tend to have a higher financial health. However, their concern about money can create anxiety about their future and prevent them from enjoying their money.

Which of these four money scripts (summarized in Figure 3.1) would you assign to me? If you chose money vigilance and money avoidance, you would be correct.

Now, let's learn about *your* money script(s). As part of the process to improve your relationship with money, having information about your money script will be invaluable. To take the *KMSI*, go to https://www.bradklontz.com/moneyscriptstest and follow the directions to complete the inventory. After you complete the *KMSI*, your results will be emailed to you. In addition to the money script findings, the report includes activities that can help you shift your money script.

Money Vigilance	Money Status
• Focus on saving and frugality • Concerned about financial health • Excessive worry may prevent them from enjoying benefits of money	• Link self-worth to net worth • Prioritize outward displays of wealth • At risk for overspending and gambling
Money Avoidance	Money Focus
• Believe that money is bad and that wealthy people are greedy • Ignore financial statements and budgets • May give money away to stay at a certain income level	• Believe that money is the key to happiness • Focus is on earning more money because you can never have enough • May put work ahead of family and may have more credit card debt

Figure 3.1 Four money scripts, adapted from Britt et al. (2015)

Reflection Time

Let's take a few minutes to reflect on your money script. Find a quiet space, and respond to the journal prompts below:

- What is your money script?
- Was the information surprising? Did the *KMSI* affirm what you suspected about your money script?
- What thoughts or feelings are coming up now that you know your money script?
- How has your money script shaped your relationship with money in the past? Currently?
- What is one action step that you want to take to address your money script?

MONEY SCRIPTS, DECISION-MAKING, AND ENTREPRENEURSHIP

The Klontz money scripts framework is an extremely useful tool to increase awareness about your relationship with money. I have been using the money scripts with my coaching clients for a number of years, and I have observed the major shifts that people are able to make with their money relationship and mindset around money. After taking the *KMSI*, my coaching clients develop major insights into their money relationships and how these scripts can impact their personal lives and business finances. For many, finding out their money script is not usually a surprise, but the knowledge helps them gain insights into their decisions about money. Your relationship with money impacts your behaviors and how you make decisions about various aspects of our business.

Here are ways that your money script may impact your journey as an entrepreneur:

> *Money avoidance:* poor money management and accounting practices; unaware if the business is profitable
>
> *Money vigilance:* saving money at the expense of reinvesting money in the business to help it grow; prefer to do-it-yourself (DIY) versus hiring an expert
>
> *Money focus:* working long hours in the business because you prioritize earning money over spending time with family and friends
>
> *Money status:* overspending and high debt to project the image of a successful business

As I shared earlier, saving money was the message that I learned early in childhood, and it definitely followed me into adulthood and into my business management practices. Here are some ways it showed up:

- Saving money by building a website instead of hiring an expert. It took a significant amount of time for me to do this because it was not my expertise, time that I could have used on revenue-generating activities.
- Having poorly organized accounting and bookkeeping systems because I avoided dealing with money. My receipts were unorganized, and bank statements were not reconciled.
- I paid my bills, but I had no idea if my business was profitable.
- I held onto the revenue I earned rather than make decisions that could grow the business.

Learning about money scripts was transformative for me, both personally and as a business owner. I was able to see clearly how my early money messages were playing a major role in how I viewed my finances and how I was operating my business. It put a spotlight on some unhealthy patterns and practices that I was engaging in as a business owner. Once these behaviors became evident to me, it was hard to unsee them. Building on that awareness, I moved into action and started to take on new behaviors. I did not want to continue with these old patterns, and I was sure that these patterns would impact my long-term success if I did not make a change. I set goals and hired experts to support me.

Making the decision to let go of unhealthy behaviors is a process. It's important to be gentle with yourself. You may consider making one change at a time so that you do not overwhelm yourself with trying to change too much all at once. There may also be a mourning period as you reflect on ways that you were exploited or betrayed with money. If you have experienced financial trauma, consider meeting with a therapist who has experience in this area.

Reflection Time

Let's take some time to reflect on your money scripts, spending patterns, and decision-making. Find a quiet space, and respond to the following journal prompts:

- Think about a major decision that you have had to make recently. How did money play a role in your decision-making process? Did you delay over making the decision, or did you make the decision quickly? What money-related factors did you have to consider?
- How did your money script impact this decision?
- Upon reflection, are you satisfied with the decision you made? What might you have done differently in hindsight?
- Notice what emotions are coming up for you as you reflect on these questions.

MONEY MATTERS: KNOW YOUR NUMBERS

Therapists and Money

During my research about money, I came across some interesting findings about therapists and money. I was reading an article in the American Psychological Association's *Good Practice* magazine and the article title immediately caught my attention: "Why Is It Hard to Talk About Money?" (Delaney, 2016). I was intrigued. The article shared findings from Klontz and his associates' research about therapists and their relationship with money. It turns out that mental health professionals place a high value on helping others (doing good) and they see money in conflict with their role as helpers. Specifically, mental health professionals believe that people with money are greedy and typically exhibit the money avoidance script (Britt et al., 2015). This was an aha moment. Britt and colleagues (2015) actually note that the mental health field, as a whole, has avoided the topic of money.

It all made sense, because I would hear this money avoidance reflected as anxiety about money from my coaching clients:

- What should I charge for [service]?
- Should I take payment before or after the session?
- If I charge $XX per session, then I wouldn't be able to see the clients that I want to work with.
- What should I do if a client does not pay for a session?
- How do I talk to a client who owes me for past sessions?
- I have a client who frequently cancels late, but I have not charged the late fee. What should I do?

Learning about my money script and the money scripts associated with therapists brought about an urgency to shift my patterns. I noticed that I also had a scarcity mindset, which caused me to set safe goals for my business. Essentially, I was happy to have started a business but did not have any financial goals beyond that. When I eventually wanted to bring in more revenue, I had no clarity about what that even meant. It was like pulling on a loose thread: the whole thing just started to unravel. I knew that if I wanted to change my relationship with money, I would need to increase my knowledge about money, and I felt empowered to do just that.

BUILDING YOUR FINANCIAL FOUNDATION: KNOW YOUR NUMBERS

The first step to changing my unhealthy relationship with money started with knowing my numbers. Any business, no matter the industry, thrives on a solid financial foundation. Although many therapists of color may not have good money role models, may still be working through various traumatic experiences around finances, or may have a money avoidant script, holding unhealthy money relationships is a recipe for disaster in entrepreneurship.

Let's explore three areas in personal finances that will start to lay a solid foundation for your business and develop your financial literacy: credit score, net worth, and budgeting for your business.

Credit Score

A credit score, typically a FICO score, captures "how well you are managing your finances" and is represented by a 3-digit number. FICO (Fair, Isaac, and Company) calculations were developed by Bill Fair and Earl Isaac in 1956 (Common Future, 2021), and in 1995 FICO was adopted by Fannie Mae and Freddie Mac as part of the credit-lending process. Your FICO score is based on five categories (outlined below), and lenders use this data to evaluate your credit risk. In essence, it captures your capacity or likelihood to repay a loan, placing you into a rating category (see Table 3.1). The three major credit-reporting companies that supply credit reports and FICO scores to banks and other lending agencies are Equifax, TransUnion, and Experian.

FICO scores are based on five categories (Lake, n.d.):

Table 3.1 FICO credit scores and meanings

FICO Score	Rating	Description
<580	Poor	Risky borrower
580–669	Fair	Many lenders will still approve
670–739	Good	Most lenders will approve
740–799	Very good	Lenders like this score
800+	Exceptional	Lenders love this score

1. *Payment history* (35%) takes into account your ability to pay your bills on time. Late payments or failure to make payments lowers your score.
2. *Credit utilization* (30%) refers to the percentage of credit available to you that you are currently using.
3. *Credit history* (15%) considers how long you have established your credit; longer credit history is better.
4. *New credit and recently opened accounts* (10%) reflect inquiries about your credit or credit checks (e.g., credit card applications, car loans applications, etc.).
5. *Credit mix* (10%) refers to the different types of credit that you are using (e.g., mortgage, auto loan, credit card).

As you may have already guessed, credit scores have been part of a financial system that has had inequitable outcomes for Black people and other people of color. Due to systemic racism and a history of discriminatory practices in lending (e.g., redlining) and in employment, people of color continue to be disadvantaged by credit scores because of low rates of homeownership, employment instability, and predatory lending practices. As a result, low scores may make it more difficult to qualify for car loans, student loans, and mortgages that help build generational wealth.

Additionally, if you are considering funding your company with a business loan from a bank, most lending companies will run your personal credit first to assess your eligibility. As you can see, your credit score is a crucial number to know, understand, and improve.

As of this writing, you are entitled to a free credit report every year from the three credit-reporting services:

Experian: https://www.experian.com
TransUnion: https://www.transunion.com
Equifax: https://www.equifax.com

Net Worth

Net worth is the calculation of your assets minus your debt. Obtaining your net worth calculation gives you a big-picture view of your finances and can serve as a guide for your financial and retirement goals (see Appendix A for a sample net worth worksheet). Finding out your net worth may serve as motivation to increase your annual salary or increase your retirement savings. In addition, if you plan to obtain a business loan to raise capital for your business, lenders will use net worth calculations in their lending decisions.

In 2015, the Federal Reserve Bank of Boston, Duke University, and the New School published a report that showed racial differences in net worth of Boston residents (Muñoz, Kim, Chang, et al., 2015). Their findings were astounding: the average net worth of African Americans was $8, compared to their White counterparts, who had an average net worth of $247,000! This report highlighted the impact of systemic racism in the United States.

While calculating your net worth may be distressing for you, it is best to know your numbers so that you can do something about it—knowledge is power. Additionally, remember that there have been systematic policies determined to keep Black people at a financial disadvantage, so give yourself grace given this history.

Budgeting for Your Business

A budget is an estimate of your income and expenses for a determined period of time. It is crucial to understand your budget as a step to entrepreneurship. When you start your business, a goal might be to cover your salary. As a result, you will need to know your monthly/annual expenses, so that you can cover those expenses. Some people have a very close eye on their budget and expenses, and others do not. Because I was high on the money avoidant money script, I did not look very closely at my numbers. I paid my bills on time, but for a long time I had no idea what my monthly expenses were. That has changed.

Now, it is time to calculate your budget. Depending on how you plan to use the budget, you can calculate a weekly budget or a monthly one (see Appendix B for a template budget calculator, which you can use with your own budget numbers).

Take Action Exercise

- Contact one of the credit score reporting agencies (see the list above) to obtain your credit score and write it down.
- Calculate your net worth and write the number down.
- What are your monthly expenses?
- What is your monthly income?
- Are you operating your business at a deficit or a surplus?

Reflection Time

Let's take a few minutes to reflect on your numbers. Find a quiet space, and respond to the journal prompts below:

- What did you learn from each of your numbers: your credit score, your net worth, and your net income?
- What thoughts and emotions came up for you as you calculated these numbers?
- What is a new action that you will commit to doing to monitor your money?

CREATING NEW MONEY MINDSETS AND HEALTHY MONEY HABITS

Money EQ, or emotional quotient, taps into your emotional intelligence and relationship with money. When I lead workshops on our money EQ, I ask participants to share a word that describes their relationship with money. Here are some of the words frequently shared:

Complicated
Anxious
On a break
On and off

Often said with honesty and a bit of humor, these descriptors indicate a negative or challenging relationship with money. There is an awareness that the relationship is difficult, but often they lack knowledge about what they can do to change it.

Redefining your relationship with money is essential for entrepreneurship. Building a healthy relationship with money not only is important personally but also is critical for the success of your business.

A great place to start in creating new money mindsets is to reflect on the feedback you received from the *KMSI*. The results include actionable items that you can follow to shift your money script. For example, for my money vigilance script, one recommendation was to have fun with my money.

Developing healthy money habits starts with understanding your patterns and learning new tools to improve them. It is about leaning in and learning more, rather than avoiding your finances. It is about developing your financial literacy and enlisting experts who can help you along the way. Your habits and mindsets will not change overnight. It will take intentional and consistent work to make the shifts, but it is essential to operating a thriving business.

PERSONAL REFLECTION: A HEALTHIER MONEY RELATIONSHIP

On my entrepreneurial journey, I've had to reflect on my money scripts and adjust my money mindsets, specifically, shifting from a scarcity mindset to one of abundance. This is still a work in progress, but being intentional about this has helped me release the tight grip that I had on my money. In 2022, I took a week's vacation to rest and restore, alone. I went back to my home country, Barbados, and instead of staying in one of my parent's homes, I booked a hotel room. And . . . I chose an ocean view, which was the most expensive option. You should have seen me doing the calculations and trying to make that decision about spending a few hundred dollars more. I could afford it, but did I want to splurge that way? In the end I did—and LOVED it! By no means am I cured, but I am on the path to a healthier and joyful relationship with money, and that feels really good.

Mindset Work

- Describe the type of relationship you want to have with money as you grow your business.
- Now that you have a different understanding of your relationship with money, is there anything that you would change or do differently?
- What are three new habits or behaviors that you want to develop around your relationship with money?
- How will these new habits or behaviors impact your personal finances?
- How will they impact your business?
- What resources will you need to successfully change these habits or behaviors?

Who Can Help?

Below is a list of the types of financial professionals and how they support clients with their financial goals and financial health:

- *Business tax accountant*: prepares and files taxes for the business and ensures compliance with tax laws.
- *Bookkeeper*: tracks and records financial transactions (e.g., purchases, payments, receipts), reconciles bank statements, and prepares financial statements.
- *Financial coach*: helps people change their behavior around money and finances by developing healthy money habits (e.g., creating budgets) and providing accountability.
- *Financial advisor*: provides guidance on investment strategy, asset management, and retirement planning.
- *Financial planner*: takes a long-term view of financial goals and plans through investments, estate planning, educational funding, insurance, and retirement.
- *Financial therapist*: supports individuals in managing their financial stress and in understanding the beliefs and behaviors that impact their financial decision-making.

For more tools and resources for money management see Appendix D.

Take Action Exercise

- To lean into wealth-building activities, schedule a consultation with a financial planner and a financial advisor to better understand what they do and how they can help.
- To organize your finances, choose at least two accounting software products to explore and decide which one(s) work for you.
- If you do not have an accountant, schedule a consultation call with at least two tax accountants.

CHAPTER 3 MOMENTUM AND MINDSET CHECK

Money, money, money. This chapter was all about money and finances and you survived. You had to explore your relationship with money, reflect on early messages and past financial trauma, and take a deep dive into your personal finances, including your credit score and net worth. The exercises focused on cultivating a wealth-building mindset and reenvisioning your relationship with your money and finances. You uncovered your money scripts and explored how these scripts influence the decisions you make about money. It's a great opportunity to make any adjustments you need before you launch your business. Even if you have already launched your business, there are likely some needed adjustments you have to make. Now, you are on your way to creating a healthier and more beautiful relationship with money. Let's build some generational wealth.

- What is one takeaway that you have as you finish this chapter?
- What is a mindset shift that you have made after reading this chapter?

You Are the Brand

Harnessing the Power of Personal Branding

* *

You are a purpose-driven brand.

BRANDING WORKS

In some form or fashion, we are all consumers. In today's retail economy, with so many objects to consume: clothing, shoes, tech gadgets, food, cars, vacations, and more. With so many brands to choose from, companies have to fight hard for our attention.

Brands want us to connect to their brand story, to recognize products quickly when positioned with competitors, and to cultivate a feeling that we cannot live without a product, or to wonder how we survived before a particular product came along. Brands want our attention, our loyalty, and most importantly, our dollars. According to a HubSpot blog post by Forsey (2024), companies that sell directly to customers (i.e., business to customer or B2C) spend about 5–10% of their revenue on marketing, which includes branding. This can translate into millions of dollars, depending on the size of the company. The marketing budget is spent to create logos, taglines, compelling brand stories, and marketing content to share information about products and services. Marketing focuses on creating brand recognition and messaging to potential consumers or a target audience to use and purchase a product over their lifetime.

Reflection Time

Let's take a few minutes to reflect on some of your favorite brands, the brands you use in your daily life. Find a quiet space, and respond to the following journal prompts:

- What is a brand that you can't live without? What makes this brand stand out for you?
- What is the story behind the brand or company?
- How do you feel when you use the product or services?

Discovering the Power of Personal Branding

As a private practice owner, you will find marketing to be an important budget consideration. While it is unlikely that you will be investing millions into branding (at least not right away), it is important for you to think deeply about how you will stand out and how people will connect with you and what you offer. You may be asking yourself, *With the demand for therapists, do I really need to do anything to stand out?* I would argue that you do, and here is why: All therapists need to have a diversified stream of income that goes beyond direct clinical services. So, while therapy may be your primary income source, ensuring that you are offering different products and services is key to growing a profitable business. For that reason, it is important to ensure that you effectively define and communicate your personal brand, since it will apply to all these potential income streams.

Now I will ask you a question that I ask every time I lead a workshop on personal branding: Do you have a personal brand?

☐ Yes
☐ No

When I am with a live audience 99.9% of people in the room respond no. And my response to them is the fact that: "you *all* have a personal brand—the key is whether you are working your personal brand to your advantage."

So what is *personal branding*? It's the practice of intentionally, authentically, and consistently *communicating your value* to people who will make decisions about you. It is the *alignment* between how you want people to see you (or your business) and how they actually see you (or your business).

I first learned about personal branding in 2009 while participating in a leadership program in Boston for professionals of color by the nonprofit organization, The Partnership, Inc. Susan Hodgkinson, author of *The Leader's Edge* (2005), was our keynote speaker. During her talk, she spelled out her "5 Ps of Personal Branding": persona, products, packaging, promotion, and permission. I was blown away by her talk because it made me think about my career and why I was not getting opportunities I thought I should be getting. All the Ps hit home. She emphasized that your perception of yourself and what people actually experience when they interact with you needed *intentional* alignment. It was clear to me that I was definitely not communicating my skills or expertise to those around me, or to those who were making decisions about me, in part because of my cultural upbringing. I was raised in a culture where talking about your accomplishments was considered arrogant, and could bring misfortune. So, I had played the humble game. (Can you relate?)

Hodgkinson's talk helped me realize that I was not sharing any of my wins with my leaders, except by written annual evaluations, and I can honestly say that people did not see me as a leader because I was dimming my light. I realized that I needed to start shining. I knew it was in my power to change some of the circumstances around me, but it would not be easy. I would have to wrestle with some cultural teachings that were no longer serving me. I would have to learn how to leverage my experiences and skills to intentionally communicate my value. I knew that I would need to realign my personal brand.

Reflection Time

Let's take a few minutes to reflect on people with effective personal brands. Find a quiet space, and respond to these journal prompts:

- Name a few people who have strong personal brands that you admire.
- What do you admire about their brand?
- What are some of their personal qualities? What makes their brand stand out?
- What words or adjectives would you use to describe their personal brand?
- What is clearly and consistently communicated to others about their personal brand?

The Oprah Effect

Without fail, when I ask people to share names of people with personal brands that they admire, Oprah *always* makes the list. Over her 50+ year career, Oprah stands out as a person with an exceptional personal brand. I'm not sure whether she intentionally started that way or what coaching or mentoring she had along the way, but when you look at her brand, you can see its consistency, intentionality, and purpose. (Maybe one day, Oprah and I will get a chance to discuss this—my 11-year-old daughter randomly told me that she believes Oprah knows me! Hoping she is right.) Oprah started out as a news reporter and leveraged her skills and talent to become a news anchor, and then host of a talk show in Chicago, which later became the *Oprah Winfrey Show*. On her show Oprah often covered intimate and deeply vulnerable topics with her guests in front of a live studio audience, which was then broadcast to millions of people around the globe. These conversations were not just for entertainment but for education. She wanted the audience to learn how to improve their lives. Oprah was authentic and vulnerable on her show. Not only did she make her guests and audience cry with her soul-baring questions (as a therapist . . . I have much respect for that), but she cried along with them. She was also extremely generous and was known as a gift giver. All these are central to her personal brand. But a true marker of the impact of her brand is the power of Oprah endorsements. If she endorsed a product or service, you could guarantee that product would break all kinds of sales records. Her personal brand is all about positive vibes, bringing people together, trusted knowledge, and an abundance of vulnerability.

Another personal brand icon is Rihanna. (Fun fact: Rihanna and I are both Barbadian, and we attended the same high school, Combermere Secondary School—yes, I will unapologetically take any opportunity to talk about my home country, Barbados, and my alma mater!) Besides being an amazing performing artist, Rihanna has established herself as a skillful businesswoman. Launching the Fenty brand, she was able to capture a market segment that was largely ignored by major beauty brands. Rihanna was named the youngest self-made billionaire in 2022 (*Economic Times*, 2022; Sauer, 2022). She has also made strategic partnerships that help to build her personal brand and her companies.

These examples highlight the clarity, consistency, and intentionality that is required to unlock the power of your personal brand. Your personal brand is your superpower and the power is in your hand to cultivate it.

PERSONAL BRANDING FOR THERAPISTS

You may be thinking: *I'm a therapist, why do I need a personal brand?* I strongly believe that developing your personal brand will elevate the work you do as a mental health professional. When you have clarity about your personal brand, your ideal clients will easily find you and will help you stand out in the field.

A mental health professional that stands out in the personal branding area is Dr. Jessica Henderson Daniel. Her consistent and intentional messaging about the power of mentoring and her intentionality about creating mentoring groups for psychology interns, fellows, and psychologists inspired me deeply. She was my first Black psychologist supervisor. In 2017, she was elected as the first Black woman president of the American Psychological Association. Dr. Henderson Daniel has been consistent and intentional about mentoring. During her American Psychological Association presidential initiative, she focused on "giving psychology away" by making psychology accessible to the general community and even created an award, the Citizen Psychologist. I am proud to have been named a Citizen Psychologist by the Massachusetts Psychological Association in 2021. Dr. Henderson Daniel also extended her trust in me when she hired me to lead workshops for one of the ALANA mentoring programs she had started. As I shared in the Introduction and Chapter 1, the personal branding workshops led me to create a private practice course for therapists, which would eventually lead to this book—truly a full-circle moment.

Reflection Time

Let's take a few minutes to reflect on personal brands of mental health professionals. Find a quiet space, and respond to the journal prompts below:

- Name one or two mental health professionals whose personal brands have inspired you or that you admire.
- What do you admire about their brand?

Defining Your Personal Brand

As I stated earlier, you have a personal brand whether you have been intentionally communicating it or not. Being able to articulate your brand will give you a wealth of information that you can strategically use in your business. For example, it will help you to identify the services/products you want to offer, give direction for designing your office space, and most importantly, how to present yourself when you meet prospective clients. So, let's spend some time getting clarity about your personal brand so that you can communicate it with intentionality and consistency to your target audience. First, you can start with doing an honest reflection of your personal brand as it stands now. Don't try to fix or change anything.

In thinking about your personal brand, consider the energy or vibe you give off. You need to be aware of how people experience you and to assess if that truly reflects your spirit. Once you know what your vibe is, you can use it as part of your brand story (more on this below). You can lean into that style when you communicate with clients. For example, people often say that I have a calm, friendly, and knowledgeable vibe. I recall there was a time when I wanted to be perceived as more flashy and gregarious, but I realized that that's not who I am at my core. If I showed up that way with clients, it would not feel authentic to me or to them. You can use the following questions to guide you.

Reflection Time

Let's take a moment to reflect on your personal brand. Find a quiet space, and respond to these journal prompts:

- What words do people typically use to describe you?
- What words do you typically use to describe yourself?
- Is there any overlap with the words people use to describe you and the words you use to describe yourself?
- What do you want clients and employees to feel when they interact with you? What is the experience that you want people to have when they are in your company?
- What do you clearly and consistently communicate to others about your brand?

Now, I wonder what would happen if you were to ask people who are familiar with your brand these same questions. Would their responses be consistent with yours? Let's find out.

Exercise: Unveiling Your Personal Brand

This crowdsourcing exercise helps you obtain feedback about the effectiveness of your personal brand. I learned this exercise during a workshop led by Jennifer Witter as part of LIWP (JoWitter, 2019; personal communication). During this exercise, you will ask about 15–20 people who know you well (friends, family members, coworkers, and even supervisors) to give anonymous feedback about your personal brand. When you receive the feedback, compile the different responses and reflect on the information you receive. This exercise will give you excellent results on your personal brand and provide insights into how you can create a stronger personal brand. It also requires you to be vulnerable and to be open to hearing what changes your friends and colleagues may suggest. I invite you to maintain a nondefensive stance if you receive feedback that does not feel good.

The goal of this exercise is to gain insights into how others perceive your personal brand. Some of the feedback may be hard to hear, but these gems will guide you in crafting *the personal brand you desire*. Keep this goal in mind as you follow these instructions:

1. Create an anonymous survey with the following questions using software such as Google Forms, SurveyMonkey, or Jotform.
   - What am I known for?
   - What are some ways that I help people?
   - What is one thing I can improve?
   - What are three words you would use to describe me?
2. Send the survey to 15–20 people (the more responses the better).
3. Compile the responses for each question.
4. To display the adjectives that describe you, create a word cloud, and make the most commonly used words larger (see Figure 4.1 for a word cloud example). This will help you see the words that are frequently used to describe you.
5. Review the data and look for themes—what similarities (and differences) do you notice?

Reflection Time

Once you receive your feedback, take some time to reflect on it. Review it looking for clarity, consistency, and intentionality in how you communicate your brand. Find a quiet space, and use the journal prompts below as a guide:

- How do people describe your personal brand?
- Does your perception of your personal brand align with how others perceive your brand? Explain.
- What are one or two suggestions for improvement?
- What were the three most common words that people used to describe you? Was it surprising? Do you agree or disagree with the words they chose?
- Was there any feedback that was hard to receive?
- How would you describe your personal brand now? What is the messaging that you want to communicate to others?

Now that you have feedback about your brand, we will use this information to continue to map out your brand in Chapter 5. But first, let's explore how personal branding fits your cultural upbringing.

Figure 4.1 A word cloud of adjectives

LOOKING AT PERSONAL BRANDING THROUGH A CULTURAL LENS

Being exposed to Susan Hodgkinson's Five Ps of Personal Branding was a defining moment in my career journey. Two of the Ps, promotion and permission, shifted my mindset in major ways because they challenged how I was socialized to show up at work. Hodgkinson defined promotion as informing people about your achievements. She explained that if people are unaware of your accomplishments, they can't help to further your career (Hodgkinson, personal communication, 2009). In essence, you have to communicate your accomplishments and contributions to people who make decisions about you. Wow! This literally flipped how I approached my career from that point forward because it helped me to understand why my supervisors were not better champions for me. I was taught to be humble and not to brag about my accomplishments. If people do not know what I was doing, how could they elevate my work?

The other P, permission, Hodgkinson defined as the "internal confidence and core belief that you have important contributions to make, and therefore don't need to wait for anyone else to invite you to do so" (Hodgkinson, 2005)—not waiting for other people to give you the go ahead to do something. This concept was empowering because it reminded me that I have important contributions to make and if I wait for people to invite me to share my contributions, it will likely never happen. It is a great message to challenge feelings of imposter syndrome. Like promotion, the concept of permission was challenging because it also conflicted with my cultural values. I was also raised to defer to elders or bosses and to not interject into adult conversations ("stay out of grown folks' business"), but after years of socialization, it was hard to flip this in adulthood. But I was learning that I would need to.

Navigating the Cultural Dilemma of Self-Promotion

While the idea of promotion was eye-opening, it was still a big hurdle for me. In Barbados I was raised to be respectful and to defer to elders, and this was in conflict with U.S. workplace culture. For example, I was told explicitly by my parents and teachers that you do not go around telling people about all the wonderful things you have done or accomplished—nope! That would be poor taste and could not only invite misfortune into your life, but would be seen as arrogant. People from my community would often "put you in your place" or remind you of the importance of being humble if you stepped out of line. Given my upbringing, I knew it was going to be challenging to self-promote, but I also saw how it could help me to advance my career. I knew I would need to find ways to share my contributions with others that also honored my cultural values. Eventually, I did find methods of self-promotion that felt genuine to me and allowed me to share what I was doing with others. I can definitely say that this shift led to some bigger changes in my career. I felt empowered to ask for things that I needed in order to be successful, either from supervisors or even from myself. As I started to be more vocal, more opportunities came my way.

Your culture likely influences how you feel about self-promotion. I have found that many people of color, especially those from the Southern United States (or those who were raised by parents or grandparents from the South) and immigrants (or who were raised by immigrants), received messages in childhood that talking about your strengths and accomplishments is bad—not only does it disregard the community's and/or family's contribution to your success, but it can cause people to be jealous of you, which could lead to people wishing you misfortune. I've also come to understand that downplaying your talents and accomplishments is the result of generational trauma from the violence of enslavement. In the face of cruel practices that involved separating family members from each other, our ancestors learned that standing out in any way ran the risk of having family members being harmed or being sold off to other enslavers. So for many, the idea of self-promotion, which triggers this deep trauma wound, may be especially challenging.

For a long time in my career I avoided self-promotion. I worked hard. I took initiative to create programs that I thought would benefit our clients, trainees, and the institution. I worked late hours, often taking work home. I assumed that people would take notice of my efforts, but it didn't happen. Because of my upbringing, I felt that some misfortune would fall upon me if I "tooted my own horn." So I stayed silent and kept working. Honestly, some frustration and resentment started to build as my supervisors did not acknowledge my hard work or contributions.

Reflection Time

Let's take some time to reflect on how your salient social identities (e.g., race, ethnicity, gender, immigration status, sexual orientations, religion) intersect with personal branding. Find a quiet space, and respond to the following journal prompts:

- What are your salient social identities and what childhood messages did you receive about sharing your accomplishments?
- If you were to share three of your accomplishments from the past year or two, what would you share?
- Who would you share these accomplishments with in your professional life? How would you share them (e.g., verbally, email)?
- How many of these accomplishments have you shared with family members? On your social media platforms?
- If you have not shared with anyone, what is holding you back?

As I mentioned earlier, the five Ps shifted my mindset about my career and helped me to be more strategic with my career moves. So when Dr. Jessica Henderson Daniel asked me to lead a workshop for psychology interns and fellows at the Harvard Medical School, I knew I had to talk to them about personal branding, because it was something that was missing from my training and my professional development. Like me, the personal branding really hit home for them. During these personal branding workshops, I often saw people struggle with the idea of talking about their accomplishments—it was undoubtedly the concept they struggled with the most. I would see people visibly cringe, tense up, give me the deer-in-headlights look, or actively shake their heads no. It was definitely not something that they normally did. Like me, their cultural values created an obstacle to sharing their achievements or contributions. But they also saw how it was holding back their career advancement. They could see the differences between people who were encouraged to talk about their accomplishments, even the not-so-big ones.

Self-Promoting Versus Bragging

One of the biggest fears that I had and that participants in the personal branding workshops shared is their worry about coming off as bragging or being arrogant.

Promoting your expertise is *not* bragging. It may feel like it, but it is not. So if promotion or self-promotion isn't bragging . . . what is it?

Let's get clear about what bragging is. Simply put, *bragging* is showing off—showing off things you have, things you have achieved, places you have been, people you have met (e.g., name dropping)—in a way to elevate yourself *over* someone else. Think back to childhood and someone saying, "I have more _____ (fill in the blank) than you." One child is letting the other child know that they have more and are therefore better. Bragging can be viewed as an over-the-top or excessive way of telling others about your achievements, often with an intention about making yourself look better than someone else. It can feel competitive. It may be a defense mechanism for people who feel insecure or need frequent validation. Whatever the reason, it is a big turnoff, and many of us worry about being that obnoxious person. I venture to say that if you are mindful of bragging and thoughtful about how to talk about your wins, it is highly unlikely that you will be sseen as bragging about what you have done.

Promotion, in contrast, is about sharing information about your contributions and achievements so that people can make an informed decision when they choose to work with you. It's about informing others of your expertise and how you can help them best. As you prepare to step into leadership or entrepreneur roles, customers need to know that you are qualified and have the expertise they need. In order to embrace the idea of promotion or self-promotion, it will be helpful to redefine how you see these concepts.

Making Self-Promotion a Professional Practice

For people who struggle with promoting or sharing their accomplishments with others, the following strategies will give you practical ways to get comfortable with promoting your achievements:

1. *Focus on client outcomes:* Focusing on how you help people, and the relief that people have felt as a result of using your product or service, is one way to reframe your thinking about self-promotion. Example: As a psychologist with over 25 years of experience working with children and families in hospital settings, I help children reduce their anxiety about medical procedures, making the process much calmer for children, their doctors/medical team and their families.

Here the experience is mentioned, but it is connected to how these experiences help clients.

2. *Focus on your story or your family story:* Document the reasons you are starting a business. For many BIPOC clinicians, it is to pay off student debt, to build general wealth for your family, to have more autonomy in your caseload, or better health for yourself. Reflecting on your purpose can serve as a reminder why you are engaged in the work and you may also notice similarities between you/your family and the clients you want to serve.

3. *Be honest about what your products/services can or cannot do:* Many times when we think of selling, we think of people who are overselling their product or are trying to take advantage of their clients. (I hope that is not your motive or intention!) If you are honest about what you have to offer, then you won't feel sleazy at all.

4. *Maintain a growth mindset:* Self-promotion is a skill you can develop. The more you practice, the easier it gets.

CHAPTER 4 MOMENTUM AND MINDSET CHECK

You have a personal brand! Hooray. This chapter was focused on techniques to help you become more conscious of your personal brand and to identify ways to bring your personal brand in alignment with how you want other people to see you. The exercises helped you articulate your vibe and use feedback from people in your network to refine your personal brand. You also explored how your cultural values can play a role in how you talk about your achievements with others. You reflected on ways to reframe self-promotion so that you can message how to let clients know your expertise without feeling that you are bragging.

- What is one takeaway that you have as you finish this chapter?
- What is a mindset shift that you have made after reading this chapter?

The Personal Branding Blueprint

It's All in Your V.O.I.C.E.

....

Find your personal brand . . . it's in your story.

BRANDING YOUR VOICE

Branding is the language you use to speak with your audience, which means it is about capturing and sharing your *voice*. It's the way that you message your values, how you speak specifically to your target audience, and how you use your story and experiences to connect with your ideal clients. That's all *your* voice! Your personal brand speaks for you. In today's market, customers want to know the person behind the brand. This can feel very tricky for therapists who are usually trained to be blank slates and to avoid publicity. Your clients and customers want to connect with you and hear your stories, which is often in conflict with your professional ethics and training. Many training programs emphasize that self-disclosure is to be avoided in therapy. However, one of the first mental health professionals that I remember breaking the mold is Dr. Phil McGraw, who hosted the television show *Dr. Phil*. It was mind-blowing to see how he challenged what our training had previously said we could not do. He opened a door that has forever changed how mental health professionals engage with the general public.

Currently, the field is going through some major shifts with the rise of therapists using social media platforms like TikTok, Instagram, and YouTube to connect with their audiences. Additionally, the decolonizing therapy movement teaches us that self-disclosure is a culturally affirming practice, and that hiding behind the cloak of "neutral therapist" (which is a fallacy) is ineffective. Bringing your full self into the therapy room actually fosters a deeper therapeutic alliance, especially when working with Black and BIPOC clients. Similarly, as you build a BIPOC-owned businesses, sharing more about yourself and your brand will help you cultivate deeper connections with your clients.

As a child, I was reserved and I often found that my voice was silenced or devalued in many spaces. However, moving to the United States started my journey of using my voice to advocate for my needs, and for others' needs too. Career-wise, I also realized that if I did not share my voice, I would be overlooked (as I discussed in Chapter 4). Sharing my voice at work and in professional spaces became a goal. I would challenge myself to speak up and to add my perspective in meetings, even if my heart was pounding in my chest. Now, as an entrepreneur, I relish the opportunities to share my expertise and to use my personal brand to advocate for mental health access and for mental health professionals. That's why the V.O.I.C.E. acronym for personal branding is especially meaningful for me.

Let's break down the five components of personal branding I developed, V.O.I.C.E.:

V = Vision
O = Offerings
I = Image
C = Clients
E = Expression

V IS FOR VISION

A vision is an idea or plan that you have about your future. As it relates to business, it is a plan or goal you have for establishing a venture to address a need or problem. I believe that your vision is the necessary foundation for the success of any business. Crafting a *vision statement*, a written version of your vision, incorporates identifying the values, overarching goals, and impact you want to make. A vision statement for your personal brand and your business can serve as a compass that will keep you focused when you are pulled off course. Your vision statement should be bold, inspiring, and focused on the impact you plan to make, now and in the future.

When I started InnoPsych, my vision was to *disrupt racial inequities in mental health by making it easier and faster for people of color to find therapists of color.* While this vision has remained the same, it has evolved to a larger goal of creating a platform that provides transformative and inclusive mental health content and experiences for individuals, institutions, and communities worldwide. I am passionate about this vision and have built a social enterprise around it.

Writing your vision statement may seem intimidating at first. However, I want to assure you that you can do it. I believe that your vision statement already lives within you. With a few targeted prompts, using a special formula that I developed for entrepreneurs, you will have a bold, inspiring, and impactful vision statement that will guide you during your entrepreneurial journey.

The Vision Statement Formula

Your vision statement is a combination of your self-fulfilling purpose in life, the values that guide you, and the goals you wish to achieve in life. Simply stated, your vision statement is the integration of your purpose, values, and goals:

Vision Statement = Purpose + Values + Goals

Purpose. Your reason for being, your motivations, aspirations, and intentions. Through the entrepreneurial lens, purpose may encapsulate what guided you to the mental health field and the impact that you want to make in the world. A few years ago, I was diving deep into learning about entrepreneurship and stumbled on a book, *Start With Why* by Simon Sinek (2009). In this book, Sinek explained that many companies talk about what they do (products/services) and how they do it (processes), but few share the why. The why can be the story that inspired you to start your business, or the impact that you want to make in the world. He explained that the why, your purpose, is a powerful way to emotionally connect to customers.

In Japan, the concept of *ikigai,* or "life's purpose," has contributed to longer life expectancy and a higher satisfaction with life (Tamashiro, 2018). We achieve our life's purpose when our passion, mission, occupation, and profession are in alignment. Figure 5.1 is an image of *ikigai* that shows its interlocking components:

- What you love: Passion and Mission
- What you are great at: Passion and Profession
- What earns you money: Profession and Vocation
- What the world needs: Vocation and Mission

I am aware that, for many therapists, the mental health field has felt like a calling—the thing that you wanted to do since you were a child. That was definitely true for me. For others, the mental health field is a second or even third career. For most of you, I can imagine that being a therapist or in the mental health field feels like a life's purpose. The following exercise will guide you in articulating your purpose.

Ikigai = Your Life's Purpose

Figure 5.1 The interconnected elements of *ikigai Source:* Charmain F. Jackman and Demp Agency, adapted from "Ikigai" by Emmy van Deurzen, licensed under CC-BY-SA-4.0

Exercise: What Is Your Life Purpose?

To help you summarize your purpose, reflect on the prompts below. Write down your answers so you can revisit them later.

- What led you to the mental health field? Who or what inspired you?
- What do you enjoy about being a mental health professional?
- How do you want to help clients? Why is this important to you?
- What is the problem that you want to solve?
- What impact do you want to make in the mental health field?
- What is motivating you to become an entrepreneur? What would happen if you didn't pursue your business idea?
- In one brief sentence, what is your purpose for starting your business?

As you reflect on these prompts, I anticipate that your purpose will start to unfold. Writing it out is essential for *you*, not just for your clients. Connecting back to your *why* is a powerful tool for growing your business and helping you stay on your journey.

Values. Values are the ideals that guide your decision-making, communication, and how you prioritize work and family responsibilities. It is important to define your core values as they will undoubtedly connect to your business. Articulating your values is a great way to gain a better understanding of what drives you and the guiding principles that will be the foundation of your business.

Exercise: What Do You Value?

Reflect on the prompts below, and write down your answers so you can revisit them later.

- Write down six core values that are important to you.
- Why are these values important to you?
- How do these values guide your decision-making?

Goals. Goal-setting is necessary for any successful entrepreneur. Goals set the direction for the business, and if followed, will help you stay on track. Consider the goals you have for yourself and your business. (Chapter 11, on growing your business, will explore how to create SMARTIE goals—goals that are specific, measurable, attainable, relevant, time-bound, inspirational, and equitable—and how to have accountability partners to help you accomplish your goals.)

Exercise: What Are Your Goals?

Dreams without goals are just dreams.
    —Denzel Washington

- What are your legacy goals? At your 90th birthday, what would you want to have accomplished?
- What are three to five long-term (5 to 10 years) goals for your business? For each goal, state why this goal is important.
- What is a goal that you want to accomplish in the next 12–15 months that will move your business forward? Why is this goal important to you?

PERSONAL REFLECTION: MY VISION

When I was about 15 years old, I created a vision for my future 30-year-old self. (Wow, 30 seemed so old back then! Oh, the innocence of youth.) My dream at 15 years old was clear: by the time I reached 30 years of age, I wanted to earn a PhD in psychology, and I wanted to work in a high school so that I could be a trusting adult that young people could come to when they were going through difficult times in their lives (*my purpose*). So when I was 32, and I landed a job working at a high school in a hospital-community partnership, I was ecstatic. But, fast forward 15 years, and I was still in the same position, with one promotion. I had a career, I was in my dream job, and it is very likely that I would have retired from that job, had I not applied to the American Psychological Association's Leadership Institute for Women in Psychology (LIWP).

As I went through this year-long leadership program, I came to realize that I had stopped visioning about my career and my life—I was stuck.

Talking to other women psychologists and hearing their journeys made me realize that there was much more I could do with my expertise. I had accumulated a host of skills and experiences, and I could share them with a broader audience. I remember vividly the last day of the LIWP program, when we wrote out our short- and long-term goals. One of *my goals* was to start a company that provided access to mental health resources for people of color. As I started to share my goals, I burst out crying because I knew that I would need to leave my 9-to-5 to follow my new vision— saying it out loud made it very real and very scary!

I was living my best life, or so I thought, in my dream job, but my dream had not progressed beyond age 30, and now I wanted more. I wanted to do more, and I wanted to have a greater impact in my community. I wanted to help people (my values) in my community find tools for healing and thriving. I had to rethink my vision and dream bigger and bolder than I did before. I had gained unique experiences, and it was time to share (my values) these experiences with the world.

You know, sometimes, you do not even realize how small your dreams are until you are challenged to dream bigger. It was time for a vision refresh.

Vision Statement. Now you have all the elements to assist you in creating your amazing vision statement:

Vision Statement = Purpose + Values + Goals

A great hack for writing your vision statement is to use an action verb related to your purpose and to combine it with the focus of your values and your desired impact, outcome, or results—your goals:

Action Verb + Focus + Impact/Outcome/Results

For example,

- *InnoPsych:* to disrupt (verb) racial inequities in mental health (focus) and promote positive mental health outcomes for communities of color (outcome).

- *Boston Children's Hospital:* to advance (verb) pediatric care (focus) worldwide (impact).
- *Google:* to provide access (verb) to the world's information (focus) in one click (result).
- *Amazon:* to build (verb) a place where people can come to find and discover (focus) anything they might want to buy online (outcome).

Now, it's your turn to use this formula to create your vision statement. Review what you have written about your purpose, your values, and your goals, and brainstorm your action verb, your focus, and your impact/outcome/results. Then collate these elements into your vision statement.

Exercise: Write Your Vision Statement

Use the vision statement equation above to write your vision statement.

1. Revise your vision statement until you feel ready to share it.
2. Share your vision statement with your network to get some additional feedback. It would also be great to obtain feedback about how it resonates with your ideal clients.
3. Use the feedback to refine your statement.

FOUR WAYS TO BRING YOUR VISION TO LIFE

Visioning is a powerful tool for letting the universe know what you want. When you are clear about what you want, ask for what you need. I have heard amazing stories from fellow therapists and entrepreneurs who have used a range of strategies to help realize their visions. See some examples below:

1. *Manifesting:* This is a way of achieving your goals, wishes, and desires by forming a communication synergy between yourself and the universe. It is about getting clear with yourself on what you truly want and then clearly, consistently, and intentionally sharing and embodying that desire (see Appendix D for some helpful resources on

manifesting). It is also a way of visualizing your vision and goals, and keeping your focus and attention on these goals.

2. *Tap into your faith*: If you are a person of faith, use your faith to share your vision with your higher power. There may also be readings, scriptures, prayers, and praises that you can tap into to feel supported with your vision and goals. For example, Steve Harvey, comedian and television show host, shared how he has tapped into his faith to achieve success by using two scriptures (Harvey, 2019; for the scriptures, see Appendix D). One strategy he suggests is to write a list of 300 things that you want in life. Harvey acknowledged that it will be hard, but he sees it as a way to build the practice of asking for what you want.

3. *Vision boards*: These are visual representations of your vision, goals, and desires using images and words of inspiration. Figure 5.2 gives an example of a vision board (for instructions on creating vision boards, see Appendix C).

4. *Synergy maps*: A type of mind map that provides a visual display of the relationships and interconnections among different business entities or products and services that an entrepreneur owns or plans to launch in the future (Appendix C for has instructions for creating synergy maps). Think family genogram, but for different services or products for your business. Purportedly, Walt Disney first created a business synergy map on a beverage napkin; and Issa Rae, creator of the TV series *Insecure*, also created a synergy map that shows how her different businesses connect and support each other (Trapital, 2020). (Images of both synergy maps can be found online.)

O IS FOR OFFERINGS

How will you solve your clients' problems? Your offerings are the solutions that will address your ideal clients' problems. Generally speaking, these are your products and services. As an entrepreneur, your offerings are your special sauce. Your clinical training plus your lived experiences (your wisdom) makes your services unique. (Sometimes, we place so much emphasis on our clinical training that we can forget that our lived experiences are valuable.) Your lived experiences enhance your clinical expertise. Your special sauce or your wisdom allows you to develop a niche area, and creating products from your wisdom will support your business's growth (more in Chapter 11).

PERSONAL REFLECTION: MY OFFERINGS

After completing my doctorate training in child and adolescent psychology, I had an opportunity to obtain additional training through a postdoctoral fellowship in forensic psychology. This was perfect for me, as my doctoral thesis explored justice-involved youths' perceptions of police officers (Jackman, 2002). During my training at the juvenile court clinic, only one multicultural training was offered, and it did not address concerns that court-involved clients were facing as they engaged with the court system. I had also just finished adapting a parenting curriculum for Haitian and Spanish-speaking families, so I had all this knowledge relevant to our work. I decided to create a workshop for our department that focused on conducting evaluations with racially and linguistically diverse clients. Additionally, in my private practice, attorneys began referring cases to me that involved Black or multiracial families because of my experience and, honestly, because of my identity as a Black woman.

Figure 5.2 Dr. Charmain's 2021 vision board

I was able to leverage my experiences in forensic psychology and curriculum development with my interest working with communities of color to create a niche facilitating workshops that address the needs of our court clinic clients. This expertise also increased my visibility and led to more referrals for evaluations and speaking opportunities on topics related to racial and ethnic diversity and forensic psychology.

Exercise: What Is Your Special Sauce?

Let's explore how your lived experiences enhance your clinical expertise—your special sauce, or your wisdom. Reflect on the prompts below, and write down your answers so you can revisit them later.

- What expertise have you gained from your clinical training?
- What client concerns do you want to solve?
- What lived experiences do you have that are relevant to your clinical expertise or to the clients you plan to work with?
- What is your special sauce? What makes you uniquely you?
- What are the solutions you plan to offer?
- Write down five ways that set you apart from other therapists, and think about how they can fit into your practice or business plan.

I IS FOR IMAGE

The brand image is the visual representation of a brand's values, mission, and vision and is used to cultivate an emotional connection with current and potential clients. Companies often use symbols (e.g., logo, colors, and fonts), communications (e.g., brand story, case studies), and customer experiences (e.g., testimonials and reviews) to foster the relationship with their potential client base. The stronger the connection, the more likely clients will purchase your goods or services and develop a long-term buying relationship.

You Are the Brand Ambassador

As the owner of the business, you are also a primary ambassador for the brand. Like it or not, people look to you as a model for the brand. Your physical appearance, how you speak, and what you say are all relevant for your personal brand.

As such, how you show up, in person and in your *online spaces*—what, where, and how you post and comment—can impact the brand image.

THREE TIPS FOR MANAGING YOUR ONLINE PRESENCE

1. *Everything is public:* When you engage online, stay consistent and true to the brand values you developed earlier in this chapter. Always remember that everything is public. Your potential clients, sponsors, and partners will research you as they decide whether or not to work with you, so keep it on brand.

2. *Audit your online presence:* I always recommend that clients conduct a web search of their name to see what images or stories pop up. You may want to close accounts that you are no longer using, upload more on-brand images, and archive or delete images or posts that no longer align with your brand. There are companies that will conduct a social media cleanup for you, so consider outsourcing this role if you think it would be helpful.

3. *Be mindful of the images you post:* When you put your images on a website or out into social media, be mindful of who can see these images and how it could impact your brand. For event promotions and directories, use a professional headshot (see Figure 5.3 for examples of good and bad headshots). You don't have to spend a lot of money, but headshots look so much better when they are done by a good photographer, either in the studio or outdoors.

   When you show up for in-person events, be aware that you represent your brand. Is there a message that you want to convey with you style? I love wearing African prints because they connect to Inno-Psych's mission.

Reflection Exercise: Designing Your Brand Image

Your brand identity helps capture those visual images that are associated with your brand. Tap into your five senses to start to visualize the look and feel of your brand.

- What images, symbols, and sounds represent your vision and values?
- What colors resonate with your values, vision, and expertise?
- What elements or symbols communicate your solutions to your clients' problems?
- What elements or symbols communicate the experiences that your clients will have when they engage with you?

There is a psychology about all the aspects that go into visual designs. Color psychology explores how different colors can impact how we think, feel, and act. For example, green conveys peace, healing, and nature, while blue conveys intelligence, trust, and productivity. Similarly, *typography*, the art and science of how text is displayed, examines how font styles impact our emotional response. For example, *script* is associated with fun, playfulness, and creativity.

Working with a graphic designer can help you create your brand ID. While designers will have their own ideation process, doing your own reflection can help you kickstart the process. For example, a *mood board* (see Figure 5.4) is a collage of elements that you identify with your brand such as images, symbols, colors, words, font styles, and patterns and that represent your brand's values, mission, inspirations, and aspirations. My mood board (below) captures elements of Africa that I wanted to center in my brand design. These elements led to the use of the Sankofa bird in InnoPsych's logo (see innopsych.com for the Story of Sankofa).

Take Action Exercise

- Create a mood board that captures the images, colors, symbols, words, and feelings that you want to communicate with your brand.
- Identify two or three graphic designers who could help you design your logo and other marketing brands. You can share this mood board with the creators you hire.
- Identify potential graphic design software you can use to brainstorm and execute ideas (see Appendix D for a list of resources).

Creating your brand identity involves spending time reflecting on the elements you will use to create a compelling visual design—this is the *what* of brand identity, to go along with the *why* of your brand story. Once you have your visual images you'll want to showcase them.

Figure 5.3 The ideal headshot. *Left:* This headshot has poor lighting, with reflections in the glasses, and a busy background. In this selfie I am not looking at the camera, and I captured someone else in the background, who is partially cropped out. *Middle:* This headshot is taken in an indoor studio. It has a neutral background and excellent lighting. I am looking at the camera, and a colorful outfit balances neutral background. *Right:* This professional headshot, taken outdoors, has a calming, neutral background. With excellent lighting, you can clearly see I am looking directly at the camera. *Source:* Middle and right photos by Alexandria Pierre-Etienne

Branding is everywhere. You can showcase your brand images on a website, business cards, social media platforms, products and merchandise, offices, video conferencing, and the list continues. The key factor here is for you to have consistency across all of your different marketing channels, so that the message is clear, consistent, and uncomplicated.

Reflection Time

Let's take a few minutes to reflect on customer experiences. Find a quiet space, and respond to the journal prompts below:

- What do clients say about their experiences working with you (e.g., unsolicited comments; testimonials and reviews [more in Chapters 6 and 12])?
- What have supervisors said about your work with clients?

C IS FOR CUSTOMERS*

No business can survive without customers. To have profits and achieve success, you need customers, plain and simple. The more specific you are about your ideal client, the more successful you can be. It is your job, as the entrepreneur, to learn as much as possible about your clients' pain points, demographics, professions, and spending habits, so that you can create an effective marketing strategy. Knowing everything about your ideal clients will help you craft engaging messages that speak directly to the clients' needs.

Here is the rub: Many newly minted entrepreneurs, in the pursuit of revenue, will cast a wide net, with a goal to just sell their products or services to anyone and everyone. On face value, this seems like a great approach—who wouldn't want everyone in the world as a customer? However, if your message is too broad, then it will not speak to your ideal client or to their experiences, and it will attract no one. As a result, you will have to work harder to convert potential clients in to paying customers.

Defining Your Ideal Client

When I first opened my practice in 2005, I had a logo, but I didn't have a brand. I cast my net wide and was open for business to anyone who found me. I was

Figure 5.4 Sample mood board

* "customers" and "clients" are used interchangeably

fortunate to get some referrals from colleagues, but overall this was a limiting sales strategy. Here's why:

As time went on, I realized there was a certain clientele that I did my best work with and whom I really enjoyed working with. I also had clients who, in retrospect, were not a good fit, but *I was chasing the dollar.* What I came to learn was that I could build a practice around the clients that I did my best work with, clients I enjoyed working with (bonus), and could still have a profitable business.

I learned the hard way that chasing the dollar and taking any client can be detrimental to your brand. Specifically, if you are not doing your best work with these "non-ideal" clients it will show, and they will not send referrals to you or, worse, may share poor reviews with people in their network or online. However, when you work with clients who are a great fit, then the client referrals will come. Your ideal clients are people who you do your best work with.

Creating a Customer Persona

When you are in alignment with your brand and are clear
about your ideal clients, the business works.

The *customer persona* is an amalgam of customers with similar interests and behaviors into one identifiable persona or avatar (see Figure 5.5). (Chapter 6 on selling discusses how to engage your ideal clients.)

As an entrepreneur, you get to decide who will be your ideal client. Having a deep understanding of the clients' problems will also help when you create the right messaging for them.

It is also important to get a holistic view of your ideal clientele. Beyond the demographics, such as age, racial identity, gender identity, you will want to learn about their values and behaviors, salary, preferred social media platforms, shows they watch, and their professional stage. You'll also want to learn personal information such as how they spend their time. For example, how do they travel to work or school; what do they listen to for entertainment, where do they like to shop, and so on? This information gives you a wealth of information about potential clients and strategies to reach your ideal clientele.

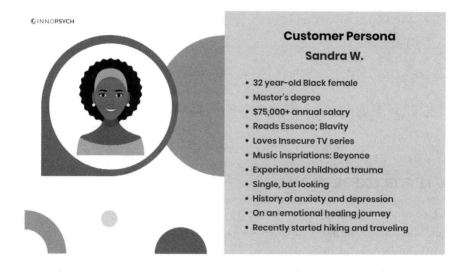

Figure 5.5 Customer profile of a potential client *Source:* Charmain F. Jackman and Demp Agency

Exercise: Describing Your Ideal Client

Think about the clients that you do your best work with or get the best results from. Who are they? Now take a few minutes to create your ideal client profile, by completing the information below. Your goal, in the end, is to be able to describe what a day in the life of your ideal client looks like.

- Age
- Racial identity
- Ethnic identity
- Gender Identity
- Language(s) spoken
- Education level
- Occupation
- Industry
- Salary range
- Geographical location
- Marital status
- Parenting status

- Number of children (ages)
- Favorite activities
- Problems/concerns
- Social media use
- Commute/transportation method
- Favorite shops
- Other:

E IS FOR EXPRESSION

Once you have all the pieces together, it's time to express your brand. Let everyone know about business—express yourself!

If the thought of that scares you, you are like 99.9% of therapists of color. However, getting comfortable telling others about your work and your expertise is a necessary skill for any business owner. In Chapter 6, we will discuss how to talk about your business confidently with an elevator pitch. An elevator pitch is a short prepared summary of your business, which is especially useful when attending networking events. In addition to talking about your business, you will have to prepare written materials such as email newsletters, a therapist statement, and website copy (all of which can be helped with artificial intelligence [AI]).

Reflection Time

Let's take a few minutes to reflect on expressing your brand to your clientele. Find a quiet space, and respond to the following journal prompts:

- How can you let people know about your expertise?
- How do you feel when you are talking about your business with family and with friends?
- Think about the clients that you do your best work with or get the best results. Who are they?
- How do you feel talking to strangers about your business?

Put It All Together: Owning Your Brand Story

Now that you have worked through all the elements of crafting your personal brand, let's put it all together into a brand story. Your brand story is the narrative that communicates why the business exists. For therapists, the brand story is *your* story. People want to get to know you. They want to know that you are someone that they can trust, that you have the skills to help them solve the concerns that they have. This applies to therapy, consulting, and even for speaking opportunities.

In developing my brand story for InnoPsych, I had to reflect on what motivated me to start the company. Unfortunately, as I mentioned in an earlier chapter, it was not a happy time in my life, which required me to be vulnerable. However, it was also the catalyst for starting my business, and it is something that resonates with others. By sharing my personal struggle with finding a therapist of color, it communicates to my target audience that I had direct experience with the problem that they are having and that I can empathize with their journey. The Personal Branding Blueprint: VOICE offers the steps needed to identify the major elements of your brand story. Now, it's time to create you own brand story.

Reflection Time

Let's take some time to reflect on your brand story. Find a quiet space, and respond to the journal prompts below:

- Why are you interested in starting this business? Include a personal connection to your business idea.
- Was there a hardship that you experienced that led you to starting this business?
- What is a challenge that you faced or that your clients faced that you will be addressing in your business (include any personal connections, words, or phrases that will resonate with your ideal client)?
- How will your business relieve a pain point for your clients?
- How did you come up with this solution, and how do you know it will work?
- What comes up for you when you think about sharing personal information about yourself?
- What information feels comfortable to share with your audience?

As an example, consider this brand story for my company InnoPsych.

INNOPSYCH'S ORIGIN STORY

InnoPsych was born from my experiences and challenges searching for a therapist. I was going through a difficult time in my marriage, and I wanted to work with a Black woman therapist. As I searched through website after website, I found there were either too few therapists listed to choose from and/or there was no way to filter the lists by race. The process was frustrating and cumbersome. When I did find someone who fit my criteria, they did not call back, were "not taking new clients," or they did not take my insurance. I just knew that there needed to be a simpler and faster way for people of color to find therapists of color, and I decided that I was going to create it! Not only did I want to create a directory of therapists of color, but I also wanted to facilitate the process for therapists of color to launch their own private practice, in order to increase the pool of therapists of color in the field.

In this description, you can see the struggle I went through to find a therapist at a challenging time in my life. I also included all the roadblocks I faced in searching for a therapist because these are also roadblocks other people have shared that they have experienced in their search. When I share this story I know that it resonates with others, which is also a major selling point.

Exercise: Developing Your Brand Story

Use these steps to develop your brand story. We will use this brand story in Chapter 6 on promoting your practice.

1. Write out your brand story in under 200 words. Revise it until you feel ready to share it.
2. Once you have completed your company's brand story, share it with your network to get some additional feedback.
3. Then use the feedback to refine your story. We will be using this brand story in Chapter 6.

CHAPTER 5 MOMENTUM AND MINDSET CHECK

Your story needs to be told. Using the Personal Branding Blueprint—V.O.I.C.E.—gives you tools that you can use to craft a compelling brand story and engage in authentic communication with your audience. You created a vision statement, developed a customer persona, curated your product and service offerings, and visualized the brand colors and logo. You are ready to unapologetically share your brand with others.

- What is one takeaway that you have as you finish this chapter?
- What is a mindset shift that you have made after reading this chapter?

CHAPTER 6

Say It Loud

Promoting Your Black-Owned Business

••

Selling is not to be feared, it is to be revered!

SALES AND MARKETING . . . MAKE IT YOUR THING

If I had a dollar every time I hear therapists talk about their disdain for sales and selling, I'd be making bank, retired, and traveling around the world. It's captured in this thought: *I just want to help people, not sell to people.*

Many therapists dread the idea of selling, or sales and marketing because they think they have to convince someone to purchase their service or product offerings. When we hear the words *sales, marketing,* or *selling,* images of sketchy car sales ads or the QVC line "But wait, there's more" come rushing in. If these are the images that you have of getting your offerings in front of your ideal clientele, then it is time for a change—a mindset shift I want you to make.

What I have noticed is that, underneath the dread of selling, lies fear. After all, you are your business, and if someone says no to your product or service, they are essentially saying no to you and your business ideas, and so the spiral begins: if my idea is worthless, then I am worthless; if I am worthless, that means I'm a bad entrepreneur who has no business running a business; and so on and so on, until you stop talking about your business and hope that the services and products just sell themselves. Can you relate? I know all too well, because I've been there . . . a few times!

Fear of promoting your business comes in many forms:

- Fear of rejection
- Fear of talking to strangers
- Fear the product or service won't work
- Fear of success

"I don't like selling" may actually mean "I'm terrified of selling my products and services." But sales and marketing has to be your thing—without it your business will not grow or thrive. You need customers and you need revenue and your sales and marketing strategy will help you to get there.

REFRAMING SELLING FOR THERAPISTS

When we think about selling, we often characterize it as something we are doing *to* customers, or we think we have to convince customers to purchase something that they don't need. If you hold this point of view about marketing and sales, you will not prioritize these business tasks and instead may avoid them without realizing how essential they are to the growth of your business. I can imagine this is especially challenging for therapists.

What is sales and marketing, anyway? *Marketing* is the strategy for building client relationships and brand awareness—informing clients about products or services that solves their problems, while *sales* include the activities related to converting prospects to customers. Together, these activities are focused on bringing in new clients, maintaining relationships with past and current clients, and completing sales transactions. If you are in tune with your customers' needs and introducing them to offerings that solve their problems, the tension around "selling" will likely disappear.

Easier said than done, I know. I have a confession: marketing is probably one of my least favorite business activities (well, that and paperwork), yet it takes up so much brain space. One part of my brain says, "You need to do more to engage your clients"; while the other part says, "You have created an awesome product, your customers should just buy it." Sales and marketing are the *actions* that bring in revenue, and products and services are not going to sell themselves. If people don't know what you have to offer, they cannot purchase your products; if your ideal clients don't know about your private practice or your expertise, then they can't seek you out. You have to share information about what you have to offer (promote) and how it will make their lives easier. Therapists, you have to reframe how you think about sales and marketing and consider it an essential function of your business. Even if you are like me and still don't like it, you will understand why you have to do it. (Just like writing those progress notes!)

MY MARKETING AND SALES JOURNEY

When I first started my private practice, there were very few marketing activities that I had to do. I had a website (which I created myself using templates on GoDaddy.com), but most of my clients came from word-of-mouth referrals from clients and colleagues. This worked for a part-time practice, though I'm sure I would have needed to do more for a full-time practice.

When I started InnoPsych in 2020, I had a marketing plan in place to build brand awareness, but I did not have a sales strategy to bring clients into a sales funnel (see Figure 6.2) or to close deals. One day, I looked at my bank account and was shocked at how low my balance had dropped. I freaked out—I like my money to be right! I knew what I had to do: For weeks, I had been putting "send emails to past clients" on my to-do list, but had not executed. That night, I got off my butt and sent a bunch of emails. I got a few hits from that round of emails. One person said, "Great timing!" and requested a meeting. It became clear to me that marketing and talking with clients had to be part of my daily practice.

Let's take some time to reflect on your feelings on marketing your expertise and selling your products/services. Find a quiet space, and respond to the journal prompts below:

- What emotions come up when you think about selling and marketing your offerings?
- What thoughts come up when you think about selling and marketing your products and services?
- What behaviors do you exhibit when it comes to selling and marketing your products and services?

Repeat the following affirmations to help shift your mindset around sales and marketing:

- I will no longer fear marketing and selling my products and services.
- I embrace sales and marketing as a core business practice.
- I respect that without sales and marketing there will be no revenue for my business.
- My offerings will actually help people.
- I am doing potential clients a disservice if they are not aware of the products/services I have to offer.
- I sell, I win.

You may wish to create one or two of your own affirmations to help you with your mindset around marketing and sales.

CRAFTING A SOLID MARKETING STRATEGY

I can hear you now: *I'm a therapist, I don't need a marketing strategy. I have a waiting list of clients.* Any successful business must engage in marketing activities that help them to:

- identify their ideal customers
- develop a relationship with their target audience
- turn that audience into paying customers

It is as simple as that. No matter what business or industry you are involved in, these are the steps to growing your sales and revenue. While sales and marketing theories can be more complex and have many steps embedded, at its root this is what you have to do as an entrepreneur.

My response to the comments above: "Even with a waitlist, you still need a marketing strategy!"

Creating a marketing strategy is an effective way to help you execute a plan to get customers, increase your revenue, and grow your business. Getting your offerings into your customers' awareness and driving sales is not a one-time affair—you have to execute time and time again.

Three Cs of Marketing

To engage your prospective clients, you need to understand your brand, build partnerships with other brands, and showcase your expertise. Crafting your

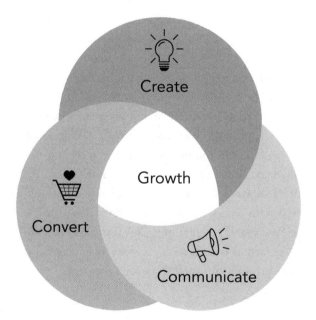

Figure 6.1 Three Cs of marketing *Source:* Charmain F. Jackman and Demp Agency

marketing strategy should include an application of the three Cs of marketing (see Figure 6.1).

1. Create your brand message.
2. Communicate your message.
3. Convert your audience into paying customers.

Each of the three Cs is crucial for sound marketing, so below I walk you through each step on your journey to becoming a Thriving Therapreneur. These three elements work together to increase global brand visibility, communicate the brand message, and substantially increase revenue.

CREATE YOUR COMPANY'S BRAND MESSAGE

In Chapter 5, you did the work of creating a brand story. While this version focused on your personal brand, there may be overlap with the story about how you started your business.

My brand story highlights the difficult journey I had finding a therapist of color, which led me to create InnoPsych. In addition to sharing my personal experience with my clients' problem in my brand story, I also include the story of Sankofa (see Appendix E), which serves as the inspiration for my company logo. Sankofa represents connecting back to our roots to inform our future. I want to emphasize the connection to healing among our ancestors, our present, and our future generations. The InnoPsych brand is about sharing healing resources that connect our ancestral roots to current and future generations.

InnoPsych's first product was the national therapist of color directory. I wanted to showcase the diversity of therapists and to create a product that would make it much easier to find a therapist of color through our search filters. A story that I often shared was launching the directory in January 2020 with a mission to address mental health among people of color, and just two months before the COVID pandemic. We all know the current focus on mental health, so it's a story that people can immediately relate to. Let's return to your brand story for a moment.

Reflection Time

Let's take some time to reflect on how your brand story, your offerings, and your clientele work together. Find a quiet space, and respond to the journal prompts below:

- Look at your brand story from Chapter 5. What is the unifying message that you want to share about your brand that will build engagement, foster trust, and cultivate brand loyalty with your target audience?
- What is your signature service or product? While you may offer a number of products or services, what is one offering that your company will be known for? How has it helped and, most important, how will it help others?
- In one sentence, what do you want your customers to know about this offering?

COMMUNICATION CHANNELS: SPREADING YOUR BRAND MESSAGE

Telling your story and talking to prospective clients, often complete strangers, is another skill to marketing your business. In the past, having a website or landing page was enough for therapists who had private practices, but that has changed. There are so many more ways to find clients and get the word out about your business, which also means that your potential clients have to sift through the noise of other colleagues to find you.

Communicating with your target audience requires you to use a variety of *marketing channels*, platforms to build awareness and to engage with your target audience—where your ideal client spends time. The following sections review several different channels you can use to share your company's brand message with your target audience:

In-Person and Virtual Networking

On a basic level, you likely understand that as a business owner you have to promote your business, even if you don't want to. Through promoting your business, you gain new customers, and most importantly, bring revenue to your company.

However, as a therapist, promoting your private practice also means that you have to promote *you*, often to complete strangers. This can be an intimidating task, but it is a necessary business strategy. (Review the section in Chapter 4 on self-promotion if you are still struggling with this.)

The Elevator Pitch. The elevator pitch is a brief introduction of your business that is usually shared in 30 seconds or less (the length of an elevator ride). It comes from the concept of using any interaction, such as being in an elevator, to give a quick, attention-grabbing overview of our business. The elevator pitch leaves the listener wanting to learn more about your business.

The elevator pitch is a great tool for in-person networking at professional meetings and conferences or when you are out and someone asks what you do. It gives you the language to confidently speak about your business. On the following page are the three central elements of the elevator pitch—I illustrate each with a hypothetical example:

1. *The hook:* This could be a question, a statistic, or a personal revelation that brings awareness to the problem, for example,
   - "Did you know that only 6% of Black males seek therapy?"
2. *The solution:* This is simply your name and a short statement about your solution and how it helps to solve a problem, for example,
   - "Hi, I'm Dr. Charmain, founder of Barber Therapy, a mental health practice that provides haircuts and therapy all in the same location. Instead of waiting around for your haircut, you can use your time to learn tools to heal. Our goal is to improve outcomes for Black men's mental health by meeting them where they are."
3. *The call to action:* This is an action step that the listener can do to learn more or to connect with you, for example,
   - "Find us at www. . . . .com to schedule your next healing haircut."

Exercise: Creating Your Elevator Pitch

Now, it's your turn to create your elevator pitch. Think of a problem you are solving for a client and respond to the following prompts:

- *The hook:* What is an interesting way to capture your audience's attention about the problem?
- *The solution:* Share your name and a short statement about your solution and how it helps solve the problem. Tell the audience what you do and how it can benefit them. You can also include how you are different from your competitors.
- *The call to action:* Ask the listener to do something to learn more about you or your business or to take some action.

Now, pull it all together and write out your elevator pitch. Consider creating a few versions for different audiences. For instance, using my example of Barber Therapy, I would create a version for potential clients, one for therapists, and one for potential investors.

Practicing Your Elevator Pitch. Now that you have written your pitch, it's time to practice, practice, practice. The more that you speak it out loud, the more natural it will become. I also encourage you to record a video of your pitch and review it. The goal is to have it committed to memory so that you are always ready, but it should also sound natural and not over-rehearsed.

Biographical Statement (or Bio) and Therapist Statement

A *bio* is a brief summary that captures your career highlights, contributions, and impact. A bio is often used by presenters to introduce you before you give a talk. It can also be used to introduce yourself to potential clients and collaborators via email. For example, when a colleague wants to introduce me to someone in their network, they will typically ask me to share a short bio so that they can better talk about my expertise. You can also post your bio publicly, such as on your website, so that it is easily accessible to potential clients. For therapists, an alternative to the bio is a *therapist statement*: a description of your therapeutic approach, the types of clients or concerns you specialize in, and how people benefit from working with you. The therapist statement is usually written in the first person, while the bio is typically written in the third person.

It is helpful to have different versions of your bio, based on which expertise you want to highlight (e.g., educator experience, child/adolescent development, and entrepreneurship). I also have versions of different lengths: short (50 words) for introductions, medium length (200 words) for continuing education applications or event advertising, and longer (250–500 words) for conference brochure. On the other hand, the therapist statement is usually written for potential clients to get to know more about your therapeutic style. Appendix F has examples of bios and therapist statements, including a template you can use to create compelling bios. It's a good idea to keep a folder with all your bios clearly labeled and up-to-date, so that you can easily access them when you need them.

Word of Mouth

The cheapest and most authentic marketing tool out there is word of mouth: past clients who tell other people about their positive experience, or people who know you share information about you and your company with people in their network. Word-of-mouth referrals are the cheapest form of marketing. Your job is to make sure that you deliver a high-quality service so that people readily share how good you are. It also means that the people in your network such as friends, family, other therapists, mentors, and coaches need to know what you do so they can share this information with people in their networks.

Blogs, Podcasts, and Vlogs

Creating content offers the opportunity to showcase your expertise and communicate your thought leadership. There are many options for content creation, and it can easily get overwhelming. One strategy I learned is to be consistent, which might mean focusing on just one platform and establishing consistency there before adding others. Here are some common examples of content creation (Chapter 11 goes into further detail on leveraging content):

- *Blogs/articles:* Writing your own articles and posting them on your website and on social media platforms offers you a premium way to communicate with your audience and to share information that can be useful to them. You can also contribute to articles for print or digital resources, or write an opinion piece and submit it to your local

newspaper. These are excellent ways to establish your thought leadership and communicate your brand message.

- *Video content:* Creating video content is becoming more and more
  popular, and a must if you are looking to attract attention and
  increase brand awareness. A number of platforms allow you to
  host your video content or embed your videos on your website and
  in emails. (See Appendix D for resources.)
- *Audio content:* Many people engage with audio-only content, such as podcasts and audiobooks. You can build your own podcast or serve as a guest.

Promoting Through Social Media

Social media is constantly changing and evolving. At the time of this book, Instagram, LinkedIn, Facebook, YouTube, and TikTok are some of the common
places therapists are engaging with their audience. Social media requires an
investment of time, energy, and money to gain the most from it. Each platform
has its unique strategy, and understanding how the algorithms work can help you
maximize your presence on these platforms.

Here is an easy way to think about social media engagement:

- *Instagram:* Connect with your audience to share updates with posts
  and captions (images and text), reels (short videos), stories (images
  or videos that disappear after 24 hours), live events, and community broadcast channels. You can also host a shop and sell products
  through Instagram.
- *Pinterest:* Share or find visual inspirations for a range of projects, such
  as home and office decor.
- *LinkedIn:* Professional networking and business connections and a great
  platform to showcase your expertise. You can also host live events,
  share events, host a blog, and create communities or groups.
- *Facebook:* Connect with your audience to share updates with text,
  images, and videos; create private or public groups; and host live events
  or webinars.
- *TikTok:* Share short video content, usually set to music or other
  audio files.
- *YouTube:* Video-sharing platform for vlogs and other video content and
  to livestream events.

Paid Ads

In addition to free use of social media, entrepreneurs can pay advertising fees to increase their reach to their target audience, usually through ads marked "sponsored." Web developers are able to promise more visibility for those who pay for advertising. Paid ads also provide more analytics for entrepreneurs using this option. Lots of people have made careers helping people create and leverage ads for their business, so consider hiring someone to help with this if your budget allows.

Therapist Directories

More and more we are seeing therapist directories as a place that practitioners can list their profiles and businesses. Some are free and low cost, while other directories are pricier. Some therapist directories are general, and some are specific for a cultural group, like InnoPsych's directory for people of color. It is important to consider the audience you are trying to reach and what the directory will actually deliver. For example, therapist directories have been around for a long time, but only in the last 5 years have directories for specific social identities emerged.

Partnerships and Collaborations

Partnerships and collaboration allow you to leverage the audience of other organizations that have overlapping interests with you or your company, so it's another great way to increase brand awareness. One of InnoPsych's early collabs was with a nonprofit founded by a radio personality well-known in the Black community. This mutually beneficial partnership helped to elevate both brands in the mental health space.

Before approaching a potential collaborator, it is important for you to conduct due diligence, to ensure that your mission aligns with the other organization. Additionally, be sure to have written agreements about how you will work together, name what deliverables will be exchanged, and how money, if applicable, will be shared. Also consider working with an attorney before signing any contract. (See Appendix D for resources on identifying a lawyer.)

Email Marketing

Email newsletters offer a great way to share curated information about your business with potential customers and clients. You can consider weekly, monthly, or quarterly newsletters to keep your audience engaged and up-to-date with the brand. Always include a call to action (e.g., "visit our website"), so that your readers clearly understand what you want them to do with the information.

Websites/Landing Page

Websites are still a frequently used method for entrepreneurs to inform the public about their businesses. Therapists will often ask me if they should invest time and money in building a website. Before closing a deal, customers will often research the company, and websites are one of the sources people will check to vet a company or to learn more about its founder and leadership. For this reason, it would be beneficial to have a digital presence such as a website or at least a *landing page*, a single page to advertise your particular product, service, or business, with limited navigation functionality. However, depending on your offerings and your target audience, you may not need a traditional website. For example, many people use Instagram or Facebook profiles for their business website.

Now, let's review the typical pages that you will need to build a landing page or website to showcase your brand:

- *Your welcome message:* This is a brief, one-sentence message that welcomes people to your site. You can use language from your brand story or your elevator pitch to create this.
- *About you:* This is a paragraph that gives visitors to your website an introduction to who you are or what your business does. For this section you can use one of the bios you created earlier in this chapter and your therapist statement. Consider putting a longer version of your bio on your website so that people can see your full expertise.
- *Services:* Provide the name, image (if applicable), and a description of the products and services you offer. Depending on the offering, you can include pricing and also provide a link for people to purchase directly from the website. It is also helpful to include some testimonials from

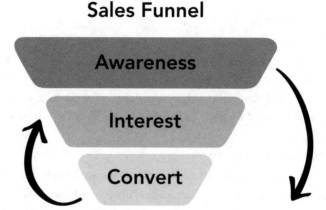

Figure 6.2 The sales funnel *Source:* Charmain F. Jackman and Demp Agency

past customers, if appropriate. *Note:* Do not ask your therapy clients for testimonials, as this is unethical and would violate their privacy.

- *Contact:* Provide your contact information so that prospective clients can reach you with any questions or to schedule a consultation call. You can include a business email and business phone number, and/ or you can embed a form that allows you to collect information from potential clients (see example at www. innopsych.com).

CONVERT YOUR AUDIENCE INTO PAYING CUSTOMERS

We have moved through the first two of three Cs of your marketing strategy: create and communicate your brand message. The last step is converting your audience into paying customers—this is how you bring revenue into your business.

The sales funnel is an excellent visual to capture how to attract potential customers, move them through your business (i.e., customer journey) and convert them into paying customers. There are many versions of the sales funnel—some have six or more stages! Here I want to keep it simple: Figure 6.2 shows three fundamental stages:

- *Awareness:* Focus is on brand visibility or attracting potential customers to their business or brand.

- *Interest:* A segment of these potential customers will want to learn more about the brand. They may do their own research such as visiting your website or social media pages, or even talking to current customers about the product or services.
- *Convert:* A smaller segment of interested prospects will make a decision to purchase. Boom! Once you have these customers, your goal is to keep them interested so that they continue to be paying customers.

Awareness

The top of the funnel, the widest part, has the goal of attracting as many people as possible—people who fit your ideal client characteristics—to the brand, by increasing brand visibility. Ideally, your messaging is geared to your target clientele so that you are gaining their interest in your product and increasing the likelihood of converting them to customers. Here are some strategies for increasing brand awareness:

- *The grand opening strategy:* Opening announcements can be designed as letters, emails, or even postcards that you send out to your potential customers or referral sources to let them know you are open for business. In these communications, you can craft a simple but engaging message informing the reader that you are open for business and what products and services you offer. It is important to provide information about the types of clients you work with or the types of referrals you are looking for. You will also include your contact information and business hours and provide a way for them to reach you (see Appendix G for a sample practice opening announcement). For example, if you are working with children, sending an announcement to all the pediatricians or school counselors within a 20-mile radius would be an excellent way to expand your reach. You may consider adding an incentive to get them to open the email or letter and to respond (e.g., a chance to win a dozen donuts for the office).
- *Open house:* If you have a physical location, another way to get the word out is to host an open house at your location. This is an opportunity for your potential referral sources to meet you and to see your space. You can market it as a networking event or educational event where you provide a workshop on a topic. Use the open house as a way to bring

people to your space. If your office is virtual, consider a virtual open house. This is a strategy to get potential clients in your sales funnel, so remember to collect names and contact information, especially email addresses, which you can use to communicate with them.

- *Offer a giveaway:* Giveaways are another easy way to get people into your sales funnel. This is especially useful when you are exhibiting at in-person events and you want to collect email addresses from visitors to your booth. People enter their name and email for a chance to win a raffle prize. You can also use this strategy with people who are already in the cycle as a way to get referrals.

- *Focus groups:* These groups provide a way to bring people together to get feedback. This could be feedback about an offering or new initiative you plan to launch. Ideally, these are groups of people who are willing to share their time and experience about a problem you are trying to solve. The members of the focus groups can easily move through your funnel because they are aware of your brand, and this new relationship can build interest and make the conversion process easier.

- *Social media:* You can use your social media channels to share information about your business, such as podcasts, blogs, and webinars. These tools help to build awareness as you can share content on multiple channels.

- *Free content:* Offering free content is a great way to build awareness, create interest, and drive people further down your funnel. You can offer downloadable materials such as an ebook, checklist, or helpful tips, and in exchange, you gather names and email addresses from potential customers. Once they submit their information, an automated email sends them the information.

Interest

We are in the middle of the sales funnel now. You have done well in capturing some potential clients' interest. They may like what they have seen so far, but they still want to learn more before they make the decision to purchase. At this stage, people have some interest in learning more about you or your company before they make a buying decision. It is really important to have a clear strategy that turns these leads into paying customers. You also want to maintain a database that captures their information so that you can continue to engage with them through targeted emails and newsletters.

- *Sales calls:* Sales calls are opportunities to speak directly with a potential client with the intention to convert them to a paying customer and bring in revenue to the company. At this stage, you can schedule an in-person or virtual meeting. *Cold calls* refer to outreach calls or emails to people you do not know and who are not familiar with your brand, while *warm leads* refer to people who may have some knowledge of your company. Warm leads can also come from introductions from clients or people in your network. Warm leads have the highest rate of converting to customers because of the familiarity with the company.

- *Product samples:* As a way to deepen a lead's experience with the product or service, you may send them a sample (think about the sample stations at a grocery store) or send a preview of the service. For example, before starting a course, I always hold a free session so that people can experience part of the product, and this also allows me to convert to customers by creating more urgency for them to purchase (e.g., limited time offer, flash sale, bonus offer).

- *Booking form:* You can increase the likelihood of conversion by creating a form that requires prospective clients to share information about why they want to work with you. If your form is done well, they would have invested time and you will have also communicated how you can assist them. This form will also give you enough information to know their readiness to purchase and to assess if they fit your ideal client parameters. Many business owners often want to convert everyone who is interested, but as discussed in Chapter 5, not everyone who wants to secure your services is the right client for you.

- *Newsletters:* As discussed above, newsletters are an email marketing strategy to keep your target audience informed about your business and the products and services you offer. You can share personal stories, which help your audience feel more connected to you. You can also offer discounts and use it for product launches. Maintaining a consistent rhythm to your newsletter (e.g., weekly, monthly) is key to building ongoing engagement and to be in direct communication with people in the middle of the sales funnel.

Building Customer Loyalty

Doing your best work with clients turns them into loyal customers.

Once a customer has purchased a product or service, and they are satisfied, it will take less effort to have them purchase again. But you need to have processes in place to make repeat purchasing seamless. Building customer loyalty requires that, first and foremost, you deliver a quality product and provide good customer service. If you have this covered, customers will not only come back to you, but they will tell their friends. Next, you want to make the buying process as seamless as possible. Ensure there are not too many steps from the product selection to checkout and offer multiple payment options. Always test out how to purchase a product on your website before making it public. Once you have a converted customer, make sure to send a thank you email (a process that can be automated), and send additional offers or product info to keep them interested. Invite them to subscribe to your newsletter to stay current on product releases and product updates.

Customer Feedback. Another strategy that fosters customer loyalty is to obtain customer feedback. Build a system that allows you to systematically collect feedback from paying customers. For example, schedule a debrief session following an engagement or job to obtain feedback from the client (a brief survey at the end of a workshop), and share data that you collected (if applicable); and request testimonials from current or past customers who have expressed satisfaction with your services. *Note*: do not ask for testimonials or reviews from therapy clients—that would breach their privacy.

Debrief Meetings. Once you have completed an engagement with a client, it can be very easy to move on to the next client. However, as we discussed earlier, keeping customers in your sales funnel is the best strategy for gaining repeat customers, and it is less expensive at this stage than having to start from the top of the funnel again. I have found it very useful to schedule a debrief call after a workshop, consultancy, or speaking engagement because it allows me and the client to reflect on the engagement and identify what worked well and what did not work well. Having the opportunity to reflect on areas that did not work is powerful and gives you the chance to discuss the obstacles or barriers together. Sometimes, there are problems that may be unrelated to you, but may get attributed to you. In these scenarios, the debrief gives you a chance to clear the air and offer ways to address any shortcomings on your end. You can also use the debrief to get testimonials if they are happy with your work, and to request warm introductions to people in their network.

Take Action Exercise

Consider an offering that you plan to market and sell to clients. Then respond to the prompts below:

- List two activities that you will use to drive brand awareness to the identified offering.
- Share two activities you will use to create interest in the offering.
- Identify two strategies you will use to convert prospects to paying customers.
- What are two strategies you will use to create urgency for potential clients to purchase?
- Identify three strategies that you will use to get paying customers to purchase again.
- Identify three strategies that you will use to convert customers into champions.

Metrics

An instrumental activity of a strong marketing strategy is tracking customer data and analytics. The data and analytics help you to make informed decisions and determine if your marketing efforts are working or not. To get the most out of your marketing activities, you want to keep a database with contact information and demographic data of your clients and prospective clients. This data is key to building your customer persona and being able to deeply understand your clients' needs, motivations, and even habits. Whenever possible, be sure to collect contact information from your target audience. Examples of the metrics you can collect include newsletter subscriptions, website traffic, email open rate (for emails and newsletters), and click rate (links within a newsletter).

Reflection Exercise: Metrics

- What are some metrics will you use to assess your marketing plan?
- What metrics will you use to assess the success of your sales strategy?

ETHICAL CONSIDERATIONS IN MARKETING YOUR THERAPY SERVICES

When I first started my business, I had a website and business cards—that was my marketing strategy. It was definitely a simpler time back then. When I was coming up in the profession, the major focus from an ethical perspective was ensuring that psychologists did not "make false or deceptive statements" about their services (American Psychological Association, 2017) and that they practiced within their expertise. Without a doubt, social media has opened more opportunities for sales and marketing, but this is an area where the ethics codes have not kept pace with practice, lagging behind the rapidly changing landscape influenced by technology. For example, a search of the most recent American Psychological Association's Ethics Codes (2017) yielded *zero* results for "social media" and "technology."

As you plan your marketing strategy or hire someone to run your marketing, check with your state licensing board and professional associations to ensure that you stay compliant with board requirements, which may include considerations such as:

- *Stay within your expertise:* Do not give advice on topics for which you have no training or experience.
- *Avoid making false or deceptive statements:* Do not guarantee results.
- *Accurately communicate your training and expertise:* If you are unlicensed, please indicate that you are not a licensed mental health professional.
- *Do not misrepresent your title or license:* Be sure to represent your credentials accurately.
- *Collect testimonials only where appropriate:* Do not ask for testimonials from "current therapy clients/patients or people vulnerable to undue influence" (American Psychological Association, 2017, p. 9). I would recommend not asking past therapy clients either.

- *Review content others create on your behalf:* It's on you to ensure that any content posted on your behalf meets ethical standards.
- *Stay current:* Keep your license malpractice insurance up-to-date.

CHAPTER 6 MOMENTUM AND MINDSET CHECK

You are ready to sell! This chapter discussed how to reframe the idea of selling as a way to help your clients. Another mindset shift for many of you. The selling mindset focused exercises that guided you create an elevator pitch, which helps you to talk about your business with confidence. You identified marketing channels that you will use to reach your target audience and how to get the word out. You explored the three Cs of marketing: creating your brand messages, communicating your message, and converting customers, and you considered ethical concerns as you market your services. You have a marketing strategy and you have identified key metrics to track the progress of your plan. Now, go sell like a boss!

- What is one takeaway that you have as you finish this chapter?
- What is a mindset shift that you have made after reading this chapter?

Launching With Confidence

Essential Pre-Launch Strategies for Success

....

On your mark, get set . . . launch!

YOUR PRE-LAUNCH MENTALITY

As you prepare to launch your business, I know that you will experience a whole host of emotions, such as excitement, nervousness, joy, self-doubt, and much more. One thing I would suggest is to embrace all the emotions—take it all in, knowing that you have been working toward this goal for some time. You're shifting your mindset, and your purpose and vision are tangible. You are truly seeing yourself as an entrepreneur and owning this role. Like sports, entrepreneurship is all about the mindset, and you are developing one for winning! There is no reason to doubt that you are well on your way to being a Thriving Therapreneur.

You will also find that there are many, many tasks to complete to get yourself ready for your opening day. Yes . . . this will happen! Every task that I share is necessary to operating an ethical and profitable practice, so don't skip any steps. My goal is to help you stay organized as you move through the steps (see Appendix H for a sample private practice launch checklist). Some tasks may take more time than others, and you may need to wait for approval from another organization (for example, applying for a business certificate or waiting on licensure). Keep moving through the chapter so that you maintain the momentum you started with, complete your reflections, and focus on the tasks that you can complete. You've made some major mindset shifts. That's the truly hard part—launching is the easi*er* part, but you still need your mind in the game.

Reflection Time

Take a moment to check in on yourself, by responding to the following prompts:

- Notice what emotions are coming up for you as you prepare to launch.
- Where in your body did you feel these emotions?
- How do you want to feel at the end of this chapter?
- Use the MINDFUL MOMENT below.

MINDFUL MOMENT

Let's take a moment to pause to connect back to your body, center yourself, and calm your mind.

Take a few deep breaths using your favorite breathing technique (e.g., box breathing, slow breathing, 4-7-8 breathing). I will use the slow breathing technique below:

1. Take a deep breath, in through your nose, on a count of three, and slowly release the breath, through your mouth, on a count of seven.
2. Repeat a calming word or affirmation of your choice or use this one: "I am building a thriving Black business."
3. Repeat for four more rounds.

Tip: You can come back to this exercise as often as you need to.

THE BUSINESS PLAN

A *business plan* is a document that outlines how a business will execute its vision. It provides a road map detailing the business idea, the target customers, and how the business will market to customers, earn revenue, and make a profit.

The traditional business plan is a pretty hefty document that lays out the business road map in the following categories:

- Executive summary
- Company description
- Products and services
- Market research and analysis
- Marketing and sales plan
- Competitor analysis
- Management and organization plan
- Operational plan
- Financial projections

This type of business plan provides a step-by-step plan of action, but it requires an investment of time, money, and energy to create. While it provides a detailed road map for the entrepreneur, it could be outdated fairly quickly, or no longer relevant if there are market shifts or if customers' needs change. As a result, the traditional business plan lacks agility.

The Lean Canvas

In a changing landscape with an explosion of startups, investing time and energy on writing a traditional business plan is not practical. In 2010 Ash Maurya developed the Lean Canvas (see Figure 7.1), a simpler, more agile process to outline a business plan (LEANFoundry, LLC, n.d.). Maurya describes the Lean Canvas as a "one-page business plan." The Lean Canvas is adapted from the Business Model Canvas created by Alexander Osterwalder in 2005 (LEANFoundry, LLC, n.d.), which changed the way business owners document their business ideas.

Figure 7.1 Lean canvas *Source:* Ash Maurya, licensed under CC BY-SA 3.0. Available at: https://leanstack.com/leancanvas

Exercise: The Lean Canvas

Look at the categories for the Lean Canvas template. Anything look familiar? You have covered many of these sections so far. Take a few minutes to complete the sections outlined below (we will cover the other sections in Chapter 9):

- *Problem:* Your ideal client's pain point/problem you intend to solve (Chapter 5).
    - Write down your ideal client's pain point or problem that you intend to solve.
- *Solution:* How you will solve your client's problem? What products or services will your offer? (Chapter 5).
    - Write down the names of the products or services you will be providing to address your ideal clients' problem(s).
- *Unique value proposition:* Indicate how your products or services will stand out from others doing similar work (Chapter 5).
    - Write down how your products or services will stand out from others.

- *Unfair advantage:* What are the strengths or resources you possess that give you an edge over your competitors? (Chapter 5).
    – Identify any special resources, connections, networks, or training that gives you an advantage over competitors.
- *Client:* Describe your ideal client persona (Chapter 5).
    – Write down key demographics about your ideal client.
- *Channels:* Write down the methods you expect to use to communicate with your target audience and ideal clients. How will you get the word out to potential clients? (Chapter 6).
- *Metrics:* How will you measure and track your success? How will you keep track of your KPIs and who will be assigned to track? (Chapter 6).

Forming Your Business

As you go through the process of forming your business, you will first need to make a decision on the business structure you will use. The *business structure* concerns how the business will be taxed, the exposure of your personal assets, who will own the company, and your business growth goals. It is beyond the scope of my expertise to tell you which business structure will be best for you because there are many factors to consider. Therefore, consulting with a business accountant and/or a business attorney can help you choose which structure will work best for you and your company. Here is some basic information that you may wish to consider and ask about:

- *Sole proprietor:* a business with one owner. This is the easiest way to form a business, but there is no separation between the owner's personal and business assets and liabilities and, as a result, provides the least amount of financial protection for you and your business. For example, if the business is unable to pay a debt, your personal assets could be used to cover the debt. One advantage is that all the profits from the business go to the owner.
- *Partnerships:* businesses with two or more owners who come together to operate a business. Within this category there are *general partnerships*, where all partners share responsibility for managing the business and all partners have unlimited liability (i.e., personal assets are exposed); *limited partnerships*, where general partners manage the

business, while limited partners invest capital but are not involved in the management and have limited liability (i.e. personal assets are protected); and *limited liability partnerships*, where all partners manage the business and have limited liability.

- *C corporation:* a business entity that is completely separate from the owner(s). Corporations can raise money from investors by selling shares of the company, and shareholders have limited liability. Corporations pay taxes, and any profits made are distributed to shareholders as dividends. Both profits and shareholder dividends are taxed, which leads to double taxation.

- *S corporation:* more of a tax status than an entity, a type of corporation that separates the owner's personal assets from the corporation and avoids double taxation. However, there are specific criteria that a company and its shareholders must meet to qualify for S corporation status (e.g., shareholders must be U.S. citizens, with no partner agreements; no more than 100 shares can be sold, and only one class of stock).

- *Limited liability company (LLC):* a business structure that combines corporations and partnerships but protects the business owner's personal assets. The LLC may opt to file taxes as a C corporation, an S corporation, or a sole proprietorship, which allows profits and losses from the business to be passed through to the business owner's personal taxes.

- *Nonprofit:* a designation for businesses that are organized for charitable or socially beneficial reasons. While nonprofit organizations may make a profit, there are restrictions on what may be done with those profits, and broadly speaking, while a nonprofit's earnings may be used to pay "reasonable compensation" to its employees, its profits may not be distributed to private individuals.

- *Cooperative:* businesses that are owned and operated by the members who are using the services. Membership is through the purchase of shares, and any profits are shared among members. All members have voting rights in how the organization is operated.

PERSONAL REFLECTION: BUSINESS STRUCTURES EVOLVED BUSINESS GROWTH

When I started out with my part-time private practice, I operated as a sole proprietor for over 15 years. My business primarily provided therapy, speaking, and consulting services. The town where I practiced did not require me to register my business, and I did not need to register with the state. However, as I shifted my business from a private practice to a start-up, I consulted with a tax accountant and a lawyer to help me decide the best structure for the company. As a result, I started a new organization as a C-corp because my goal was to eventually raise external investment. However, as I learned more about the venture capital landscape, and that only 0.34% goes to Black women (Kunthara, 2021), I knew I needed to pivot. I spoke with my accountant again, and we made the decision to apply for S-corp status.

As you can see, I have had a number of business structures since starting my private practice almost 20 years ago. As your business evolves, plan to review the business structure with your accountant or attorney to make sure that you have the right structure in place that matches your business' current situation. (See Appendix D for resources on business structures.)

NAMING YOUR BUSINESS

Naming a business can be like naming a child—there's a lot of pressure to get it right. Naming my first business took some time. I was looking for a word that captured the insight that you get from therapy. I did a brain dump of words and collections of words. I would then do an online search to see if any other businesses had a similar name. I finally landed on InPsych, a play on insight. Years later, as I was changing my business structure, I decided to rebrand. I changed the business name to Innovative Psychological Services, which I shortened to InnoPsych. As you can see, I did not veer too far from the name of the first business.

Naming Strategy

As you consider the name for your business, bring your creativity and excitement. Try to release the pressure of trying to get the perfect name and enjoy the process.

Here are some strategies to help with your naming process:

- *Personal name:* If you have an established presence, using your name is a great way to extend your personal reputation to your business (e.g., Jackman Consultants, Jackman Psychological Services, Dr. Charmain Jackman).
- *Inspired name:* With this strategy you can select a name inspired by a work of art, artist, book, or symbol or that serves as an inspiration for your clients (e.g., Thriving for the Future, Bloom For You).
- *Product or service name:* Using the name of the service or product provides an advantage when potential clients conduct their search (e.g., Trauma and Recovery Services, D.E.I. Professional Consultants Inc.).
- *Tribute/legacy name:* Business owners use this naming strategy when they are inspired to name their business to honor a family member who holds significance in their life.
- *Growth name:* Business owners can select a name that they will grow into. They may start out as a solopreneur, for example, but have a vision to grow a bigger business (e.g., Jackman Global Consultants, Jackman Well-Being Enterprises).
- *Geographical region:* Choosing a name that includes the geographical area can be helpful to signal to potential clients where the business is located. However, if you move locations, it may no longer feel relevant (e.g., Boston Therapy Services, Trauma and Recovery Services of Massachusetts).

Using a Trade Name or "Doing Business As"

Some organizations use a trade name with customers that is different from the legal business name. A *DBA* (doing business as), also known as the *trade name*, is the public-facing name or name used with customers. It is an alternative to the *legal name*, the name used to register with the state (or states) where the business operates. For example, before my businesses merged, the legal name for one of my businesses was Thriving Therapy Space, Inc., and the DBA was InnoPsych. So even if you have a legal name, you might wish to look into whether in the state or states where you do business permit therapists to use a DBA and, if so, you can choose a different name that might connect better with your customer base.

Take Action Exercise

Naming your business can feel like a lot of pressure, but it does not have to be. I encourage you to approach the process with openness, curiosity, and patience.

If you do not have a name for your business, you can use the process below to help you develop one.

1. *Brainstorming:* Find a favorite spot in your home or outdoors where you can have uninterrupted time to brainstorm possible names. Try using a space that fosters your creativity.
    a. Reflect on the following (reviewing your notes from Chapter 5 will help):
        – Your vision or mission
        – Your brand story
        – Your product/services offerings
        – What inspired you to start your business
        – The impact you want to make
    b. Let the ideas flow: Set aside 20–30 minutes to brainstorm a list of 30 possible names (feel free to keep writing if the creative juices are flowing).
2. *Narrowing your list:* Now that you have a list of viable names, it's time to cut out names that will not work.
    a. Name search: Do an internet search to see if any of the business names you choose are already in use by another company. Check to see if the business is listed in your state or in another state. Eliminate any names that are already being used, especially if they are in the same state as you are located, to avoid any trademark issues. If the company is located in the same

   state, this can create confusion for potential clients, and they
   may end up going to the other business.

    b. Domain search: Conduct a domain search to check if the
   domain name you would use is available. Again, this may not be
   a reason to cross the name off the list, but it gives you information. If the domain name is taken, you can consider alternative
   extensions (e.g., .org, .co, and .net), but using a domain that is
   already taken but with an alternative extension could be con-
   fusing for potential clients, and people may end up at the other
   company. Again, this is something to consider as you choose
   the final name.

3. *Crowdsourcing*: Now it's time to get your family and friends involved.
   Share your list of names, and ask people to rank the top three names
   and what they like about them. You can send this as an email or a
   survey, but you should also talk to some people directly—you want
   to hear how they would pronounce the names and how they feel
   about the name.

4. *Choosing the name*: Ideally, these steps have helped you narrow
   down your list to 10 names or less. Now, rank the names on your list.
   What are the top three names?

5. *Try on the names*: Spend a few days "trying on" the top three names.
   Think about how they sound, how they are spelled, how would people pronounce them, how you might abbreviate them.

6. *Make the decision*: Now, all that is left is to make the final decision. The final decision is with you. Select the name that resonates
   with you and communicates your values and your vision. You got
   this . . . name that baby!

You did it! (High five from me . . . now do a happy dance!) Guess what?
Now it's time to share it with others.

REGISTERING YOUR BUSINESS

Now that you have your business name, it's time to register your business. Generally speaking, most businesses have to be registered with a municipal or state
agency for reasons including consumer protection and tax purposes. Registering

your business helps the agency track business data, establishes your business's identity, and ensures consumer safety.

1. *Tax identification:* The Employer Identification Number (EIN) establishes your business's identity and is like an individual's Social Security Number (SSN) but for your business. It's the number the government uses for tax identification purposes. You will use your EIN on any applications or forms that require a tax identification (e.g., invoices, W-9 tax forms, ACH forms for deposits). I have noticed that many therapists who are sole proprietors use their SSN on invoices and when conducting business, which is ill-advised. You can get an EIN even as a sole proprietor, and applying is, as of this writing, **free** and takes about 15 minutes . . . super easy (while you may wish to consult with your accountant or other tax or legal advisor, do not get scammed by companies that charge a lot of money to do this). As of this writing, you can apply online during business hours at https://www.irs.gov/formss4. Alternatively, you can submit an EIN application by mail, but it takes much longer. See Appendix I for a list of information needed as of this writing for online or mail-in application.

2. *Registering with your city/town:* You may need to register with the town where you are conducting business, depending on your business structure, the type of business, and the town's rules. It is very easy to call the town hall, check their website, or walk in to ask a question. Even if registering in the town is not required, it may have some advantages (e.g., access to certain programs for small businesses and historically excluded business owners).

3. *Registering with the state:* Most businesses, often with the exception of sole proprietorships, will in most states need to be registered with the state/states where they operate. LLCs, corporations, and nonprofits will have filing fees or other fees to register the business, and there may also be annual fees, such as an annual report filing fee. These requirements and associated costs will likely vary by state.

Getting Certified as a Diverse Business Owner

Many states and larger cities offer the opportunity for Black/BIPOC, veterans, LGBTQ, and women to get certified through a diversity supplier program. Obtaining this diversity certification status, sometimes called Certified Underrepresented Business Enterprise (CUBE) status, will likely offer an advantage if you plan to conduct business with governments and corporations. To provide access for small and economically disadvantaged (historically and systematically excluded) business owners to do business with them, many government agencies and businesses set aside a certain number of contracts for diversity or underrepresented business owners.

Check which certifications you may qualify for, such as:

- *Minority Business Enterprise (MBE)* is majority (often at least 51%) owned, operated, and controlled by an individual(s) who identifies as Minority (e.g., Black/African American, Asian American or Pacific Islander, Hispanic, or Native American).
- *Woman Business Enterprise (WBE) or Woman-Owned Small Business (WOSB)* is majority (often at least 51%) owned, operated, and controlled by an individual(s) who identifies as a woman.
- *Veteran Business Enterprise (VBE)* is majority (often at least 51%) owned, operated, and controlled by an individual(s) who is a veteran.
- *Lesbian, Gay, Bisexual, Transgender Business Enterprise (LGBTE)* is majority (often at least 51%) owned, operated, and controlled by an individual(s) who identifies as lesbian, gay, bisexual, transgender, or gender nonconforming.

Diversity certifications are relatively easy to obtain, but the required documents can make it challenging for some. The issuing entity needs to make sure that you are eligible based on the diversity criteria and that you are indeed the true owner of the company.

Organizing your documents, so that you can find them when you need them, will go a long way to simplifying the process. Here are examples of supporting documents that you will likely need for your application (see Appendix P for a diversity business certificate checklist).

- *Proof of ownership:* You may need to provide a paper trail showing how you acquired the business. For example, if you purchased a business with a loan, you will provide a copy of the loan agreement. If you started with personal funds, you may need to provide bank statements showing where the funds originated.

- *Proof of business formation:* You may need to provide all the documents that you created when you formed the business, for example, business certificates, articles of incorporation, bylaws, partnership agreements, and list of board of directors (if applicable).
- *Proof of business activity:* You may need to provide financial documents to show the financial activity of the business. Typically you may need to provide tax returns for the past three years, or for the duration of the business, if the business is younger. If you have not filed taxes, you will need to submit financial statements (e.g., income statements and budgets).
- *Proof of expertise:* In order to demonstrate that you have the expertise to operate the business, you may need to provide a resume or curriculum vitae (CV), a requirement for individuals who are the primary owners.
- *Proof of identity:* To verify your identity, you may need to provide a government-issued identification.
- *Attestation:* You may need to attest that your identity meets the requirements of the specific certification.

You should check to learn about the specific requirements and programs in the town and state where you do business. Be sure to check if your city offers reciprocity with the state or vice versa (i.e., if you register with one entity, you only need to show proof of that registration to the other entity to obtain the same type of certification).

Getting registered at the federal level has additional steps and scrutiny. For example, the owner(s) must be a U.S. citizen. Some companies have made a business out of helping people get their businesses certified and will do the process for you—for a fee, of course. Some cities and states offer free resources to help business owners set up these certifications, so be sure to check out what is available in your area. Additionally the Small Business Administration (http://www .sba.gov) is a great resource and will help you through this process for free, but you will need to pay any relevant filing fees.

Take Action Exercise

Let's take some time to plan how you will get these tasks completed:

- Plan when you will obtain your EIN by setting a date in your calendar.
- Visit the website for your town/city to find out the process for registering your business and the information you will need.
- Visit the website for your state to find out the process for registering your business and the information you will need.
- Visit your state or city website to learn more about the process for getting diversity certifications for your business and plan when you will embark on this process.
- Create a folder to organize your business formation documents, opening bank documents, and business certificates so that you have them close at hand when needed.

PREPARING TO OPEN YOUR BUSINESS

Opening a new business is an exciting milestone. As you prepare to open your business, there will be a number of tasks that you have to complete to ensure that all is in order. Writing your tasks in a checklist format is a great way to help you stay organized and on track. In this next section, I will highlight some of the tasks that you may need as you start your business. Please note that this is not an exhaustive list and your tasks will depend on the type of business you are forming. This is a good time to connect with colleagues who own similar businesses and ask about start-up costs and tasks. In addition, in Appendix H, you will find a sample checklist of tasks that you may need to complete. You can use this template to create your opening task list.

Opening a Business Bank Account

Once you have an EIN number you can open a business bank account. Entrepreneurs will typically have a checking account, which is needed to pay bills. However, you can also consider opening a savings account, which you can use to start an emergency fund (more on finances in Chapter 9). You will want to consider minimum balances and transaction fees (e.g., low balance, number of monthly transfers) as you consider your options.

Finding the Right Office

Before you open your business to the public, you will have to make a decision about whether you will need a physical location or whether you will operate virtually or hybrid. Before the COVID-19 pandemic, most therapists saw their clients in physical locations. However, the number of clinicians offering virtual therapy dramatically increased during and after the pandemic. According to Mulvaney-Day, Dean, Miller et al. (2022), the number of claims for teletherapy jumped from 1% in February 2020 to 53–59% in May 2020; by the end of 2021 the number of claims had dropped, but only down to 40%. As you can see, a large number of therapists have maintained their virtual practices; some have opted to remain as virtual-only practices, while others operate as hybrid practices.

PERSONAL REFLECTION: MY OFFICE SPACE

Prior to the pandemic, I had a physical office and engaged in telehealth on a very limited basis—usually snow days. I did have one client who requested telehealth because it worked best with their schedule. My preference was for in-person sessions—after all, that was how I was trained. However, after the pandemic, I opted to stay remote. By that time I was reducing my therapy practice and expanding my consulting and speaking practice, so I no longer needed a physical location. I could lead workshops from the comfort of my home office, or travel to my clients for in-person workshops and speaking engagements. While I like the quiet and minimal external distractions that come with working from home, I do miss socializing with others during breaks. To address that, I've created opportunities to connect with colleagues by scheduling walks and coffee/tea dates, forming accountability groups with other entrepreneurs, and attending educational and networking events.

As you weigh your decision regarding the type of office space you will need, you may want to consider factors such as your personal preference for in-person sessions, the type of services that you will be providing, your desire for socializing during the workday, the cost of physical spaces, and other personal factors such as commuting time, caregiving responsibilities, and the associated costs.

To find office spaces, contact a local real estate agent, use your town's or professional association's classified ads, try a search engine, or ask your colleagues about subleases or vacant offices. If you will be leasing an office space be sure to read the lease agreement carefully to make sure that you are complying with the rules and understand what you are entitled to as a tenant. For example, if you plan to sublease to other therapists, you will want to make sure that this is allowed.

OFFICE SPACE OPTIONS

Physical Office. A physical office provides clients withe the opportunity to obtain therapy in a neutral location. You may have coworkers or officemates if you share space with other therapists, which would have the added benefit of reducing professional isolation. Depending on the size of your practice, you may need to budget for an administrative assistant to receive clients and take payments, and of course, you'll need to decorate your waiting room and office.

- *Location:* Think about your commute, where your target clients live and work, cost of office spaces in your preferred location, and availability and cost of parking.
  - Do you want the office to be near your home, in the same town you live, or farther away? What radius or how many miles are you willing to travel from your home base? Do you mind running into clients at the grocery store or other places?
  - What is the maximum commute time you desire (e.g., hours spent driving or taking public transportation)?
  - Are there particular neighborhoods where your ideal clientele live, work, or attend school?
- *Accessibility:* You will need a location that is accessible and easy for clients to navigate. For example, is it accessible by public transportation? Does it have a ramp and an elevator to reach higher floors for clients needing assistive devices for walking?
- *Size:* Will you need an office with only one therapy room or with multiple meeting spaces? Will you be doing testing or assessments, offering groups or hosting events? Will you plan to sublease to other clinicians?
- *Amenities:* What additional features would you like the office to have

(e.g., waiting room, kitchen/kitchenette, bathroom within the office, ample free or metered parking)?

- *Staffing*: Will you need to hire an administrative assistant to receive clients? Will you need a cleaning service?

Home Office. A home office can offer a great deal of flexibility as it reduces your commute time. You will need to consider the impact on people who may live with you and to put measures in place to ensure your clients' privacy and confidentiality, such as using headphones when in therapy sessions and putting a *Do Not Disturb* sign on your door when you are meeting with a client. You will also need to consider soundproofing or noise reduction devices such as a white noise machine. Be sure you set up correctly for a home-based therapy office, by consulting with an attorney, a tax accountant, and an insurance professional. Additionally, be sure to implement safeguards to protect your clients' identity (more to come in Chapter 8, which covers ways to protect your business).

On-Demand Offices. On-demand offices offer flexibility, allowing you to use offices only when you need them. You may pay an hourly or monthly rate depending on the number of hours you need. Some companies have offices in multiple cities, states, and even countries, which offer the business owner greater location flexibility if needed. Many on-demand offices may also have amenities such as administrative support, cleaning service, mail services, and snacks and beverages, which adds additional value.

Coworking Spaces. An office location that allows users to share office space and amenities. They are typically designed with a variety of common spaces and private office spaces of different sizes to accommodate various meeting configurations. Most coworking spaces operate on a monthly membership rate and will likely have tiered options depending on the frequency of use. Traditionally, coworking spaces have not been HIPAA compliant, but that is changing: a few coworking spaces have been created specifically for therapists to address the needs for privacy and confidentiality. These are great options for solopreneurs as they offer you the potential of a built-in community.

Alternatives to the Office. Some people also opt to see clients in the clients' homes (in-home therapy), which can offer great flexibility for clients, especially clients who may be home-bound. Also, ecotherapy or nature-based therapy uses the outdoors, such as parks, arboretums, and walking trails as the "office." Before engaging in these alternatives, ensure that you understand the risks, have consulted your malpractice insurance provider, and communicate them to your clients.

Reflection Exercise: Alternative Office Spaces

Think about the alternative options for office space (virtual, coworking, on-demand, home office, outdoors).

- What is your preference? Why?
- What is your second choice? Would you consider a hybrid, combining some of these options?
- Is working out of your home an option? If so, what will you need to do to confirm that it offers privacy for your clients and that you are properly insured?
- Would you consider an on-demand office? If so, what amenities would you need?
- Would you consider coworking spaces? Why or why not?

Designing Your Office Space

If you opt for a physical space, you will also need to think about the interior decor of the space, and how much you are able to change it. This is another key difference among your choices in type of office. Coworking spaces may not allow you to make many changes, whereas a home office offers you greater flexibility.

Beyond the typical office furnishings such as chairs, couches, waiting room furniture, filing cabinets, coffee tables, lamps, rugs, and desks, also consider how you want clients to feel when they enter your space—the atmosphere you want to provide for them. Below are ways to attend to confidentiality, representation, and comfort for your clients.

- *Wall decor:* Consider wall decorations that will resonate with your clients. You may opt for such items as framed art, quotes, or murals.
- *Waiting room activities:* Think about how clients can occupy themselves while they wait for their appointment. If you have a waiting area,

you may want to have toys and art materials for a range of ages, for children or families, and subscribe to magazines that resonate with your clients.

- *Snacks/beverages:* Consider providing beverages such as water, tea/coffee/hot chocolate, and light snacks such as granola bars, mints (freshens everyone's breath), and candy.
- *Nature:* Plants and other natural elements such as sand and rocks are a great way to bring nature into your space, and also provide a calming environment.
- *Sensory tools:* You can help your clients feel comfortable by engaging the senses beyond the visual decor. For example, blankets, pillows, stuffed animals, and fidget tools engage the sense of touch. Mints can provide taste, and diffusers and unlit candles (no open flame) can provide scents—be sure to ask about allergies or scent sensitivities, because some smells can trigger allergic reactions.
- *Soundproofing*: Be sure to test the space to make sure that noise does not bleed from one office to another. If it does, you will need noise reduction devices to provide soundproofing.

Reflection Exercise: Office Decor

Describe the decor you want for your ideal office from the moment a client steps through your door.

- What is the vibe or feeling you want to communicate? What are some elements to project that?
- Draw an image or sketch of what your ideal office will look like.
- What is your budget for your office decor?

ORGANIZING YOUR BACK OFFICE

To get your business up and running, you will need tools to get it organized and keep it organized: tools for the back-office, behind-the-scenes tasks. Your business operations are core tools and processes that keep your business flowing and growing. With all of the technology advances, you can operate most if not all of your business with computer-based or cloud-based software. While these tools are intended to save time, improve efficiency, and offer flexibility to operate from anywhere, they can quickly add up in terms of cost. With a plethora of product options to choose from and the potential costs for monthly/annual subscriptions, do your research before you purchase or subscribe.

Below are categories of practice management software that you can use (see also Appendix D for a list of resources):

- *Electronic health records:* As the name implies, an electronic health records (EHR) system allows providers to document sessions with clients in a digital format. An EHR eliminates the need for paper charts and increases legibility of session notes and patient orders. Providers can also access an EHR from anywhere, which makes it easy for care coordination among providers in the same organization or for providers who work at different locations. Most EHRs are now part of a practice management software package (see below).

- *Practice management software:* A practice management software (PMS) system integrates a number of operational and administrative tasks into one system to simplify tasks and improve efficiency for providers and administrative staff. Most PMS systems will include electronic health record keeping, appointment scheduling, billing, invoicing, electronic consent forms, session documentation, payment collection, secure messaging, and telehealth services. This software usually offers ways to automate parts of the operation such as appointment reminders, charging a client's credit card after a session, and automatically sending invoices and receipts to clients. Some companies offer only one or two features, while other companies offer a collection of features. It is unlikely that one platform will solve all your needs, so you will have to do your research to assess what will work best for you.

- *Monitoring patient outcomes:* Using measures to monitor and track client progress, or *measurement-based care*, can improve the client therapy experience. Outcome data can be used to request reimbursement from insurance payers, offer clients insight into their progress in real time, and monitor individual therapists' performance.

- *Customer feedback:* Using software to obtain feedback from patients and customers gives you information about the strengths, areas for growth, and needs of your clientele. For example, if you regularly lead workshops, ensure that you have a system for collecting feedback from attendees.

- *Accounting software:* You will need to keep accurate and up-to-date financial records as a good business practice and to track finances for tax purposes and other financial reporting obligations that you have. Most accounting software will help you organize the business with a chart of accounts, generate invoices, print financial documents with a few clicks (e.g., income statement, balance sheet, and cash flow statements), and sync with your business bank accounts for more accurate and timely tracking of transactions.

- *Project management:* As an entrepreneur, you will have to manage so many tasks, keeping track of projects, payroll, client leads, and other tasks of the business—it is easy for some things to get lost. Project management tools help you keep track of to-do lists and projects and monitor how your team members are moving on their projects.

- *Scheduling:* Using calendar/appointment software to automate or streamline scheduling can save you time and the hassle of going back and forth with emails. Some software has features that let you offer a range of times, allow clients to schedule directly on your calendar, or allow people to vote on their preferred meeting time. Other scheduling software allows for creating automated workflows to streamline scheduling processes by sending details of meetings directly to everyone's email and calendar, which is great for consulting and coaching practices. Other automated workflows can include sending reminder emails and even collecting payments.

- *Artificial intelligence (AI):* AI software has become fully mainstream and can be useful in many aspects of a private practice or business, such as writing initial drafts of therapy and meeting notes, coding qualitative research, revising drafts of letters, and generating ideas and content for marketing. AI tools are very popular because they make certain day-to-day demands of entrepreneurship very easy to deal with, such as chatbots for customer service. However, be sure to verify information provided by AI tools, to modify results for accuracy, and to make sure that anything you share reflects your VOICE and doesn't violate your ethics and licensure mandate.

- *Customer relationship management:* A customer relationship management

(CRM) system is a tool or database that businesses use to collect and maintain customer information, such as customer communications, pipeline status, customer engagement with the business, and other data to better understand customer behavior and the customer journey.

- *Social media scheduling:* Most businesses use at least one social media platform to communicate with target audiences and increase visibility. Being able to plan out your content ahead of time and schedule it to release on a regular schedule is an ideal strategy to regularly and consistently communicate with your audience, and there is software that can help with that.

- *Graphic design creator:* To create engaging visual content that will accompany your social media posts, presentations, and product branding you will need graphics or assets that resonate with your audience. While a graphic artist can help you design templates, a number of software design apps can help you create beautiful and engaging content for your social media platforms.

Getting your back office organized is a priority before you start to see clients. There are many options to choose from, so do your research. You can also find online resources that have published product reviews, compared different products, and summarized the pros and cons of different tools. Also, talk to others to find out what tools they use and why they like the particular tool. Take note that while these software products can help save time in the long run, they usually take time at the front end to set up and to get familiar with, so be patient with yourself and the software.

It can be easy to fall into decision fatigue, so try your best to assess the software product, and then make a decision. Some tools will have a free option, a free trial, or a product demo. Take advantage of them to try out software before fully committing. If you realize a particular product is not effective for you, then try something else. It can be overwhelming to try to adapt to all these software products right away. Think about which software you want to prioritize and which ones can wait.

Take Action Exercise

- List the software tools that you want to research or try out for the various aspects of your business. What jobs will they do for you?
- What are the monthly costs? and benefits?
- Which ones will you prioritize, and which will you add on later?

CHAPTER 7 MOMENTUM AND MINDSET CHECK

Preparing to launch your business includes many, many steps, but stay with it. This chapter was designed to help you to attain the information needed to start your business and to serve as a guide for the many decisions you will have to make as an entrepreneur. We discussed forming your business structure, naming your business, and documenting your business plan using the Lean Canvas template. You also were able to visualize the type of office you want and to consider the interior design. Last but not at all least, we explored the vast types of technology tools available to therapists to make their practices operate more efficiently, including practice management systems, accounting software (getting your finances organized), and even using AI to streamline some of your tasks. Be sure to use the launch checklist to help you keep track of the tasks you'll need to complete.

- What is one takeaway that you have as you finish this chapter?
- What is a mindset shift that you have made after reading this chapter?

Protecting You and Your Business

Risk Management for Thriving Practices

Protect your business so that you can stay in business.

PROTECTING YOU AND YOUR BUSINESS

As an entrepreneur, you must take critical steps to protect your business by protecting your assets, ideas, data, property, products/services, employees, and, of course, *you*. In business as in life, many things will go right, but at times things will go wrong. It's the cycle of life. Having the right protections in place can make a difference in how your business survives any misfortune.

Business Insurance

Business insurance is a risk management strategy that helps an entrepreneurs cover the often high financial costs associated with legal defense, injury or damage caused to clients, employees, or property, medical expenses, and much more. Failing to have insurance coverage or adequate coverage will mean that you may have to pay for these liabilities from your business assets or personal assets, depending on your business structure—which could mean the close of your business. You can protect your business in several ways. Below I will share common insurances used to protect therapists and their businesses.

Malpractice Insurance

Malpractice insurance, also known as professional liability insurance, is typically used by health-care professionals to protect against claims that your services caused harm to a client. Depending on the insurance plan and coverage you purchased, malpractice insurance will typically cover all or part of your legal defense fees and damages or settlement costs. As you consider your options, you will have to make some important decisions (see below). You should consult with an insurance advisor to guide you.

- *Coverage amount:* As of this writing, typical minimum coverage for solo mental health practices is usually $1M/$3M, which means that the insurance company will cover $1 million per claim and $3 million for the length of the policy (subject to various limitations and requirements). The coverage amount for your business will be determined by the number of employees, the type of practice, and the level of risk.
- *Coverage type:* You will need to choose among several options for malpractice coverage.
  - *Occurrence-made* provides coverage whenever an insurance claim is made, as long as the policy was active at the time of the alleged event. For example, if the alleged event occurred while you were insured by Company A, but you are now insured by Company B when the claim was made, Company A will still be responsible because it was the insurer on record when the event occurred.
  - *Claims-made* provides coverage as long as you are actively insured with a particular company whenever a claim is made. Claims-made policies are often less expensive than occurrence-made policies, but with this type, if you change insurance companies, you may not be covered—unless you purchase tail insurance:
    - *Tail insurance* is an assessment that a company will charge if you were insured with a claims-made policy and you are changing insurance companies or closing your policy. Tail insurance covers you in the event that your old policy is inactive but a

claim is made. For example, if a past client files a claim for an event that happened while you were insured with Company A, but you now have claims-made insurance with Company B, you would not be covered by either company unless you have tail insurance with Company A. It may well be worth the cost to purchase a tail if you are closing a claims-made policy. Some insurance agents will offer to cover the cost of tail insurance as an incentive for switching to their company.

— *Students:* Typically, graduate programs will provide malpractice insurance, which covers any services you provide in your role as a student (e.g., research, practicum, and internships). If you plan to engage in any professional activities on your own while you are a student (e.g., consulting, speaking, volunteering, or product creation), it is critical that you look into the scope of what the school's insurance covers in terms of those activities, and purchase your own malpractice insurance to cover any gaps for your business activities.

General Liability Insurance

Commonly referred to as slip-and-fall insurance, general liability insurance protects against claims due to bodily injury (i.e., physical harm), personal injury (e.g., libel or slander), or property damage caused by your business. Subject to limitations and requirements, these policies typically cover medical expenses, legal costs for defending a claim, and any associated damages or settlement decisions. For example, if a client sustains an injury on your property and then files a lawsuit for medical costs and emotional damages, the insurance would support you in defending the lawsuit and cover associated medical costs, with some exceptions, like intentional harm or damage.

If you are purchasing, leasing, or renting a building or office, you will likely be required to obtain general liability insurance as part of the purchase or lease agreement. If you are subletting an office from another therapist, they may not ask you to get general liability insurance, but it may be in your best interests to do so. In addition, some health insurance companies require proof of general liability insurance as part of the provider credentialing application process (more on provider credentialing in Chapter 10).

Business Personal Property and Commercial Property Insurance

General liability insurance typically would not cover the contents of your office or the building. As a result, you will likely need to purchase personal property insurance to cover items up to a certain value inside the office building, such as your computers, furniture, art, and other items. If you are planning to purchase a building, you will need to obtain commercial property insurance, which typically protects your business's physical assets from damage due to fire, theft, storm, and vandalism.

Cybersecurity Insurance

If your business is engaged in online activities, such as collecting online payments, or stores personal information or protected health information about your clients, such as their name, date of birth, mailing address, phone number, or credit card information, your business is vulnerable to a cyberattack. Cybersecurity insurance covers or defrays the costs associated with damage and loss caused by cybersecurity incidents (e.g. a data breach), such as notifying customers about a data breach and monitoring their credit history for a period of time after. If you have been the victim of another company's data security breach, you may already be familiar with the resources that are often offered to the targets of cyberattacks and their customers.

Key Person (Key Man) Insurance

This involves taking out a life insurance policy for the owner or a key executive of the business to protect the company financially in the event of death or disability of key personnel. Key Man insurance provides funds to help pay off any debts, support the business due to financial losses incurred by the employee's absence, or pay the family of the deceased for their interest in the business.

Income Replacement Insurance

In the event that you become ill and are unable to work, income replacement insurance cover a portion of your income for an identified period of time. If you've ever worked for a company and had to take medical leave, you may have had short-term disability or long-term disability, depending on the length and severity of your illness.

For self-employed therapists, replacement coverage is a priority. We all get sick at some point in our lives, and we can never predict what illness might befall us or how long it will take to recover. Income replacement insurance can offer peace of mind and allow you the time you need to fully recover without having to return to work prematurely.

Workers' Compensation Insurance

Workers' compensation insurance, or workers' comp, covers medical costs and compensation for employees who are injured on the job and is required for any business with employees. Depending on your business structure and the state you operate in, you may or may not be required to have workers' comp even if you are the only employee of the business. However, as you think about protecting *you* as a key asset of the business, think carefully if you opt out of this type of insurance.

Health Insurance

Health insurance provides cost savings for medical expenses and can protect you from the exorbitant financial costs should you have a major or even minor medical issue. In some states health insurance is required for its residents, and in others it is not. As a business owner, you must take care of your health and attend to your routine health appointments—this is crucial to the longevity of your business. However, the truth is that health insurance in the United States is very expensive compared to other developed countries. Finding options for lower-cost health-care insurance is necessary because you don't want to skip routine health appointments in an effort to save money. One way to reduce this business expense is to check with your local or specialty professional association, or your local chamber of commerce for discounted group pricing. You can also contact an insurance broker to obtain an estimate of premiums, covered services, and out-of-pocket expenses.

A Note About Purchasing Insurance. This is not an exhaustive list of the different forms of insurance that you can use for your business. Be sure to consult an insurance broker who can help you identify the types of insurance that will adequately protect your business. You can also talk to entrepreneurs who operate similar businesses to identify the types of insurance that they have used for their business.

With any type of insurance, you want to be clear about what is covered and what is not. Read the policy documents carefully, including the fine print, and ask questions. Obtain a few quotes so that you can compare the coverage options and costs, and discuss differences with your insurance broker.

Most of all, remember that insurance is there to protect you and your business. Without insurance coverage, your out-of-pocket expenses for legal representation, medical costs, and any damage you incur could wipe out your business . . . that's not worth the risk.

Take Action Exercise

- Identify two or three business insurance and health insurance brokers that you will reach out to.
- Identify two or three business entrepreneurs you will ask about the types of insurance they have for their business.
- Make a list of the types of insurance you will need for your business.

PROTECTING YOUR BUSINESS WITH CONTRACTS

In running a business, it is important to have contracts for any business relationships with employees, vendors, and clients. A *contract* is a legally binding agreement between two or more parties that outline, usually in writing, the terms of the relationship and obligations related to some type of exchange.

Therapist Contracts

As a therapist, it has probably been drilled into you that you need to provide an informed consent document when you are starting with a new client. The informed consent document provides clarity for you and your clients about the therapy services that you will offer, including your approach, confidentiality, mandated reporting, explanation of fees, social media policy, and much more. If you are using a practice management software, it is likely it has templates of contracts you can use—you may need to tweak them to fit your practice, but the outline is there.

Contracts for Therapy Practices. General operations of a therapy practice require various contracts on a regular basis, which are outlined below:

- *Informed consent* is a document that outlines the role of the therapist and the client, including client rights, confidentiality and exceptions to confidentiality, fee structure, cancellation policy, potential risks and benefits of therapy, emergency coverage (if you are on a leave of absence), record keeping, social media policy, and working with minors.

- *Medical record release form* is a legal form authorizing you to release or receive protected health information and medical records for a client.
- *Telehealth consent* is an agreement provided to a therapy client that provides information about using telehealth services, including what is required to have a stable connection, what happens if the connection is lost, and emergency procedures.
- *Good faith estimate* is a document explaining the costs of health-care services clients are receiving from a provider. As of this writing, a reasonable estimate of costs and services is required for clients who are uninsured or are not using health insurance (Centers for Medicare and Medicaid Services, n.d.).

Business Contracts. As a business owner, you will need to use various contracts whenever you are entering into arrangements with a colleague, client, vendor, or employee. Here are some examples of contracts that you will likely need (see appendices, I provide some illustrative samples of contracts):

- *Contract for services/consulting contract:* This contract with a customer outlines key terms, such as the scope of services, compensation and payment terms, termination clause, and work product ownership (see Appendix J).
- *Speaker contract:* This typically clarifies with your client the summary of your topic, date of event, fees and payment terms, cancellation policy, and any requirements that you may have for the event, such as parking, sound/tech check, or recording (see Appendix K).
- *Offer letter:* This is a letter businesses often provide when offering employment to a job candidate that outlines their role, compensation, and benefits being offered, and sometimes includes basic terms and conditions. (I suggest that you consult with a knowledgeable human resources professional, such as an employment lawyer, before sending an offer letter to be sure that you understand when an offer letter might be viewed as a contract.)

- *Employment contract:* This contract between the employer and employee outlines the job title, job description, salary/wages, work schedule, and other information pertinent to completion of the contract.
- *Nondisclosure agreement (NDA):* This agreement establishes a confidential relationship or confidentiality regarding sensitive information. The party who signs agrees to hold information in confidence for a specified period.

Terms of Service Agreements. If you offer a technology platform, app, or other form of technology, you will also be well-advised to provide a terms of service agreement. This type of agreement outlines the rules for visitors to your platform, users of your app, or users of other technology. It aims to limit your legal liability while also protecting against issues such as copyright infringements. If you have used another business's app or web-based product, you likely had to read the terms of service before proceeding. Terms of service agreements are usually long documents filled with legal language and so-called "fine print" that many people skip to the end of and agree to proceed without actually reading the terms. While you may be among those who skip terms of service as a consumer, do not want to skip this as an entrepreneur. Also, as your app, platform, or other technology changes, you will need to update your terms of service.

Disclaimers. Depending on the products or services you are offering, you may also need to include a disclaimer statement in offering those products/services to the public. A disclaimer statement would assert your lack of responsibility and/or liability in situations such as a potential consumer using your products or services and claiming to be harmed.

Working With a Contract Law Attorney

Working with an attorney to create solid contract documents is an important step to protect you and your business's finances and intellectual property. While seeking legal counsel can seem pricey, it's one of those things, like insurance, where a mistake can be more costly. It is fairly easy to obtain contract templates from online sources (and starting from a template might save some money; as the attorney does not have to draft each document from scratch), but you will want an attorney to review your documents to ensure that they comply with any relevant state or federal laws. You can also look for free or low-cost legal services in your area (e.g., law school clinics; small business programs).

PROTECTING YOUR BUSINESS WITH ESTATE PLANNING

Estate planning involves creating a plan that articulates how your personal affairs should be handled if you become incapacitated due to severe injury or physical or cognitive impairment, or in the event of your death. (I'm not trying to be morbid here, but we are mortal beings.) It requires identifying how your assets will be shared or distributed, naming who will make medical decisions on your behalf if you fall ill (sometimes called a medical proxy), and who will handle your financial and legal affairs (sometimes referred to as an executor).

Professional Will

A professional will is a document that lays out how your business affairs will be handled in the event of your death or incapacitation. It's like estate planning, but for your business. For therapists, this is particularly important, given the confidential nature of our profession as a therapist's practice. A key purpose of a professional will is to assign an executor who understands the importance of HIPAA compliance, often another therapist, who will ensure that your clients' protected health information is confidentially maintained (this may also be someone you can use for emergency/vacation coverage; see below). The executor will need access to all areas of your business to ensure a smooth transition for your clients and to ensure your ethical obligations as a mental health professional are maintained. Of particular importance, in the event of your death or incapacitation the executor will need to contact your clients to inform them of your status and make a plan for referring them to another provider. In addition, you will want to include a plan for how the executor will be paid for these services.

The American Psychological Association (2003, 2004, 2014a, 2014b) has outlined the main elements that go into creating a professional will:

- *Assign an executor and provide access to the following:*
  —Current and past client caseload and client contact information

> > —Practice management software (including usernames and passwords)
> > —Appointment calendar
> - *Access to physical office:* location of office, keys to office, filing cabinets, archived medical records, and information for anyone who can assist (e.g., landlord, business manager)
> - *Technology:* usernames and passwords for computers, telephone number, voicemail, email accounts, and other software
> - *Storage:* name and location of any off-site file storage
> - *Business documents:* insurance policies, bank accounts, billing and financial information

You would be well-advised to consult with an attorney to create your professional will, ideally one who has experience with estate planning and mental health law. You will also want to consult with an attorney to create a trust and/or will for your personal assets.

PROTECTING YOUR INTELLECTUAL PROPERTY

Intellectual property is a term that refers to any original works or inventions that you may create. As a mental health professional, consultant, or speaker, you will likely create content based on your expertise. Taking the steps to establish or document ownership and protect that intellectual property adds value to your business and enables you to license and make your products available to others while maintaining and protecting your ownership.

As a Black/BIPOC entrepreneur, I really want to emphasize this area. We have seen stories after stories of BIPOC creators whose financial success was limited because they did not own the rights to their original work. Sometimes in our haste to get our work out to others, or to get a contract, we skip the steps to secure ownership. And sometimes people may bank on your naivety and rush you to sign away your rights. Always carefully read all contracts before signing, and even better, have an attorney review them first.

Copyright
A copyright establishes ownership of an original work such as books, photographs, worksheets, models, frameworks, blogs, presentations, and much more.

A *copyright notice* is a mark that you can affix to any original work that you created: copyright symbol ("C" inside a circle), year, and name of the creator, like this: © 2024 Charmain Jackman.

Copyright infringement occurs when a copyright-protected work has been reproduced or made into derivative work without the permission of the author (unless a copyright exception or defense such as fair use applies). Registering your copyrights may be beneficial, as registration serves as a public record and it may put you in a stronger legal position if infringement occurs (and may be necessary for a legal case).

Works for Hire. Generally the person who creates a work owns the copyright. However, an exception to this occurs with "works for hire." In this situation, a work is prepared by an employee within the so-called "scope of their employment," or someone commissions you—or you commission someone—via a written contract to create a product for them which falls into a category such as instructional text or a contribution to a collective work. If you create something in a works for hire situation, you cannot claim copyright ownership of the work and the person that employs or hires you is the copyright owner (something which may be negotiated except in the employer/employee context). As you enter independent contractor relationships, this may be a condition of the contract. Again, read your contracts carefully.

Trademark

Trademarks are words, phrases, and symbols associated with a business or product such as business name, product or service name, logo, and tagline. Even when you have not registered the trademark, you can show that you claim to own a trademark by using ^{TM} for products or ^{SM} for services. However, this may not protect your mark if someone registers the mark before you do. With trademarks, the first person to file the trademark application may be significant. Registering a trademark can be a complicated process, particularly if there are similar names being used by individuals or businesses in the same or a similar field. In addition, trademarks must fall in one of 45 classes or categories used to organize products (e.g., food, movie, clothing, education, coaching). Unfortunately, I had to learn the hard way how important it is to apply to register a trademark in a timely manner.

Registering a trademark has a number of steps, and there are associated fees. The U.S. Patent and Trademark Office (USPTO) reviews the mark to ensure it is not a word used in everyday language, does not include profanity, is not already in use at the state and national levels, or, can not be confused with a similar mark. Sometimes businesses will register a mark before they are ready to use it, and if they do not use it within a specified period of time, they run the risk of losing the opportunity to keep their trademark. When filing your mark, you have to determine the appropriate class—the 45 categories the trademarks office uses to organize goods and services—for your product or service.

When application for a registered trademark has been approved by the USPTO, you can use the registered trademark symbol, ® (i.e., "R" in a circle) in connection with the use of the now-registered mark. For example, the name Thriving Therapreneur was approved as a trademark in 2023 in class 44 and can now appear as Thriving Therapreneur® in promotional materials.

Patents

A patent is a designation allowing the exclusive use of an invention for a specified period of time. Patents are usually reserved for machines, medicines, chemical compositions, and technology processes and designs. For people in the mental health field, this might include an app you invent to diagnose, treat, or monitor mental health conditions; designing technology to facilitate therapy sessions (e.g., telehealth), or creating an AI-assisted chatbot to provide mental health support. *Patent pending* alerts others that a patent application has been filed, but the invention has no legal protection until the patent has been approved—only then can you include *patented* on the product.

Working With an Intellectual Property Attorney

If you decide to pursue copyrights, trademarks, and/or patents, you will find it helpful to work with a specialist intellectual property attorney. While this may come at an additional expense, you will know that the process is done correctly. Recall our discussion about operating within your expertise—while you may "save" money by doing it yourself, you may lose time, money, and your intellectual property if you make a mistake.

Take Action Exercise

Identify two or three attorneys, with contact information, that you can consult with for the following tasks:

- Business structure
- Contracts and agreements
- Estate planning
- Intellectual property

PROTECTING YOUR BUSINESS BY PAYING YOUR TAXES

There's a quote about death and taxes: two things in life that are certain. Paying taxes is a necessary part of operating any business, and understanding the taxes that go along with your business structure will ensure that you are prepared to remain in compliance with tax requirements. If you have products and employees, your business will be responsible for paying beyond the basic taxes you may be familiar with. Failure to pay your taxes can create problems and cause you to incur additional financial and other burdens, such as penalties, late fees, reduction in credit score, liens on personal assets, garnishment of wages, and in the worst case, imprisonment.

Below are some common categories of tax you can expect for your business:

- *Income taxes:* All businesses are required to file federal and state income tax returns.
- *Estimated quarterly tax payments:* Businesses often pay Social Security, Medicare, and income taxes quarterly. Businesses must pay taxes quarterly if their expected income meets a certain threshold. If you do not pay or underpay your quarterly taxes, you could have a penalty.
- *Payroll taxes:* If you have employees, you will withhold taxes from their paycheck each pay period for their contribution to Social Security and Medicare. The amount of income tax the employer withholds is based on the employee's earning and the information the employee uses to complete the W-4 form (withholding taxes).
- *Employment taxes:* This is an employee's contribution to Social Security and Medicare (the employer pays a portion), and all of their Federal Unemployment Tax.

- *Self-employment tax:* This is assessed for sole proprietors, independent contractors, and members of partnerships to cover the portion of their Social Security and Medicare taxes that an employer would withhold for them if they were employees.
- *Sales tax:* If you have a product that you are selling to customers, you will have to pay a state sales tax (except for states with no sales tax). If you are operating an e-commerce business or do business in other states, you will also be required to pay sales tax to the states where purchases or business occurs.
- *Corporate excise tax:* If your business is formed as a corporation, it may be subject to corporate excise taxes. In addition to federal tax requirements, the laws governing how various businesses will be taxed vary from state to state.

Qualified business expenses are deductions that you can take for certain expenses you incur as part of running your business. For example, travel to a client's home, professional services, or office supplies may be qualified business expenses. Talk to a tax professional about expenses that qualify.

For more information about taxes and your tax liability, consult with a business tax accountant. Personal taxes and business taxes are different, plus the tax codes change every year, so working with a business tax accounting professional who understands business taxes is recommended. For business structure and information about tax categories, visit https://www.irs.gov/businesses.

Take Action Exercise

Identify two or three business tax accountants, with contact information, that you can consult with for the following tasks:

- Business structure
- Estimated quarterly taxes
- Qualified business expenses
- Identify two bookkeepers to discuss their services and how they can support your business.

Protecting Your Business During Vacations and Medical Leaves

One last area to consider is how to protect your business when you have to step away for an extended period of time such as vacation or medical leave. When you have a planned or unplanned leave, it is important to identify and obtain permission from at least one therapist who will serve as a backup when you are away. This mental health professional may also be the person you identify as the executor for your professional will.

For planned absences. Plan ahead and provide clients with information about the start and end of your absence, and offer the name and contact information for the covering therapists that they can contact if they need support while you are away. Explain what circumstances are appropriate to contact the covering therapists, and what they should do if they are having a mental health crisis: call 988 for mental health crises and 911 for medical emergencies.

For unplanned absences or emergencies. Two steps will help smooth any emergency absences that may arise:

- Be sure that you have completed a professional will (see above), so that an executor is in place with information needed to access your practice.
- Your informed consent document (see above) should include what clients can do if you experience an emergency and are not able to contact them right away.

Take Action Exercise

- Schedule a call with at least two therapists to ask if they would be able to serve as back-up coverage when you are on vacation or leave. Once you have a therapist identified, you can include this information in the informed consent document.

CHAPTER 8 MOMENTUM AND MINDSET CHECK

Bubble wrap your business. While building your business, be mindful to take steps to protect it. This chapter outlined the broad list of services and products that business owners use to protect their businesses, such as insurance, taxes, copyrights, and trademarks. It sounds quite expensive, but it is important to consider that these expenses will help you and your business survive and thrive should there be any legal or taxation issues. Consult with an expert to help you prioritize which services you will need right away and which once you can add as you grow. Remember, there are a number of community resources that offer free or discounted professional services, so check what is available in your community.

- What is one takeaway that you have as you finish this chapter?
- What is a mindset shift that you have made after reading this chapter?

CHAPTER 9

Passion to Profit

Taking Charge of Your Financial Future

··

Get cozy with your numbers.

YOU CAN DO GOOD AND MAKE MONEY

You are getting into business to make money, right? The only correct answer here is *yes*. Even if you are launching a social impact company that has a mission of addressing a social problem in your community or in the world, you will need money to do it. Regardless of the business structure, making a profit is a good thing, even if it is a nonprofit organization. Profit ensures that you can carry out your mission, expand your team, make an impact, and have funds to reinvest in your business. *Don't shy away from making a profit.*

Let's take a moment to make a distinction between profit and exploitation. When you think about profit, maybe what comes to mind are those companies that use their profits to distribute exorbitant bonuses to the CEOs and other senior level leaders but do not to pay their frontline employees living wages. This inequitable distribution of profits where company's leaders are driven by greed, not a mission, and have no problem exploiting their employees—that is exploitation. I hope that is not the type of business you plan to run. Nonetheless, growing a business that allows you to cover your expenses, pay fair wages, and execute your mission requires you to make a profit.

My goal is to help you launch and grow a business that is profitable, that meets your needs, and that gives you the freedom to do the things you love (in and out of your business). As a therapist and business owner, thinking about money can feel extremely uncomfortable. As discussed in Chapter 3 on wealth-building mindsets, ways that we were raised and ways that we were socialized into the mental health field can make talking about money feel taboo. I hope the exercises in Chapter 3 have helped you shift your mindset about money and have made you feel more comfortable and confident in money conversations. If you have not completed those exercises, *stop here* and go back to Chapter 3—after you do the work in that chapter, you will find the work in this chapter much, much easier.

REVENUE AND PROFIT

Simply put, *profit* occurs when revenues are greater than expenses:

$$\text{Profit} = \text{Revenue} > \text{Expenses}$$

Revenue, or money coming into the business, must exceed *expenses*, or money going out of the business, in order to make a profit. When your expenses exceed revenue, your business is operating at a *loss*:

$$\text{Loss} = \text{Expenses} > \text{Revenue}$$

These are simplified equations—in reality, finances can be more complex. However, at the center, these equations offer a quick and easy way to figure out how your business is doing. Ideally, your goal is to get your business to a profitable stage as soon as possible. When your business earns a profit, this will allow you to start achieving the goals you have established.

When I first got into business, I focused on revenue, revenue, revenue. I had these large revenue goals, with no clear plan on how to reach them. While revenue is important, it is not the only metric to watch. If you are generating a high revenue but your expenses are more than what you bring in, guess what: your business will not be profitable. At the end of the day, your profits, not just your revenue, matter for the sustainability of your business. This does not mean that profits are the only marker of success—your people and your mission matter, especially if you are operating a decolonized business (see Appendix Q for strategies to build a decolonized business). However, your business will not last if it does not make a profit.

UNLOCKING MULTIPLE REVENUE STREAMS

Revenue is the income or money you receive for performing a service or selling a product. Most private practices offer individual therapy, which provides a steady stream of revenue. Private practice relies on a one-on-one model, with interactions between a therapist and an individual client, couple or family. This model, what I call "on the hour for the dollar," is limited because of the person power needed to grow revenue. It is not sustainable for a successful solopreneur because your revenue will be limited by your time—the number of hours in a day or week that you can see clients—which is also a recipe for burnout. Even with a group practice model, you will always have to add more providers, which will increase your expenses, to expand your revenue. While group therapy offers a one-to-many model, you still spend time recruiting individuals and making sure that they are a good fit for the group. To prepare businesses for growth, I strongly advise all my coaching clients to *diversify* their revenue streams with activities such as consulting, professional development programs, speaking engagements (workshops, keynotes, and panels), writing, and product development, in addition to traditional therapy and assessments. (These will be addressed more fully in Chapter 12.)

Establishing a therapy practice is one of the most common types of therapist businesses, likely because of the ease and low cost to set up. Some therapists, realizing the limits of their time, will consider expanding to a group practice model to meet the increased demand for their services (e.g., long waiting list) and to grow revenue, by hiring other therapists. Therapists have historically used therapy as the primary revenue sources, with occasional workshops and speaking gigs. Given your training as a therapist and your lived experiences, you have many ways to leverage your expertise and an infinite number of revenue streams you can tap into—you simply need a strategy for doing so.

As a business coach for therapists over the past 10 years, I get so excited when my clients realize how much of their expertise they have not tapped into and how much money they are leaving on the table as a result. Plus, diversifying your revenue allows you to have a steady income stream when there are ebbs in certain segments or at certain times of the year. For example, the summer months can be slow in some regions because clients are on vacation. What do you do then? You could, for example, organize a summer retreat or consult with a summer camp to have revenue flowing all year, or you could plan your vacation during those slow periods. In addition to offering services, you can diversify by creating products, an excellent revenue source because they typically generate passive income.

As you think of diversifying your income, remember that you do not have to start each service or product at the same time. You can map out which service(s) you want to start with and add others later. Also, do not limit yourself only to services that you are comfortable doing—be bold and step out of your comfort zone. Yes, it will feel risky, but it can also expose you to a source of revenue that you did not anticipate.

PERSONAL REFLECTION: LEAPING OUT OF MY COMFORT ZONE

When I first started my private practice, my primary services were therapy, psychological testing, and forensic evaluations. Then I started consulting with an organization that led parent/caregiver workshops. While I was open to providing workshops, it *terrified* me—seriously! Fear of public speaking, or *glossophobia*, is more common than fear of dying! But instead of running away, I leaned in. It was definitely hard, and my anxiety was high when I was in front of an audience. However, the organization provided training, and I received feedback, which I used to help me improve. Now, I've spoken at hundreds of events in front of small and large audiences and I can proudly add a TEDx speaker to my title— something I would never have imagined achieving when I started my business. I could have easily walked away from speaking because of my fear and anxiety, but I saw how my colleagues used their speaking platforms to grow their brands and businesses. I approached it with a growth mindset and knew that I would get better the more I did it. Public speaking offered me an opportunity to reach a larger audience and to increase my revenue, with a lower investment of time and effort.

Tracking Your Business Expenses

Expenses are the costs associated with operating a business. Every business will have expenses—you cannot avoid it. As you prepare to launch your business, you will have expenses that are solely associated with getting the business started (e.g., furniture for an office, fees to register the business), and there will be ongoing costs with running the business. You can check out Appendix B for budget considerations for your business finances.

Startup Costs. These are initial costs or expenses that you will incur when you open a new business. These are typically costs that you will have one time and they are not recurring. For example, when you are leasing an office, you may have to pay a security deposit, installation costs for the internet, purchase new furniture and interior design, and costs for build-out if you need to change the layout of the space.

Operating Expenses. These are the ongoing costs you incur as you operate your business. They typically include rent, payroll, taxes, marketing, and insurance. Some of these costs will be *fixed expenses*, which means that the costs are the same each month (e.g., rent and some utilities), regardless of how many sales you generate. On the other hand, *variable expenses* will change or fluctuate depending on particular criteria, such as the volume of your business. For example, hourly wages and credit card transaction fees may fluctuate depending on employee schedules and online sales, respectively.

Costs of Goods Sold (COGS). COGS are the direct costs associated with delivering a product or service. Calculating COGS is an important metric because it allows you to assess your profit margin. For products, it may include manufacturing, labor, and shipping costs. For service businesses, COGS could include labor costs and material costs for that specific service. Unfortunately, some business owners price their products without considering the actual costs of the product or service that they are delivering, which will be misleading and could lead you to underprice your products or services, impacting your profit.

Payroll Costs. Depending on your business, you may have employees who are hourly or salaried and receive a W-2 form and independent contractors who receive a 1099 form. The payroll costs for W-2 employees, people under your direct supervision, include not only the hourly or wages that you have agreed to pay but the payroll taxes such as Social Security, Medicare, and unemployment insurance. *Independent contractors*, people you contract to independently, execute their roles with limited direct management from you, may include people you contract to provide services such as (depending on the circumstances) bookkeeping, accounting, graphic design, and social media management. Independent contractors receive 1099s from your business at the end of the year and you do not have to pay payroll taxes for independent contractors.

Take Action Exercise

You can use the template in Appendix B as your guide.

- Given the type of business you plan to launch, what are some start-up costs that you anticipate?
- What are some operating expenses that you anticipate? What are your variable expenses? Fixed expenses?
- What are the costs associated with making a product and getting it to your customers or of delivering a service (cost of goods sold)?
- How many employees (W-2 employees) do you employ currently or plan to employ? What will be their hourly rate or monthly salary?
- How many independent contractors will you bring on? What will be their fees?

Put You on the Payroll

One of the most concerning statements I often hear from entrepreneurs of color is that they are not taking a salary from the business. It's sometimes said as a badge of honor. I want to disrupt this thinking right here, right now. *If your business cannot pay you, it's not a business, it's just a hobby.* Ouch! These were words a number of mentors and coaches said to me as I was building InnoPsych. Those words hurt, but they were true, and I needed to hear them. What it meant was that I had no clue what *I* cost, and that my "profit" was misleading if it did not include the cost of my time. In fact, many Black and BIPOC therapists who I have coached or who have attended my workshops have told me that they never thought about the salary they wanted to earn because they are accustomed to being told what they will get paid.

Not paying yourself is like riding a bike but never taking off the training wheels. Just as you will never know if you can ride on your own if you keep on the training wheels, you will never know if your business will survive if you do not pay yourself. Paying yourself forces you to truly evaluate your business model, your pricing structure, and your expenses.

When you run a business, you are putting in time, sweat equity, and expertise, and likely investing your own capital. However, if the business is not able to sustain what you cost, it will not be profitable. While you may forgo taking a salary for a while as you start your business, there has to be a clear period of time after which you start to take a salary. If the business cannot afford you, then those are numbers that you have to pay attention to.

PERSONAL REFLECTION: PAY YOURSELF FIRST

When I started InnoPsych, I was still working full-time and I did not see a need to pay myself, as I had a salary coming in. I erroneously thought that I was helping the business by not taking a salary. *Wrong!* As I was not taking a salary, I had not given *any* thought to how the business would support me when I would eventually leave my 9-to-5. Knowing what I know now, I would have realized sooner that the business was not making a profit at the time, and I would have explored other sources of revenue much earlier.

Reflection Time

Take a moment to check in on yourself, by responding to the following prompts:

- Have you thought about paying yourself? Why or why not?
- How are you sitting with the idea of paying yourself? Do you agree or disagree?
- What salary do you want to earn from your business?

Appendix B has a template budget calculator that lets you estimate revenue sources, business expenses, and gross and net profit. An interactive version is available at www.innopsych.com.

Exercise: Lean Canvas

Let's revisit the Lean Canvas template in Figure 7.1 and respond to the following prompts:

Under *Revenue*:
- Write down three of your expected highest revenue-generating activities.
- Write down your projected revenue for the first three years.

Under *Expenses*:
- Write down the top three highest expenses that you will likely incur.
- Write down the expected expenses for your first three years.

Under *Metrics:*
- Write down the metrics what will help you track the financial success of your business.

GET COZY WITH YOUR NUMBERS

Developing financial literacy to understand the finances in your business and your businesses financial health is paramount to being a successful entrepreneur. Again, the research shows that mental health professionals prefer to avoid numbers, and my experience coaching therapists has borne that out. And if I can be honest with you, it was my experience too. *We don't like to talk about money.* But guess what: if you intend to be a successful entrepreneur, then getting cozy with your numbers is a must. Yes, it will be uncomfortable, it will make you feel raw and vulnerable, and you may even shed a tear (or two), but it is necessary.

Three Financial Statements You Need to Know

There are three financial statements that all entrepreneurs need to review on a regular basis. These statements help you assess whether your business is operating at a profit or a loss, understand how cash is flowing in and out of your business, and track how your business is managing its assets, debt, and equity. You can check these financial statements as often as you like, and you can compare months, quarters, and years to see how your business is performing over time. In addition, you can create these statements on your own, use accounting software (for examples of such software, see Appendix D), or work with a bookkeeper or accountant to generate them for you.

Table 9.1 Sample P&L statement from a part-time private practice (Year 1)

Profit and Loss

January–December 2022

Category	Amount
Income	
40300 Sales of product revenue	**9,369.08**
Speaking engagements	4,000.00
Therapy services	90,205.96
Total income	**$103,575.04**
51000 Cost of goods sold	703.32
Total cost of goods sold	**$703.32**
Gross profit	**$102,871.72**
Expenses	
60000 Advertising and promotion	189.75
60400 Bank fees and service charges	149.85
62000 Continuing education	1,700.00
62300 Dues and subscriptions	1,494.61
64200 Charitable donations	1,015.00
64300 Meals and entertainment	2,295.91
64600 Software expenses	1,021.38
64900 Office supplies	1,040.62
65000 Independent contractors	27,640.00
67000 Postage and delivery	168.37
67100 Legal and professional services	6,523.00
68400 Transportation and travel	6,074.19
68700 Communication	139.19
68800 Taxes and licenses	190.00
69000 Event rental	531.60
Total expenses	**50,173.47**
Net income (gross profit – total expenses)	**$52,698.25**

Profit and Loss Statement. The income statement, or profit and loss statement (P&L), provides a snapshot of your business's revenue, costs, and expenses for a specific time period (month, quarter, year, etc.), and it shows *net income* (revenue minus expenses)—whether the business is operating at a profit or loss—for the specified period. Table 9.1 shows a sample P&L from a part-time therapy practice. Its revenue sources include speaking and therapy services and the expenses include office supplies, rent, professional fees (i.e., accountant, marketing), meals, and contractors. The net income for the business shows a profit.

Balance Sheet. The balance sheet captures a company's *assets*, or what a company owns (e.g., cash/money on hand, property, inventory, investments, accounts receivable/money owed to you); *liabilities*, or what you owe to others (i.e., loans, wages, payroll taxes, income tax); plus *equity*, or the value of the company and what the owners and shareholders actually own—what is left after a company's liabilities are paid (e.g., retained earnings or profit that is kept in the business, stock investments). The balance sheet is based on the formula

$$Assets = Liabilities + Equity$$

and as the name implies, both sides of the equation must be balanced. In the sample balance sheet shown in Table 9.2, total assets equal total liabilities plus equity, so the account is balanced as expected.

Cash Flow Statement. The cash flow statement shows how money or cash is flowing in and out of your business based on the operating activities (e.g., therapy services, consulting, and speaking), investment activities (e.g., buying or selling equipment assets), and financing activities (e.g., debt payments or new loans). In the example shown in Table 9.3, the entrepreneur is comparing the four quarters for 2019. You can see that quarter 1 (Q1) had a loss (net income = –$1,779.77), as more money was going out than coming in. Q2 had the highest net income ($15,960.33), which was a profit, and in Q4, had the highest cash withdrawal ($7,711.17), which resulted in the lowest quarterly net cash increase that year ($1,295.10).

Reviewing the cash flow statement can provide insights into how you invoice clients. Are you billing your clients routinely? How quickly do you get funds once you send an invoice? What strategies can help you ensure timely payment? These questions are explored in Chapter 10 on charging your price with confidence.

FINANCES FOR THE TRANSITION

Now it's time to talk about how you set up your finances for your transition to private practice. Many therapists start their private practice while working a full-time job, while others make the leap into private practice right away. Regardless of which approach you choose, considering how to prepare from

Table 9.2 Sample balance sheet from a part-time private practice (Year 1)
Balance Sheet
As of December 31, 2021

	TOTAL
ASSETS	
Current Assets	
Bank accounts	
10200 Checking account - 0001	14,434.80
PayPal Bank	55.44
Total bank accounts	**$14,490.24**
Accounts receivable	
11000 Accounts receivable	7,240.630
Total accounts receivable	**7,240.630**
Total current assets	**$21,730.87**
Other current assets	
12200 Inventory	0.00
12600 Undeposited funds	0.00
Total other current assets	**$ 0.00**
TOTAL ASSETS	**$21,730.87**
LIABILITIES AND EQUITY	
Liabilities	
Bank credit card	$5,400.00
Total liabilities	**$5,400.00**
Equity	
32000 Opening balance equity	0.00
37000 Retained earnings	16,330.87
Total equity	**16,330.87**
TOTAL LIABILITIES AND EQUITY	**$21,730.87**

Table 9.3 Sample cash flow statement

Statement of Cash Flows

January–December 2019

	JAN–MAR 2019 (Q1)	APR–JUN 2019 (Q2)	JUL–SEP 2019 (Q3)	OCT–DEC 2019 (Q4)	TOTAL
OPERATING ACTIVITIES					
Net Income	–1,779.77	15,960.33	5,119.17	9,100.69	$28,400.42
Total adjustments to reconcile		–1,500.00	277.15	–93.83	$ –1,316.68
Net cash provided by operating activities	$ –1,779.77	$14,460.33	$5,396.32	$9,006.86	$27,083.74
FINANCING ACTIVITIES					
Net cash provided by financing activities	$13,672.00	$ –2,317.26	$ –270.79	$ –7,711.76	$3,372.19
NET CASH INCREASE FOR PERIOD	$11,892.23	$12,143.07	$5,125.53	$1,295.10	$30,455.93

a financial perspective will set you up for success as you make the transition to entrepreneurship.

Your Costs of Living

A question that I ask entrepreneurs is: "what do you cost?", so I'll ask you too: *How much do you cost?* As I mentioned above, putting yourself on the payroll helps you have clarity about your business's true financial picture. As a result, knowing what you cost will help determine your salary and what the business needs to pay you.

In figuring out what *you* cost, consider what your current annual salary includes:

- *Benefits:* paid time off, sick time, insurance premiums, and 401k
- *Household expenses:* rent/mortgage, car/transportation, utilities, food, and so on

- *Costs associated with the lifestyle that you want:* vacation costs, gym membership, childcare/adult care costs, private chef, monthly massages, and so forth.

Charting Your Ideal Lifestyle

As you consider your time in your business, remember to include time spent on indirect activities such as back office and administrative tasks, consulting with bookkeepers and accounting, marketing and content creation, attending professional conferences and networking events. It is also crucial to think about your time away from the office: your personal time, sick time, and vacation days. When you work for a company, your time off is typically decided with no input from you. As an entrepreneur, you get to decide your time away from the business, which makes it necessary to plan ahead. This time away, when you are not actively generating income, must be included in your calculations.

In order to make an informed decision about the lifestyle you want, you will calculate the impact that these decisions (e.g., time off and weekly hours) will have on your net income. For example, the hourly rate you charge and how many hours you work per week will impact your bottom line. You may opt to work shorter hours per week and charge a higher hourly rate or, alternatively, take less time off. As I was trying to figure out the math for my business, I came up with this session fee calculator that manipulates session fee, hours worked per week, and weeks per year. If you want to play around with your

Table 9.4 Jackman session fee calculator

A. Hours worked per week	30	30	25
B. Session fee (per hour)	$100	$125	$250
C. Percentage increase	0%	25%	150%
D. Weekly gross income (A × B)	$3,000	$3,750	$6,250
E. Weeks off per year	6	6	6
F. Weeks worked per year	46	46	46
G. Annual gross salary (D × F)	**138,000**	**172,500**	**287,500**
H. Estimated expenses	$50,000	$50,000	$50,000
I. Net salary (G – H)	**$88,000**	**$122,500**	**$237,500**
J. Percentage increase	0	39%	170%

numbers, you can find an interactive version of the session fee calculator (Table 9.4) at www.innopsych.com.

Emergency Fund

Money you set aside for unexpected emergency expenses as you operate your business might cover, for example, a broken computer, loss of revenue due illness, or delayed receipt of payments. Having this fund to draw from allows you to meet emergency financial obligations without needing to use high-interest credit cards or to borrow money from family and friends. While there is no magic number, people typically reserve an amount that will cover at least 3 months of business expenses (including your salary). Of course, you have to know your monthly expenses—that's why "Budgeting for Your Business," in Chapter 3, covered this topic in detail. Depending on your tolerance for risk, you may want to accumulate 6 months or more, or only 1–2 months, but I would recommend no less than 3 months. It's best to create a separate account for your emergency fund, so that you are not tempted to use it for your operating expenses.

Take Action Exercise

Take a few minutes to write down your desired numbers in Table 9.4. As you do, consider these prompts:

- What do you want your annual salary to be?
- What will your work–life balance look like?
- How many days/weeks of vacation do you intend to take each year?
- How many sick days and mental health days will you allot for yourself?
- What lifestyle amenities do you want to have for your life?
- How many hours do you want to work each day? Each week?
- How many clients do you want to see daily? Weekly? Monthly?
- How much money (how many months of expenses) do you want to set aside for your emergency fund?

Committing to Retirement Planning

Some entrepreneurs get so caught up in launching and operating their businesses that they forget to prepare for retirement. One of the most heartbreaking stories I've heard was from a Black small business owner who spent his career as an entrepreneur, but when he was ready to retire, he had no buyers for his business and no retirement plan. It may feel like an unnecessary expense as you are starting out, and you may figure you'll get to it eventually. However, time can go by quickly. Putting that money aside sooner rather than later gives your money more time to grow, so it is something you need to attend to. Trust me, you do not want to get to the end of your working age and find your retirement savings won't support your lifestyle.

In deciding on a retirement strategy, you will need to talk to a financial professional (see Chapter 3 for the types of financial professionals you can choose from). It is helpful to interview a few people before deciding so that you can be sure that they will help with your goals, and not just try to sell you a product. Ideally, try to find an agent who can offer an array of financial products (such as investment, life insurance, retirement, and education savings) to meet your specific needs. Below is a brief overview of the types of retirement payment vehicles that are currently available for entrepreneurs and others:

- *Simplified Employee Pension (SEP) IRA:* Entrepreneurs may, as of this writing, contribute a portion of their net income, with a cap that is adjusted regularly.
- *Savings Incentive Match Plan for Employees (SIMPLE) IRA:* This allows small business owners to match their employees' retirement contributions, currently up to 3% of employee's salary. As with SEP IRAs, the SIMPLE has contribution limits, which are determined regularly.
- *Traditional IRA:* Entrepreneurs contribute pretax dollars to traditional IRAs, and the money is taxed at withdrawal, when their income may put them in a lower tax bracket. Like the other plans, there are contribution limits.
- *401(k) plans:* With these company-sponsored retirement plans, employees decide how much they want to contribute per year, and a corresponding portion is withdrawn from their paycheck. Some companies may match the contribution. As a side note, if you are looking to access capital, using 401(k) business financing (also known as Rollovers for Business Startups, or ROBS) may enable you to tap into your retirement account and use that money to start or buy a business or franchise. However, using this vehicle would mean reducing the amount

in your retirement plan, so you will want to think carefully about this option and consult with a financial professional.

- *Solo 401(k):* This plan is similar to a 401(k), but you cannot add employees.
- *Roth IRA:* These individual retirement plans allow people to contribute after-tax dollars into an investment account. As of this writing, if the money is withdrawn after 59.5 years of age, there are no penalties or taxes paid on what the investment account earns.

In addition to these retirement savings plans, if you have worked in the United States and you and your employer have contributed to the Social Security Administration, you will likely be eligible to receive Social Security income when you reach a certain age (currently as young as 62). To find out an estimate of your monthly pension, visit https://www.ssa.gov/prepare/get-benefits-estimate and create an account. You will be able to calculate how much money you will be eligible to receive starting at the current Social Security eligibility ages. The rates are based on past tax returns and how much you estimate you will earn in the future. If you are unable to work, you may also be able to apply for Social Security disability benefits.

Reflection Time

Let's take a few minutes to reflect on your retirement planning. Find a quiet space, and respond to the journal prompts below. These questions may feel very hard to answer right now, but I invite you to give them some thought now. Answer what you can, and then make a plan to come back to them at a later time.

- At what age do you want to retire? Why is this age important to you?
- What does a retirement life look like for you? What would your monthly expenses be?
- How much money do you need to have saved by your retirement?
- What are the steps that you need to take now to make this retirement plan a reality?

Take Action Exercise

- Make an appointment with two financial professionals in your area to assess which one will help with your retirement and wealth-building strategy. You can discuss:
- Retirement planning for you as an entrepreneur
- Investment options
- Wealth-building strategies

CHAPTER 9 MOMENTUM AND MINDSET CHECK

Are you feeling cozy with those numbers yet? The focus of this chapter was to expand your financial literacy, to deepen your understanding of the difference between profit and revenue, and to examine the three key financial statements: profit and loss, balance sheet, and cash flow, which capture the financial health of a business. Being able to understand, track, and make decisions from your numbers is a boss move!! Most importantly, you saw that looking at profit is more relevant to the growth of your business than simply looking at revenue. Finally, we looked at how to prepare for the transition to entrepreneurship through a financial lens, including your lifestyle costs, retirement planning, and growing an emergency fund.

- What is one takeaway that you have as you finish this chapter?
- What is a mindset shift that you have made after reading this chapter?

Pricing With Purpose

Charge Your Worth

....

At the root of pricing dilemmas lies your self-worth.

Many BIPOC therapists become therapists because they want to help their communities. They may see their work as a calling and experience internal conflict when faced with pricing decisions and charging for their expertise. They may worry that charging too much will make it difficult for certain clients to afford their services and finding that "just right" price may feel like a mystery because there is no pricing formula.

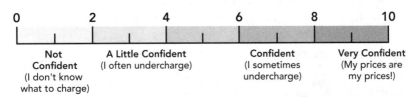

Figure 10.1 Rating scale on pricing confidence *Source:* Charmain F. Jackman and Demp Agency

Reflection Time

Before we get started, let's do a quick pulse check:

- How confident do you feel about pricing now?
- Using the rating scale on pricing confidence shown in Figure 10.1, indicate your level of confidence. Which number best describes your confidence level?
- What feelings are coming up for you as we start to explore pricing?

CRACKING THE PRICING CODE

Without a doubt, pricing was one of the toughest aspects of being an entrepreneur that I have had to deal with, and it may be the same for you. If you are experiencing feelings of confusion, anxiety, dread, and avoidance about navigating pricing, you are not alone—these feelings are absolutely normal. Time and time again I get anxiety-riddled questions from therapists about how much to charge for their services, whether for therapy, speaking, or consultations. There is no formula for pricing, and as I mentioned at the beginning of this book, many of us have never had conversations about pricing during our training programs. The added factor for Black therapists, and other therapists of color, is that we were told in more ways than one that our skills and expertise were not worth much. Plus, we got into the field to help others, and making money doing it feels contradictory (Walter, 2016). As a result, we don't see the value of our expertise and, worse, believe (consciously or unconsciously) that other people have the power to dictate what we should be paid. It's time to understand our value and unapologetically charge what we are worth (Kohatsu, 2018; Jones, 2019a).

PERSONAL REFLECTION: BEING UNDERPAID AS A TRAINEE

Most of my graduate internships were either unpaid or severely underpaid learning experiences, and this is still true in many graduate programs. You are expected to pay for school and then to work for free on practica and internships. I recall the disappointment I experienced

> when I learned how much I would be paid for my predoctoral internship. After completing 4 years of graduate coursework along with 4 practicum experiences, my salary would be a mere $18,000 (that was in 2000, which would be about $31,000 in 2024). I don't even know how I survived on that extremely low salary, especially in an expensive city like Boston, but I made it work. There was no opportunity to negotiate. The salary is a standard offer, and I had to take it or leave it.

"I don't know what to charge for my services. I've worked for a university, and I'm used to doing stuff for free or taking what people offer me." This comment, from a licensed provider who has significant experience in their area of expertise, expresses a very common theme among therapists, even therapists with significant experience in the field. Here are some of the top questions I have received about pricing:

- What should I charge for a therapy session or speaking engagement?
- Should I take the fee before the session or after?
- I was invited to speak at an event, but the organizer did not bring up the speaker fee, so I don't know if it is a paid opportunity or not. What should I do?
- How will I know when to increase my rate?
- What if I increase my rate and my clients can't afford it?
- What should I say if they ask me to lower my rate?
- I did X service but the client didn't pay—what should I do?
- I'm not licensed, so should I charge for my speaking or consulting services?
- I've only been licensed for X years, so I shouldn't charge market rate for my services, right?

It is very hard for me to see these questions now, but the truth is, I had these same questions as I was starting out, and I did not know where to turn for help. I had no guidance from professors and no mentors that I could ask as a beginner professional, and I didn't even dare ask a supervisor because I thought that would be impolite. In many cultures, talking about your salary and how much you make is taboo. To top it all off, none of my classes or supervisors discussed pricing our services—there were literally zero conversations about pricing. Looking back, it just seems unfathomable that this happened: that we would be given degrees but no information on how to earn from our expertise.

Ultimately, pricing is intricately connected to the success of your business—it can make or break your business. Pricing determines your revenue and profits and affects your bottom line. Your pricing strategy impacts how many hours you will work, your lifestyle, and your retirement. As an entrepreneur, you want to make sure that your prices are attractive to potential clients while also ensuring that you are covering your expenses and ultimately making a profit. If you price your services too low, you may have volume in clients, but you will be putting in more time and energy than is necessary to earn your desired revenue. On the other hand, if your ideal clients view your prices as too high, it could take you longer to reach your revenue goals, or it may cost you more to convert potential clients into paying customers. These are all considerations to keep in mind as you create your pricing strategy.

As we delve into this chapter, a major focus will be on helping you recognize the value of your training *and* your lived experiences because these make you uniquely *you* and contribute to the value that you bring to your ideal clients (recall Chapter 5 on branding). Until you understand the value that you bring, you will likely undervalue and underprice your offerings. I have seen the satisfaction and even joy that therapists experience when they understand their value and are comfortable setting their rates—it is liberating! It also allows you to enjoy the work and your relationship with clients. When you undercharge, it is very easy to feel resentful when you are putting in work that you know is not being adequately compensated, so do yourself and your clients a favor and charge right!

PRICING AND IDENTITY

Believe it or not, our identity can actually impact how we price our services and how people react to our pricing. Socialization, cultural upbringing, and stereotypes about us can all enter into the pricing equation. For example, groups who tend to undervalue their services and charge much lower than they are worth include women (Brown, 2015), Black business owners (Xiong, 2024) and therapists (Britt, Klontz, & Tibbetts et al., 2015; Delaney, 2016). Xiong (2024) notes that a number of factors contribute to Black entrepreneurs undercharging or not increasing their prices due to lack of business support, lacking information about pricing models, and customers perceiving lower value of their products—all due to systemic racism.

The Pink Tax

The pink tax is a practice of charging higher prices for retail goods that are marketed for women (Moshary, Tuchman, & Bhatia, 2021). For example, dry cleaning costs for women's shirts are much higher than for men's shirts. Also, women tend to charge less for their services due to a lack of confidence, lack of knowledge, or fear of being disliked (Hudder, 2023; Mohr, 2014). One of the most revealing moments I had on pricing was viewing the TEDx talk *Know Your Worth, and Then Ask for It* by Casey Brown (2015) who shared how her imposter syndrome around pricing had caused her to lose revenue because she was underpricing her services, and she was a *pricing consultant!* She knew she had to increase her prices but was terrified to do so. In many ways it was a relief to discover her journey as I was struggling with pricing myself—it was actually validating.

BIPOC and Immigrant Entrepreneurs

If you identify as Black, Indigenous, a Person of Color (BIPOC), or come from a collectivist culture with a greater focus on sharing, pricing may also present a challenge. In general, we are socialized to take care of our families and to look out for people in our communities. Growing up in another country, I also saw people operate businesses through a cooperative economics framework. People bartered and, when they had excess, shared with the community. Business owners also allowed customers to purchase "on credit" long before credit cards existed. Additionally, entrepreneurs would often throw in something extra as appreciation for supporting their business. Again, these are ways we practice being in community while doing business. This is very different from the standard way capitalist economies operate, and I observe that some Black entrepreneurs struggle with doing business in a capitalist society while also honoring their cultural values.

The Brothah/Sistah Hook-Up

The *brothah/sistah hook-up* is an expectation that a customer who is known to you or feels a sense of community may ask for a deal or discount on your products or services. However, you can see how quickly a business could get in trouble if they are regularly discounting their prices or not collecting payments, which can translate to giving away your products or services for free. You may struggle to set your rates or to maintain your rate if people ask for a deal, but it could impact your ability to run a profitable business.

As a therapist with a speaking platform, you may find that people are very interested in your expertise but may expect you to work for free or close to free. One of my mentors often advised me to charge for my services, even if it is a small fee, because *people will appreciate your time more when they have to pay for it*, so I am passing on this advice to you as well. There is also a national conversation about a practice of asking BIPOC professionals to speak but not pay them or pay them a lower rate than other speakers. I am not saying that you should *never* do pro bono (free) work—I actually do my fair share. However, if you did pro bono every time you were asked, it would be challenging to run a thriving business. Later in this chapter I share strategies for making decisions about pro bono opportunities.

TACKLING PRICING FEARS

Pricing is not a one-time affair—unfortunately, you don't "set it and forget it." Decisions about pricing will come up again and again in your business. As your company grows, as you add new services or products, as you target a new audience, as you move to a new year, as the economy shifts, as you expand your team, and and on and on, you will have to reevaluate your prices. Every transition in your business will bring financial implications that will require you to examine your pricing structure.

Deciding on the right price can cause indecision, avoidance, confusion, fear, and many more emotions. In essence, pricing can be stressful. It may trigger past financial traumas that you have personally experienced or that were passed on to you. When we are stressed, we often feel threatened or under attack and go into flight, fight, freeze mode. *Do not be surprised* if these types of feelings and reactions come up as you prepare to price your services and products. Often the biggest perceived threat to pricing is losing money due to lowballing your services—removing that fear and avoidance is critical to shifting your mindset about pricing.

My Pricing Journey

When I started my private practice, people did not openly talk about rates, and were actually prohibited from posting their rates in our professional association's email listserv due to antitrust laws (designed to protect the public by preventing groups from colluding to unfairly set their prices). However, this created so much fear within our profession that I think people believed that they could never discuss fees for their services or post them on their website for clients. I learned to do my own sleuthing to obtain prices and pose questions to people who seemed open to sharing their rate. As I figured out the rate that more senior professionals charged for therapy and forensic evaluations, I landed on a rate that was lower than their rate because I was newer to the field. I did not consider my costs or expenses, and I clearly felt that I needed more experience to charge the top rate. If I could go back in time, I would tell my younger self to value my training and experience and to charge the top rate too. I eventually started to charge the top rate when I understood the value that I brought to the work. I was learning to own my prices and made some important changes. For example, I would decline work that was not a good fit or that was not paying enough; I started to increase my prices at the start of the new year; I ended my contract with a particular insurance payer because the reimbursement rate was literally half what I was being paid by another insurance payer. And while I felt guilty because it meant that I would be unable to work with some low-income BIPOC clients, it just didn't make mathematical sense (I would find other ways to contribute to my community) and I could no longer continue a contract that felt exploitative.

Once I started to do more longer-term consulting, my stress about pricing resurfaced. I felt uncomfortable asking colleagues their hourly rate or to see a sample proposal because I worried I was overstepping or assumed they would not want to share their hourly rate. I recall submitting an awesome proposal (or so I thought) for a consultation opportunity, but when my sister, a contracting expert, looked at it, she noticed that I had only included direct costs and had omitted indirect costs such as virtual assistant costs, and other expenses related to executing the contract. This meant that I had severely underpriced the project. Luckily, the contract did not go through, but I learned a lot from that experience: consider all your costs and tap into your network of experts in and outside the mental health field. My money script (see Chapter 3) definitely played a huge role in how I engaged in conversations about money with potential clients. When a potential client would ask about my fees, I absolutely avoided the issues by telling them that I would create a proposal and send it to them later. In my mind, I thought I was so clever, until a mentor told me to stop, explaining that it is best to present the price in the meeting because I could see the client's reaction and could discuss any budget constraints. Additionally, this strategy would save me tons of uncompensated time and energy that I would invest in creating a proposal that might never lead to a contract, and eliminated weeks of pricing torture I would endure trying to come up with the right price on my own. I know that I lost some business because I never got back to some potential clients with a proposal because I was too overwhelmed. But having the conversation in person? *Whoa!* That was going to be tough too.

Pricing brought up a lot of anxiety for me, so I invested in a business coach, and we spent about 6 months working through my anxiety around pricing. I did not realize how deep my feelings of self-doubt about my value as a professional impacted my pricing decisions. My coach assigned me a task of creating a pricing chart, and I practiced having these conversations using role plays with her. I still feel some anxiety from time to time, especially with new, high-priced services. Indeed, these were hard lessons, but they helped me to realize what I didn't know and what I needed help with. I needed to own the value I bring to clients and to the products and services I offer, and feel secure in setting my prices.

Reflection Time

Let's take some time to reflect on your feelings about pricing. Find a quiet space, and respond to the following journal prompts:

- When you think about pricing your services, what emotions come up for you?
- What experiences in childhood or adulthood have you had that might impact how you approach pricing?
- How might your identity impact the way you price your services?
- If someone told you they could not afford your prices, how would you proceed: discount your price, or stay firm? How would it make you feel to lower your price? How would it feel to stay firm?

PRICING WITH CONFIDENCE

Pricing is definitely a hot topic for any entrepreneur, especially for therapists who prefer to avoid conversations about money. Pricing is about understanding your value—the sum of all the experiences you have gained so far. But the trickier part is separating your price from your identity as an entrepreneur. If someone does not want to pay your prices, that is alright—it shows they know their budget, and there is nothing that you need to do. You do not need to feel guilty or change your price to fit their budget. Do not worry about other people. If someone cannot afford your prices, fear and scarcity behaviors show up, and you feel the need to get that contract at whatever cost. No, you do not! Gaining the confidence to calculate, communicate, and charge the right prices can be done in the following three stages.

1. CALCULATING YOUR PRICES WITH CONFIDENCE

Calculating your price comes from knowing your business's finances: what it costs to create a product or deliver a service, understanding what your potential clients are willing to pay for that product or service, and the value that your products and services offer your clients (Harris, 2024; Finer, n.d.). Conducting customer discovery calls or talking to potential customers using focus groups or surveys are great ways to learn what they are willing to pay for a particular product or service (see Appendix M for a customer discovery script for a phone call). In surveying your potential customers, you can ask about their pain points and what they would be willing to pay for effective solutions.

Entrepreneurs outside of the mental health field use a number of pricing strategies to calculate their prices (Beltis, 2022; Harris, 2024; Finer, n.d.; Forbes Coaches Council, 2020; Stobierski, 2022). Below I outline five pricing strategies that are most applicable for private practices and wellness businesses.

Below is an overview of the five pricing strategies that I think are most relevant for therapy and wellness businesses. Additionally, I have organized these strategies by type of business (i.e., service-based businesses and product-based businesses).

Service-Based Business Pricing

Market Pricing. The most popular strategy that therapists use to price their services is to follow what other therapists (i.e., market) are doing. Conduct research to see how other providers in your area or market are pricing their services, by visiting therapist websites, checking therapist directories, and asking colleagues or mentors for price ranges. However, consider that simply matching the market price does not take into account your expertise or expenses, or the value that you will be giving to clients, but it does offer a guide. You may opt to charge an average of the rates, keep it the same, or even charge a higher rate. When charging higher than market rates, be sure that you are delivering a high quality service or product.

Dynamic Pricing. This involves setting different prices for the same product or service based on what you think the customer will pay. The airline industry regularly engages in dynamic pricing. Many therapists offer a sliding scale, which typically involves charging different rates for a session based on a client's income (more on this below). Speakers may also have a different rate based on the organization's size or type (corporate and nonprofit). *Value-based pricing* is a type of dynamic pricing based on the perceived value that a customer attributes to their products or services and how much they are willing to pay. It is a great option for consulting and speaking services.

- *Speaking:* While I have a standard rate for professional workshops, keynote speeches, panels, and moderator roles, the market shows significant variability depending on the type and size of the organization, which makes dynamic pricing easier. For example, speaker fees can range from $0 (pro bono, i.e., free) to $10,000 or more, depending on the platform, the event, and your speaker profile. When calculating your fee, consider not just the time needed for the event itself, but also your preparation time, meetings with the event organizers, and debrief meetings.
- *Consulting:* Consulting requires you to harness your training and lived experience to help a client address a problem or particular constellation of challenges, which is priceless. However, you do need to put a price on it! To calculate your price for the consultation, it is critical that you understand the scope of work and deliverables that are expected.

Typically, I start with an hourly rate to help me gauge the costs for direct services, and then I take into account planning time, labor costs, research, evaluation, and other expenses (such as administrative costs, transportation, and materials) that I will incur as I execute the project. For me, multiplying my therapy rate times 1.5 or 2 gives me a standard consulting rate. However, like speaking, the rate I set will depend on the size of the organization and the complexity of the consultation, which is why dynamic pricing works well for this service. You have value—if you are going to share that expertise, please *charge your worth!*

Product-Based Business Pricing

Cost-Plus Pricing. This strategy considers the production costs (e.g., manufacturing, marketing, packaging, and shipping) associated with developing and marketing a product or service and then adds a percentage on top, called the *markup*. This is typically the profit that a company receives. Cost-plus is frequently used for consumer products.

Penetration Pricing. Companies using this strategy to introduce a new product or service to the market at a low price and then raise it later. One potential drawback is that, once you have introduced a low price, you are communicating a lower value to your product or service, and you may have a harder time converting clients at the higher price point later on.

Price Skimming. This strategy is the opposite of penetration pricing: companies introduce a new product or service to the market at a high price and then reduce the price or offer discounts (e.g., percentage off, flash sales) when sales are slower, when they want to incentivize people to purchase, or when they are trying to offload inventory. However, this can also have the effect of devaluing the product or service.

Third-Party Determined (TPD) Pricing

There will be times when an entity, someone other than yourself or a client, determines the price for you and you have to decide whether that price will work for you or not. For example, health insurance companies dictate the rate that providers will receive for therapy sessions and assessments; state and federal agencies set the rate for disability evaluations and other assessments. While third-party determined rates can offer consistent income, especially as you start up your business, the rates tend to be lower than market rates, and there is typically no opportunity to negotiate, especially as a solo business owner.

Take Action Exercise

Now, let's spend some time considering the pricing for the many services that you will offer. You can use the service offerings template in Appendix N or the pricing checklist below. As you work on your pricing, consider the following questions:

- Research the typical hourly rates in your geographic area.
- Determine the ideal hourly rate that you want to charge for therapy sessions and consulting.
- Identify a specialized service that you can offer that will allow you to charge a higher rate.
- Research the typical rates that providers with similar expertise charge.
- Decide whether you will offer a sliding scale for therapy clients.
- Decide the rates you will charge for workshops (take into account different lengths of workshops and the audience).
- Brainstorm some products ideas.

Now use the template below to create a pricing chart for your products and services:

- Therapy: Hourly rate and sliding scale rate
  - Psychological assessments: Hourly rate and Sliding scale rate
- Keynote speaker (up to 1 hour): Flat rate
  - Corporations
  - Nonprofits
  - Other
- Workshops: 60 to 90 minutes: Flat rate
  - Corporations
  - Nonprofits
  - Other

- Workshops: 90 to 120 minutes: Flat rate
  - Corporations
  - Nonprofits
  - Other
- Panelist: Flat rate
  - Corporations
  - Nonprofits
  - Other
- Moderator
  - Corporations
  - Nonprofits
  - Other
- Half-day rate
- Daily rate

You may use the session fee calculator in Table 9.4 to estimate the fees you want to charge and manipulate how different rates will impact your salary and revenue. You can revisit your pricing chart frequently as you review and revise your prices. Remember, pricing is not a one-time activity—you will have to assess your prices frequently.

2. COMMUNICATING YOUR PRICES WITH CONFIDENCE

While calculating your prices may be tough, communicating your prices can bring another set of challenges. Communicating your price is actually about how you see yourself as a business owner and how much value you place on your products and services—there, I said it. If this is an area of struggle, you will have to practice talking to potential clients and sharing your prices with them. Practice in the mirror, with friends, and eventually with people in your target audience. Once you do this a few times with potential clients, it will get easier for you. That first *yes* may not come right away, but when it does, you will be overjoyed! Do your happy dance and then document what you did that worked. Then repeat, repeat, repeat.

Depending on your business and the products and services you offer, you may have opportunities to communicate your prices publicly (on a website) (Kirk, 2013) and during sales calls.

- *Public posting:* Posting your prices on your website not only offers transparency, but allows potential clients make purchasing decisions without your involvement. This is ideal for retail products and therapy services with standard rates. If you are using a dynamic pricing model and intend to post your prices, an option is to use such language as "Starting at" to give flexibility and avoid getting locked in to a particular rate.
- *Sales calls:* As we discussed in Chapter 6, making sales calls is a revenue-generating activity that allows you to build a mutually beneficial relationship with potential customers and to communicate the value and benefits of your services and products M (see Appendix M or a sample sales call script). Be prepared to answer any questions that may naturally come up, including questions about your pricing.

PERSONAL REFLECTION: MY BUSINESS IS NOT MY IDENTITY

To gain confidence in communicating my prices with potential clients, I had to make a major mindset shift. I had to separate my identity, and the work I did building my business, *from* the business. I had to learn that if a potential client declined to sign up for my services, it did not mean that they did not see the value in my services. I had to reframe what *no* meant—it could mean *maybe later*, because it was not the right time for the organization, or they did not have the funds in their budget. *Maybe later* meant they stayed on my call list and I would check back in at a later time. I had to believe in the quality of my services and not let potential client's responses be tied to my identity or how I viewed myself as a business owner. As my business evolved, these responses truly became "maybe later," as clients would check back when the timing was right for them.

Summary of Strategies for Communicating Prices

Before we move on, let's recap the communication strategies:

- Create a price list—and stick to it
- Develop a sales script (see Appendix M)
- Practice with colleagues and friends
- Share your prices during customer calls

Dealing With Low Client Budgets

Inevitably, you will have a client who wants to work with you, but your rates and their budgets don't match. Here are some strategies to deal with misaligned budgets:

- *Start the conversation with your rates, not their budget:* Avoid starting the pricing conversation by asking: "What is your budget?" While knowing their budget can help narrow down what services you can offer them at what price points, asking this question first puts you in a defensive stance. Knowing their budget might cause you to feel guilty about charging outside their budget. (I know my therapists!) If a client's budget is too low, avoid thinking: *Some money is better than no money.* Trust me, not always. Too many times I've had coaching clients complain that the clients they reduced their prices for often caused them the most headaches. Here are your options for navigating conversations with clients who share that your services are out of their budget range:
  - stay firm with your price
  - help them to problem solve ways to gain additional funding (e.g., partner with other departments or organizations)
  - offer to revise your proposal to a modified/reduced program with their budget limitations in mind. *A word of caution:* Be careful not to dilute your services to meet an unrealistic budget, as you can end up delivering a subpar service trying to meet their budget, or you may go over budget (uncompensated work) because you want to deliver a quality service. Cutting back your ideal service will likely not get them the results they want, and in that scenario no one is happy. It can even impact future business if this leads to low or poor reviews.

So think hard before cutting back your services to meet a lower budget, and if you do, be very clear about the results that the client will get with the scaled back offering.

- *Client does not share their budget:* Sometimes potential clients do not want to share their budget with you, and that's alright. There is no need to fight with them to get this information; rather, this gives you information about the client, possibly indicating that they are not a good fit for your business. As one of my mentors shared, *all money isn't good money*—it's OK to leave some money on the table because the aggravation you experience in working with a difficult client is not worth the headache. If a sale does not work out, that's alright—you move on to the next call.

Discounting Your Rate Without Discounting Your Value

As an entrepreneur, it is likely that you will encounter clients who ask you to discount your rate or even deliver a program for free. When you discount your rate, you risk devaluing your products and services. There is also the concern that people will continue to expect a lower rate for your services. If you are a Black or BIPOC entrepreneur who is engaged in community work, it is very likely that some of the organizations you want to work with may not have the funds to pay your top rate, or they may ask you to volunteer your services. As a savvy entrepreneur, it is important to always communicate the value of your products or services, even if you decide to give a discount.

If you discount your rate or deliver a service for free, you can communicate your values by asking the client to sign a contract for services. In your contract, communicate what you will be doing and what the original cost/value would be for the services you are providing. It would also be wise to include some asks for the organization so they have some skin in the game. For example, showcasing your work on their website or social media pages, providing a testimonial, sharing the attendees' email addresses, Offering a sponsorship level for an upcoming event, or listing your organization as a partner. Remember, you do not have to give a discount to everyone that asks, and you can limit how many times you will give pro bono (free) services per year. Establishing a clear policy to use when deciding on discounting your rate will hopefully make the decision-making process much easier for you and your team. Before you offer a discount, ask yourself the seven questions in the box on the following page.

BEFORE OFFERING A DISCOUNTED RATE, CONSIDER THESE SEVEN QUESTIONS

1. Is the organization aligned with my business's mission?
2. What will it cost me to discount the rate or to deliver the service at a discounted rate?
3. If I decide to discount my rate, what can I ask from them in return (e.g., testimonial, access to an email list, sponsorship level at one of their events)?
4. Has the individual/company been a champion of my business? Will they become a champion or will this lead to a deeper partnership?
5. Instead of lowering my rate, is there a bonus (or gift) that I can offer?
6. Will I feel resentful if I give this discount?
7. What is the worst outcome that would happen if I do not give the discount?

When someone requests a discount, you do not have to answer right away. Let them know that you need to discuss with your team (even if the only person on the team is you!). You can ponder the questions above and give them your answer after you have had some time to think about it. Additionally, consider creating a policy guide that you can share with organizations that request a discounted rate (see Appendix O).

While some entrepreneurs believe that negotiating your prices devalues your work, in some cultures, negotiation is a part of the language of commerce. It does not mean that you do not understand your worth, but you may accept negotiating because it aligns with how you were raised. In this context, negotiation is not a devaluing of your skills or expertise. The lesson here is for you to be very clear with yourself about whether you will discount your rate, and under what conditions.

A Word of Caution: Making the decisions to discount your services is one that I want you to seriously consider. You do not want to get stuck in a cycle where discounting your rates slows or halts your business success. Unfortunately, some business owners are so focused on taking care of the community that they do not take care of their businesses. The reality is that you can't help your community if you have to close the doors to your business.

Take Action Exercise

Let's take a few minutes to consider how discounts can fit into your pricing strategy. Find a quiet space, review the sample discounted rate policy in Appendix O, and respond to the following:

- Indicate the type of organizations you will offer a discount to (e.g., non-profits, community-based organizations, organizations with a certain number of employees or specified annual revenue).
- Decide what will you ask for in exchange for the discounted rate.
- Determine how much time will you need to review the discounted rate request.
- Generate the questions will you include on the request form.
- Review the policy and consider anything else that you plan to add to the Discounted Rate Policy.

Communicating Price Increases

Many therapists operate their business on a fixed price: they set the price and they never look back. Or, even worse, they decrease their prices. This will inevitably happen if you do not make market adjustments to your pricing due to increasing costs over time. For those accepting third-party payments, the third party controls the pricing, and I have seen situations where the rates are lower than the previous year. Unfortunately, it is not feasible to have a profitable business with decreasing rates.

Being attuned to changes in the market, your costs, and your team will help you understand when to increase your prices. I have noticed that therapists worry about losing customers with price increases. It is alright to lose some clients who are unable to afford your prices, as this will make room for clients who can pay the higher rate. For therapy clients, you want to make sure that you give them ample written and verbal notice of the price increase, at least three months' notice (more time is always better), in case your new price is no longer financially feasible for them. This will give them time to find a new therapist. You also want to communicate this information in writing and ver-bally and provide them with several reminders. Typically, I use the new cal-endar year as a signal for price increases, which means that I have to provide notice to my existing customers by October for any price increases coming in January.

Exercise: Pricing Affirmations

As I shared earlier, pricing can be stressful and it will be something that you navigate for the life of your business. However, feeling empowered around your pricing, will reduce this stress and allow you to enter pricing conversations with confidence. To build your confidence, try out some of the affirmations below or create your own:

- I will no longer approach pricing with fear.
- I will confidently price my products and services.
- I will revisit my prices every quarter to ensure that I am on track with pricing.
- Right pricing allows me to deliver high-quality services and products to my clients.
- Right pricing is about protecting my peace.
- Knowing the value my business brings is essential to pricing my prod-ucts and services.

3. CHARGING YOUR PRICES WITH CONFIDENCE

Once you have created your price list and communicated your price to a client, now it's time to proceed with charging your client so that you can get paid and bring in that hard-earned revenue. Getting payment for your services can some-times have delays, which will affect your cash flow. To keep that cash flowing, be sure to bill for your services and send out invoices promptly. You must also understand the time and terms of payment. For example, some clients will pay *after* the service is complete, and that might be 30 days, 60 days, or even more. (Payment terms are discussed in detail on the following page.) Take advantage of automation to collect payments and send payment reminders.

Payment Sources

Health Insurance Payers. For therapy practices, you may consider getting on insurance panels, or *getting credentialed.* Getting credentialed is a process that insurance companies use to vet potential providers who want to provide therapy and assessments to their members. The credentialing process includes verification of your education and training and confirming your practice address and malpractice insurance. Getting credentialed with insurance payers offers a reliable and steady revenue stream. According to the U.S. Census Bureau, in 2022 about 92.1% of the U.S. population was insured at some point during the calendar year (Keisler-Starkey, Bunch, & Lindstrom, 2023). Undoubtedly, most people who have health insurance prefer to use their health insurance benefits to cover the cost of medical services.

Once you are credentialed, you can start to bill the insurance company for services rendered. The insurance payer system is a *fee-for-service model* paid a flat rate for identified services only. Additionally, you are paid after the service is completed and after you submit a claim for reimbursement. Many insurance companies have a time limit for when you can submit your bill (e.g., within 90 days), and after that time, they will deny your claim, so it is important to bill regularly to prevent interruptions in payment. You also want to be aware of *clawbacks*, when an insurance company has paid you for a service but they later find an error and ask you to return the money (Holt, 2024). At the writing of this book, there are some states with wide-ranging time limits (such as 3 years), which means that insurance payers could ask for the money back at any point within that time. (Wild, right?) Massachusetts has successfully passed legislation that imposes clawback limits of 12 months after claim submission, which is still a long time. As always, to ensure timely payment, check your claims for accuracy and submit within the submission timelines.

Getting Credentialed. Many insurance companies use a clearinghouse to collect the required credentialing information, such as the Council for Affordable Quality Healthcare (CAQH), which provides a portal to collect all data needed for the credentialing process. (This wasn't available when I was going through the credentialing process—I had to submit applications for each insurance company separately and by paper.) This makes the process easier, as you can input your information and upload your documents just once and insurance companies can retrieve your information from this database. Some insurance companies may have additional requirements that are not part of the CAQH requests, such as a letter of intent.

CREDENTIALING DOCUMENTS

Credentialing is a vetting process that health insurance payers use to ensure that providers are qualified to provide a particular set of services to their members. As part of the credentialing process, you will likely need to submit the following:

- *Educational history:* documentation of degree, transcripts, courses taken
- *Supervision documentation:* practicum/internships hours, placement, and supervisor degree and licensure
- *Proof of licensure:* documentation of your license to practice as a mental health professional
- *Proof of insurance:* documentation of malpractice insurance coverage, and possibly general liability insurance (described in Chapter 8)
- *Practice location and hours:* mailing address, practice hours, and practice location address if you will see clients in a physical location rather than virtually
- *Building accessibility:* availability of handicap-accessible services such as ramps and elevators
- *Peer reference:* name and contact information of a clinician who is already credentialed by the insurance company and who can speak to your clinical skills
- *Emergency coverage:* name and contact information of a clinician who is available to provide emergency coverage for you (discussed in Chapter 8)
- *Letter of intent:* an outline of the types of clients you intend to see and the geographic location, if required. (Insurance panels have done this to assess whether you have special skills to offer their members.)

Deciding on which insurance companies you will accept into your practice is up to you. You will likely consider which payers are in your geographic location, their reimbursement rates and what insurance your clientele are most likely to have. Some payers have a reputation for an easy and timely reimbursement process while others may take a long time or have a high rate of denials. These are important factors to consider as you want to avoid hassles in getting paid. You will also want to consider how many different insurance companies you want to work with.

Ask therapists in your area which insurance payers are most common and what their experiences have been working with the different insurance companies. In short, do your research.

Take Action Exercise

Now, let's spend some time considering the credentialing process for the many services you will offer.

- List the insurance companies in your area.
- Rank them in order of your preference.
- Talk to three therapists who are in private practice in your state and ask about their experiences being credentials with the different health insurance companies in your area.

Insurance Versus Self-Pay. Some clients will pay fees from their own funds for therapy or assessment services, instead of using insurance benefits. The client may not have insurance, the therapist is out-of-network, or the therapist is not credentialed by the insurance company. A fair number of providers are opting for self-pay practices only and are not taking insurance, primarily due to low reimbursement rates, burdensome paperwork, and hassles getting paid on time.

Self-pay can create a dilemma for BIPOC therapists, because many clients cannot afford to pay the full hourly rate for therapy, especially in these economically challenging times. Black and BIPOC therapists often worry about meeting the needs of their community while still having a financially viable business. As a result, some providers offer a *sliding scale*, a reduced fee usually based on income, to accommodate clients who cannot afford to pay their full fee. Not surprisingly, some therapists have shared that they have gotten stuck at a discounted rate when offering a sliding scale even after the client's financial situation improved because they usually felt uncomfortable bringing up the money conversation with the client. Other therapists have had elaborate systems with multiple session rates for different income levels, and others ask for proof of income (e.g., tax forms or pay stubs) for eligibility and to determine the session rate.

If you choose this route, it is ideal to have a written policy that outlines the sliding scale, who is eligible, the time period for the discount, and how they should notify you when their income increases again. When I coach therapists on sliding scales, I recommend keeping sliding scales as simple as possible. For example, it works to have just one or two discounted rates—more than that and the time spent tracking and monitoring is not worth it. Also, I caution against collecting tax forms or pay stubs because it can become burdensome to collect and store this information. Plus, it also signals that you do not trust clients before you have even started working together.

Payment Options

Collecting payments is an essential part of the success of your business. If you do not collect payments, you do not get paid, and your business will suffer, simple as that. To get paid you will provide an invoice to the client that itemizes the services or products, costs for service or product, total amount due, your business info: organization's name, address, EIN number, and payment instructions (e.g., banking information for direct deposit or address for paper checks). It is good practice to submit an invoice for every service provided or product sold, as this creates a paper trail that your accountant or bookkeeper will need to reconcile your accounts. Additionally, most companies will request that you submit a completed federal W-9 form to all new business clients you are working with. Additionally, working with large organizations and corporate or government entities, you may need to register on their online *vendor enrollment system*, which allows you to input your business information, banking information, company verification information, and preference for payment, as well as upload documents such as W-9 and invoices.

Once you submit the invoice to the client, you can offer the client a variety of payment options:

- *Cash:* Nothing beats cash—just make sure that you document your payments. This will be typically for in-person transactions such as therapy or products that you sell at events or in a store.

- *Credit card:* Collecting payments through credit cards allows you to get your money right away, but there is a cost for that convenience. There are a number of credit card processing companies, but they all have transaction fees, calculated as a percentage of the transaction plus an additional per transaction fee (for example, 2.9% + $0.30 per transaction). You will also need to order a point-of-sale tool that will allow you to capture the credit card information.
- *Electronic funds transfer (EFT) or direct deposit:* Direct deposit allows clients to pay you by sending funds directly to your bank account. This is usually the easiest way to get paid for consulting and speaking clients. To activate direct deposit, you will likely complete an Automated Clearing House (ACH) form, which includes information necessary to execute payment, such as your name, business name, bank name and address, and bank routing and account numbers, plus your signature; or submit your information virtually.
- *Insurance reimbursement:* For therapists who take insurance, it is important to have a system in place to bill the insurance company, by submitting claims on a regular basis. You either do it yourself (DIY) manually through your practice management system or the insurance payer's online billing system. If you are doing your own billing, it is important to have a system in place for submitting your claims with a degree of regularity to ensure a smooth cash flow and that you don't miss claim submission deadlines. If you feel that the billing may be an added stress for you, there are many companies who will take care of the billing for you. Of course, you will still need to track your sessions, but they can help you get better organized and ensure that you are submitting claims on a regular basis. They often help with claim denials and other issues that could come up with the billing. The billing company usually takes a percentage of the total claim as a fee, usually in the range of 3–10%.
- *Mobile payments:* These are apps such as Apple Pay, Google Pay, Venmo, PayPal, and Cash App that allow you to transfer money through a smartphone. Given that people rarely walk around with cash or use personal checks, mobile payments offer a fast and convenient way to get paid and are great if you are selling products. However, mobile app payments are not ideal for therapy clients because they can violate

privacy. For example, some apps allow people to see who has paid you and for what, and this public setting would violate your clients' right to privacy. If you choose to take these payments from therapy clients, I strongly advise that you consult with an attorney with experience in mental health law. Also, it is quite unlikely that organizations you contract with for speaking or consulting will use mobile payment options.

- *Personal checks:* Personal checks come with a risk of a bounced check—if someone does not have the money to cover a check, you will not get paid. Some businesses will issue a paper check for payment, and these are more reliable than personal checks. With so many payment options available, fewer people and businesses use checks to pay for services.
- *Postal orders/money orders:* These checks, issued by a post office (postal orders) or a bank (money order) for a specified amount of money, have the advantage of guaranteed money and will not bounce like a personal check.
- *Purchase orders (PO):* A PO is a document that a company or government entity will issue when it is buying services or products from a vendor. The PO details the payment terms (see below), quantities to be purchased, agreed-upon price, and delivery instructions. It becomes a legally binding document when the vendor accepts the PO.

Take Action Exercise

- Identify two or three credit card processing companies that you want to consider and document the associated fees.
- Identify the mobile payment options that you want to consider for consumer products.

Payment Terms

Payment terms set the time frame for which a company will pay its vendors following the receipt of the invoice. For example, a 30-day term or "net 30" means that payment will be issued 30 days after the invoice has been received. Ideally, you want to get paid as close to the delivery of services or sale of products as possible, as it impacts your cash flow. Some companies may have term policies for paying vendors after the service or product has been delivered. Before signing a contract, get clarity on terms and ask whether you can submit an invoice ahead of a service being delivered. When creating your contract for services, include your requested payment terms. You should always try to negotiate for shorter terms, but the reality is that some larger companies and government institutions will not negotiate.

Payment terms can impact the cash flow of your company, especially when you do not receive funds in a timely manner. Imagine delivering a service but not being paid until 60 days later (net 60) and you have already "spent" that money (e.g., paying contractors or other overhead costs). That can put your business at risk for not meeting payroll or other expenses. I've definitely been in situations where a payment was delayed and my business really needed that payment. Being aware of payment terms is critical when you contract with government and corporations: If the payment terms would put your company at financial risk, you may want to decline that opportunity or explore financing opportunities that can help with cash flow.

Here's a **pro tip**: Submit error-free and timely invoices and follow up with reminders to ensure that you get paid on time. Also, when you submit a contract for services to a client, include the invoice at the same time, which can save time.

A *retainer fee* is a payment model where you as the vendor collect a portion of your payment up front and then deduct money as you deliver services. You can collect a partial payment (e.g., half) or an estimate of the full cost of services. You need to communicate with the customer verbally and in your contract that a retainer is required. If you are requiring a retainer, do not start work until you have received the retainer payment. Retainers benefit service providers because it gives them cash in hand as they are delivering services. Retainers, often used by attorneys, can protect the business from delayed payments or clients who may struggle to pay once the service is delivered.

Payment Plans, Late Fees, and Collections for Nonpayment

Nonpayment is another challenging situation that entrepreneurs will have to deal with. In your contracts, clearly document your process for dealing with payment plans, late payments, and nonpayments. For example, if you plan to charge additional fees for late payments, make sure that it is documented in your contracts and invoices. Additionally, I recommend consulting with a mental health attorney to ensure that the language in your client agreement contract is appropriate.

- *For business clients:* Include late fee structure on invoices. If you will offer payment plans, outline the structure and payment terms and send requests for payment based on the plan. If you can automate these within your accounting or practice management software, that would be ideal.
- *For therapy clients:* Set up a system to ensure that you are collecting fees (e.g., copays or self-pay rate) at the time of service. Many practice management software systems will charge the credit card on file automatically for appointments and even for no-shows. If you use such a system, be sure to turn on this function—it is worth it. This can eliminate some potential issues with late payments and nonpayments. If a client requests a payment plan, put the terms in writing and discuss how you will handle late payments and nonpayments.

In addition, you will also have to make decisions about whether you will continue to see a client if they have accumulated a balance. As a result, consider ahead of time how you will deal with complicated situations, for example, if a client loses a job or their health insurance benefits and is unable to pay, or they are having a financial hardship due to divorce, a new baby, or some other issue—how will you handle these scenarios? These are issues to discuss with an attorney.

Collecting outstanding balances from therapy clients can be tricky. If you do decide to enlist a collections agency, ensure that they are appropriately licensed to collect for the health-care industry so that you do not violate any HIPAA laws or your client's protected health information. You also want to be aware that hiring a collections agency for a current therapy client could create a rupture in the therapeutic relationship, so consider it only as a last resort.

Reflection Time

We have discussed a range of topics related to pricing your services. Let's take a moment for another pulse check:

- How confident do you feel about pricing now?
- Using the same rating scale on pricing confidence in Figure 10.1, which number best describes your confidence level now?
- What feelings are coming up for you now, after exploring ideas around pricing?

CHAPTER 10 MOMENTUM AND MINDSET CHECK

Yes—you are pricing your worth! You are thriving and taking on new mindsets about pricing. You have expanded your knowledge on ways to confidently calculate, communicate, and charge your prices. You understand the value of your products and services, and you will confidently communicate your prices to potential customers. While you explored the obstacles to confident pricing, such as fears and lack of knowledge, you have developed a mindset that shows you understand your numbers and your value. Pricing can be tricky, but it directly connects to the success of your business. You are ready to price your passion to profit.

- What is one takeaway that you have as you finish this chapter?
- What is a mindset shift that you have made after reading this chapter?

CHAPTER 11

Abundance Awaits You

Glow as You Grow

··

Your trust fund lies in the wisdom of your ancestors and the
promise of the next generation . . . it's your time to bloom.

Let's pause and take a few deep, cleansing breaths. You have done some amazing work getting here. You may be thinking, "I'm just getting to launch my business. Now you want me to think about growing it?"

Yes, you have to think about growth, and this is the time to do it!

PLANNING FOR GROWTH

When I started my private practice, growth was the furthest thing from my mind. It was enough to figure out all the things to get my business going. I was satisfied with the supplemental income that I was receiving. I knew I could take on more clients when I needed to, but that is definitely not a growth plan, especially if the growth solely relies on the owner seeing more clients. Now, I am keenly aware of the need to put growth at the forefront of my mind at the very early stages of business, and you will be too. My goal is to help you create businesses that will help you build a legacy and allow you to work smarter, not harder.

For a long time, the supplemental income was really nice. It allowed me certain luxuries, such as international travel, elegant dinners, monthly massages, and a beautiful home, but once my family started to expand, the math was not mathing. To afford my lifestyle, I would have to work more hours, which I did for a while, but it definitely caught up with me. Overworking and infants do not sync up, and I was left feeling tired and burned out. I could not work any more hours and live to talk about it (to learn more about this part of my journey, check out my TEDx Talk: "Reclaiming Well-Being in the Workplace" (Jackman, 2024). So, I changed some things around. But, instead of thinking of growth, I thought it would be easier to cut back. As I shared in Chapter 2 on thinking and acting like a Thriving Therapreneur, instead of looking at what was bringing in the most money, I made the decision to cut back on a high-revenue service because delivering part of that service was demanding and time-intensive. When I made this decision, I did not have a growth plan and had not considered the trajectory of my private practice. I made the choice based on my emotion rather than looking at my financial data or metrics. In retrospect, I wish I had made a plan for growth—but alas, I did not have a business coach at the time and did not think to ask any mentors. I made the decision in isolation. My hope is that with this book and the additional resources listed herein, it will be very different for you.

Reflection Time

In Chapters 2 and 3, you spent some time defining what success and thriving will look like as you launch your business. You've covered many business concepts since then, so this is a good time to revisit what you outlined as success.

- What does thriving look like to you now?
- How has your definition of *thriving* evolved?
- How do you define success?

Clarifying Your Vision for Success

As you think about growing your business, you have to be clear about what you want.

My definition of success is defined by impact, goals, and lifestyle. I want to do good and I want to have a business that will allow me to serve my community, provide for my family, and afford an abundant lifestyle where I can travel, enjoy the finer things in life, and engage in philanthropy. I have visions of being a multimillionaire, and it does not feel dirty to me, not anymore.

In Chapter 5 on branding your V.O.I.C.E., you outlined your vision, impact, and the goals you want for your career. Like a compass, that vision has to remain front and center as you grow your business. You want a vision that is big enough to grow with you. You want a vision that is high level but still keeps you on track. We are living in a world where people express wanting to help others, but their actions do not follow.

During my journey, a coach asked me to think ahead to my 90th birthday party and to envision who would be present and what would they say about my career and life. This was a very challenging exercise at first—I had to first imagine living to 90 years old and then to reflect on the things that I would want to accomplish.

So I will pose this same question to you: *What impact do you want to make on the field, in your community, and in the world?*

MY BOLD (BIG, OUTRAGEOUS, LUXURIOUS, DARING) VISION FOR INNOPSYCH

My vision is to grow InnoPsych to be the premier platform for inclusive mental health resources worldwide. Imagine this: when you think of anything related to emotional well-being, mental health, and behavioral health that centers people of color and the global majority, InnoPsych will be the first resource that comes to mind. InnoPsych will be like Amazon for mental health and well-being. I envision that InnoPsych will grow exponentially with employees around the world engaged in delivering well-being activities to heal the global majority. We will also have retail stores that feature well-being products and will nurture the next generation of mental health professionals through continuing education, mentoring programs, and well-being experiences. We will provide scholarships for middle school, high school, and college students to begin a career path in mental health. InnoPsych will provide innovative programming to support Black and BIPOC therapists who want to launch startups and small businesses, and we will invest in these businesses to help them grow. We will create luxurious healing centers around the world to ensure that people have access to the tools and wellness experiences they need to grow, heal, and thrive. Most important, InnoPsych will be instrumental in helping people of the global majority reclaim their right to well-being.

Many of us entered the mental health field to help people . . . simple as that. However, as you are reading this book and completing the exercises, you may already be noticing a shift in your thinking. You might be coming to the realization that you want more. It is OK to want more—it is more than OK. It means that you are shaking those limiting beliefs.

Wanting "more" will look different for everyone and can include many things:

- You intend to earn more money so that you can pay off your student loan debt and start living the life you want.
- You yearn for more flexibility with your schedule so that you do not feel drained and burned out at the end of the day.
- You desire a life of luxury—and there is nothing wrong with that.
- You are shifting the way you think about private practice and entrepreneurship.
- You plan to create a healthy workplace environment that values your contributions and is free of toxicity and identity stress.
- You intend to generate more revenue to build generational wealth.
- You desire to make a significant impact in the world with your business.

Reflection Time

Now it's your turn to think about your vision. Take a few minutes to write about your vision and desires:

- If money and time were not a concern, what would you want in life? How would you spend your time?
- Now, write down your BOLD vision for success. This vision should feel scary to you.
- How have your vision and desires evolved since you started reading this book?

Maybe you have more clarity or want to make a bigger impact than you originally imagined—I celebrate that. Maybe your desires now appear grander *and* achievable. I want that for you, but most importantly, I hope that you want that for yourself.

CREATING VISUAL REPRESENTATIONS OF YOUR VISION

Keeping your vision front of mind is essential to growing your business. One way you can do this is by creating a visual representation of your vision such as a *vision board*, an inspiring representation of your vision and goals using images, quotes, and empowering words, typically created using items cut out from magazines. Vision boards inspire you and can help you stay engaged with your goals. They have become quite popular, and people will often host vision board parties where they can come together to create vision boards.

I have a circle of friends who have met for the last three years to create vision boards together. We usually meet first to discuss our goals; then over the following weeks we create our vision boards, and come back together to share our final product. I admit that I used to be intimidated by the process because I am not an "artist." However, I have found that no art skills are required to create impactful vision boards. The process of creating is very calming and meditative, as well. If you have never created a vision board, I encourage you to try it—you will be surprised by the results.

OVERCOMING OBSTACLES TO YOUR GROWTH

Growing a business will feel like hard work . . . because it is. It will require you to do things that you have never done before. It means taking your wildest dream and executing it knowing that you don't have all the answers. It will feel scary, but you are now a part of a community of entrepreneurs, so you are not alone.

The blocks to growth can come in many forms, but it is usually due to missing one or more of these essential building blocks to success: a bold vision, a well-articulated growth plan clear and specific goals, operational processes, a solid team, a support system, and strategies to address self-sabotage and limiting beliefs.

This rang true for me during my first business accelerator, Babson Women Innovating Now (WIN) Growth Lab. It was September 2020, and as part of the program, we had to write down our 3-month and 6-month goals. They encouraged us to dream big. I can admit that I was timid as I approached my goals, but then I challenged myself. My mentor later reviewed and shared, "You can dream bigger than that." If she had only known what it took me to get to that point! It was clear that, even though I was wildly stepping out of my comfort zone and creating a company that I had never dreamed of . . . even though that felt really big for me, I was still limiting my potential. For me, overcoming limiting beliefs is a daily task because it was ingrained in me.

Reflection Time

How much confidence do you have in each of the categories below? Which ones are your strengths? For which ones would you want to obtain support?

- Vision
- Plan for growth
- Clear and specific goals
- Processes
- Teams
- Support systems
- Strategies to address self-sabotage and limiting beliefs

Challenging Limiting Beliefs

As an entrepreneur, one of the biggest hurdles I had to confront—and I believe this is true for many therapists—is overcoming my limiting beliefs, beliefs that I did not deserve more, that I will never have more, that what I have is more than enough, or that money is dirty. My coaching clients regularly share experiences that have led them to develop scarcity mindsets (see Chapter 3 on wealth-building mindsets). We worry about losing what we have, about being "too much," about wanting too much in life (for fear of losing it). We believe that a desire for money is bad (we see it used to exploit people all the time), and of course, we have to always remember where we came from—to avoid being accused of forgetting where we came from. We have seen or heard stories of people from the community who succeeded and then lost it all or people who succeeded and forgot about their community. These extreme examples become cautionary tales that stifle our dreams and hinder our success.

Here are more examples of limiting beliefs:

- What I have now is more than enough.
- If I strive for more money, I will lose it.
- I do not deserve to have more.
- Money is dirty.
- People who have a lot of money are greedy (bad people).
- Success (wealth) means forgetting about your people.
- I cannot forget where I came from.
- What if I fail?
- Success (money) only brings more problems.
- I wouldn't know how to manage my success (money).

Mindset Work

One way to overcome limiting beliefs is to recognize that they are not truths. They are just ideas that were taught to us and it is up to us to release them. They were other people's worries that got transferred to us. Here are some examples of affirmations that can help counter beliefs that may no longer be serving you.

"My past does not predict my future."
- Even though I struggled with managing my money in the past, it does not mean that I will struggle with money in the future.

"The opposite is true, for me, now."
- I did not have the tools I needed to succeed, but I do now, or I know where to look and who to ask for help.
- People use money to exploit others, but that is not who I am or what I would do.

"Yes . . . , and . . ."
- Yes, I am committed to helping my community, and I can make a significant difference when I am in a better financial place.
- Yes, I am worried about failing, and if I do fail, I will have amazing lessons that will help on my next venture.

Reflection Time

- What are examples of scarcity mindsets that you experienced or witnessed from the people around you?
- Do you continue to struggle with a scarcity mindset at times? If so, how does it show up in your life now?
- How does it show up when you have to make decisions?

SOARING TO NEW HEIGHTS: SETTING GOALS TO GROW

There are many ways that you can grow your business. This chapter goes through a number of strategies to consider, such as processes, people, and capital. You do not have to tackle these all at the same time, but it is great for you to consider as you imagine where you want your business to go and grow in the next few years. This section focuses on goals, which can help to keep you on track as you implement your growth strategies.

Goal Setting

As therapists, you routinely create treatment goals with your clients. You most likely set goals for yourself that led you to your current role in the mental health field. Likewise, setting goals is an essential practice for any entrepreneur because they provide direction during your journey. Imagine taking a road trip to a new destination but not ever looking at a map or GPS to get directions about where you are going. You may eventually get there, if you stop and ask for directions along the way, but it will take much longer and cost you more too. Goals also help you make a plan so that you can anticipate what resources and support you will need. As you grow and scale your business, goal setting helps you project out how you envision the long-term trajectory of your business. Having this vision articulated will allow you to map out the steps that you will need to reach your goals. As the owner of the business, you get to determine what those goals are—fun! Setting goals does not mean that everything will happen in the exact time frame that you plan or desire, but they are there to help you move in the right direction.

Without goals it is very easy to get distracted, unfocused, and sidetracked, which can cause you to jump at "opportunities" that are not aligned with the direction of your business or the impact you want to make. Before becoming an entrepreneur, I could never imagine that I would be constantly bombarded with ideas for new businesses, products, and services. Oh my goodness, these new ideas often come with a ferociousness that demand my immediate attention and execution, especially when I'm feeling stuck or not getting traction with a current product or service. I know how tempting it can be to abandon your current business plan to chase down a new glittery idea, but let me tell you, it is usually not worth it (unless you have exhausted the viability of your current business plan). While I do not recommend chasing distracting ideas, I *do* suggest that you write these ideas down—it might not be the right time now, but it may be viable later.

Even with goals there will be periods when you feel lost, as unexpected things come up, but goals, like a map or compass, can get you back on track and help you refocus. Goals also help you make decisions for your business. When you are faced with big or small decisions, review your goals first and consider how the outcome will get you closer to your goals. Additionally, when you are presented with a "really great opportunity," look to your goals to help you make the decision. Some opportunities actually distract you and take you further away from your goals. I've learned that opportunities have a way of coming back around, so stay on course.

SMART and SMARTIE Goals

The SMART (specific, measurable, attainable, relevant, and time-bound) goals framework is an established format for setting goals. It ensures that your goals are clearly written and that it is easy for anyone to assess whether you have successfully achieved the desired outcomes. An updated version has added an I (inclusive, implementation, inspirational, interesting) and an E (equitable, exciting, emotional) to form SMARTIE goals. I love this new adaptation because I believe that goals are meant to bring you joy and help you achieve outcomes that are fair and just.

SMARTIE GOALS

Specific: Write goals as concrete as possible and avoid ambiguity. Anyone reading the goal should be able to understand what you are trying to achieve. Does it make sense to a fifth-grader?

Measurable: Goals must be quantifiable, so that even someone who does not know your business can determine whether you have reached your goal.

Attainable: Set goals that are realistic to achieve given your resources and time. You can still set ambitious goals, but ones that you can achieve with your time, resources, and finances.

Relevant: Will these goals actually help move your business forward or are they disconnected from your north star? Are they actually goals or just tasks (see below)?

Time bound: Include the time frame for when you want to see outcomes. Goals without a time frame lack accountability and urgency.

Inspirational: Make the goals interesting and inspirational for you and your team. You will put quite a bit of time and effort into your business, so create goals that will keep you motivated, especially when times get tough.

Equitable: As you grow your company, consider how your company will address structural racism, mental health inequities, and other forms of oppression that impact your clients.

Examples of SMART and SMARTIE Goals

Sample *SMART* Goal. To reach our annual revenue goal of $300,000 for 2025, we will increase Q2 revenue by $50,000 by rebooking three past clients and securing two new corporate clients for workplace well-being services at $10,000 per contract.

Sample *SMARTIE* Goal. To reach our annual revenue goal of $300,000 for 2025, we will increase Q2 revenue by $50,000 by rebooking three past clients and securing two new corporate clients to lead a Racial Trauma in the Workplace series to members of their Black affinity groups tools to navigate microaggressions in the workplace.

Take Action Exercise

Now it's your turn. Use the SMARTIE framework to write or rewrite one of your business goals:

- Specific:
- Measurable:
- Attainable:

- Relevant:
- Time bound:
- Inspirational:
- Equitable:

How does this framework work for you? Review your initial goals from Chapter 5 (see "The Vision Statement Formula"). Does the SMARTIE framework capture your goals and vision?

Are Those Goals or Tasks? In writing goals, it can be very easy to confuse goals and tasks and create a task list instead of goals. Let's get some clarity on the difference: *goals* are the *results* you desire, whereas *tasks* are the *actions* you take to get those results. See examples of goals and tasks in Table 11.1.

While you need to complete tasks to get to your goals, it is very easy to spend all your energy and effort doing tasks that are not connected to a larger goal. Trust me, I have been there. It is very easy to spend hours checking tasks off the lists only to find that you are nowhere closer to your goal. Be clear about how the tasks are connected to your big goals and who should be assigned to complete them. Avoid spending too much time on tasks that are not revenue generating, and consider who else on your team can do these tasks.

MEASURING YOUR SUCCESS: KEY PERFORMANCE INDICATORS

Don't confuse movement with progress because you can run in place.
—Denzel Washington (2019)

Once you have your goals outlined, it's time to track and measure your progress, just like you do with clients' treatment goals. Using relevant metrics, or key performance indicators (KPIs), will help you stay focused on your goals and track your progress—the *measurable* part of SMARTIE goals. Metrics can serve as a baseline to understand your business, and later you can use these metrics to track and inform your growth goals. Which KPIs to track will depend on your business and your goals, but you want to select metrics that will help you see

Table 11.1 Examples of goals and tasks

Goals (Results)	Tasks (Actions)
Increase monthly revenue from product sales to $10,000 by December 30 Action Item: Create new program offering [Assigned to: CEO]	• Send emails to 100 potential clients each week [Assigned to: Sales associate] • Revise marketing strategy for a new customer segment [Assigned to: Business development] • Create job descriptions for sales lead and sales associate positions [Assigned to: HR consultant] • Extend offers to two new sales associates by June 30 [Assigned to: CEO/HR consultant] • Check email inbox [Assigned to: Virtual assistant]
Expand into government contracting by securing 1 government contract by October 30, 2025 Action item: Submit three new bids in 2025 [Assigned to: CEO]	• Gather the required paperwork and put in a [Assigned to: Virtual assistant] • Complete MBE/WBE certification as a minority and woman business enterprise at the state level [Assigned to: Virtual assistant] • Submit MBE/WBE paperwork to the state and city, and review city and state websites for potential contracts [Assigned to: CEO Business development]
Decrease monthly expenses by 10% in 6 months Action Item: Review financial statements to identify areas [Assigned to: CEO/Bookkeeper]	• Review budget and monthly expenses statement • Discontinue software that is no longer being used • Consolidate business credit cards • Identify lower interest loan

how the business is performing and what aspects of your business you may need to adjust. These KPIs should also be easy for you to gather and to share with your team. Reviewing the KPIs on a regular basis (e.g., daily, weekly, or monthly) will also help you notice patterns, identify changes that you need to make, and make informed decisions based on data.

As you set your goals, consider the KPIs you will use to measure progress. You can choose from a multitude of KPIs to track your business success. Here are some examples of metrics specific to therapy:

- Number of self-pay customers
- Average insurance reimbursement rate per patient
- Monthly collections or monthly revenue
- Late cancellation/no show rate
- Percent of late cancellation fees collected
- Referral conversion rate
- Weekly bank balance
- Profit margin
- Monthly expenses

Other metrics used by a wide range of businesses include the following:

- Website views
- Click rate for email marketing
- Average session duration
- Number of sales
- Average order value

MONEY SCRIPTS AND KPIs

When I started my first business, I was deep in avoidant mode when it came to tracking metrics. The only metrics I tracked, using an actual handwritten ledger, were: total monthly revenue, total annual revenue, and year-to-year revenue comparisons. I did not have any growth goals and was happy just to have some extra revenue. I had no real strategy for obtaining new clients (relying solely on client referrals) and I had no way of knowing if my business was profitable. I recall occasionally taking a look at my bank balance and freaking out at times when my balance dropped too low for my comfort. At those moments I would hurriedly send an email or make a call to bring a new client in. While that may have worked for a part-time practice, it would not be an effective practice for a full-time business. I realized that having a practice of looking at my bank account on a daily basis served as a reminder to focus on business development.

Reflection Time

Let's take some time to reflect on your own goals and KPIs. Find a quiet space, and respond to the journal prompts below:

- Given your business goals, what are three KPIs that you want to track? Why are these metrics important to track?
- What questions will these metrics help you answer about your business?
- How will you use the information to further your growth goals?
- How might your money script impact how you engage with your KPIs?

Take Action Exercise

Start a daily practice of looking at your metrics so that you understand how your business is working and how to make informed and real-time decisions. Table 11.2 offers an example of a "CEO dashboard" that can help you keep track of your KPIs. Of course, you will want to look at the dashboard regularly to stay focused.

DEVELOPING PROCESSES FOR GROWTH

Your business cannot grow if routine business functions are not automated or if the business requires your involvement for every aspect of decision-making. Developing *written* processes is an essential strategy for growing your business. Documenting your processes allows you to delegate to others so that they can carry out tasks you no longer need to do. It also identifies gaps and inefficiencies and, in turn, allows you to focus on visioning and growth. Written processes are necessary as you grow your team, and the magic is that it gives you back time.

Now, let me talk real quick to the people who have a hard time giving up control and turning over tasks to others: *If you want to grow, writing down your processes is the way to go.* When we tell people how to carry out a task, whether orally or in writing, we often make assumptions about what the other person knows, which can cause us to leave out crucial pieces of information. Writing out your processes, and having people use them, provides clarity for you and your team.

Have you ever done the PB&J challenge? This activity focuses on oral

Table 11.2 Sample CEO dashboard

Goal #1	Result	KPI	How will you track?	How often will you track?
Example: Increase annual revenue by 20%	$100,000 annual revenue	1. No. of monthly contracts	1. Contract database	1. Monthly
		2. Avg. $$ per contract	2. Submitted invoices	2. Weekly
		3. Referral conversion rate	3. Marketing software	3. Monthly
		4. Bank account balance	4. Bank account	4. Weekly

communication and demonstrates how easily miscommunications can occur between people. The first time I did the PB&J challenge was in 1995, when I was working at a residential program and was cofacilitating a girls group. It was a fun activity and it highlighted how much we take for granted when giving people instructions to complete a task.

Your goal is to have a process for every aspect of your business, so that you are not needed to carry out the day-to-day activities. These processes can eventually become part of the operations and employee handbook for your business so that team members can be trained the same way and understand how to execute their roles. As you build out your processes, consider the workplace culture that you want to cultivate.

Here are examples of some processes you could develop:

- Onboarding new clients
- Hiring new employees
- Onboarding new employees
- Invoicing clients
- Moving referrals from waitlist to active clients
- Fulfilling a product order
- Designing marketing materials

- Giving performance reviews for employees
- Tabling at community events
- Responding to requests for reduced speaker fee

Now let's do a quick check-in: what are *one or two* words that describe how it would feel for you to have all your processes documented, so that other people on your team can take over tasks that you have been doing, but no longer need to do?

My word is *freeing*! It was a tedious process that took time to fully develop, and it was also scary because it meant letting go of functions that I loved doing but had no business still doing. These tasks may include keeping track of data, onboarding new contractors, or designing slide decks. I hired an intern and it saves me time. It also meant letting go of some things that I was happy to give up!

Take Action Exercise

Write out a list of 10 processes that you need for your business, such as new client onboarding and client invoicing.

- Choose one of the processes and outline all the steps that are needed to complete the task.
- Ask someone to review the steps and see if they can execute the task like you would.
- Make any necessary edits.
- Work your way through the remaining processes, eventually, you will have an operations handbook.

Expanding Your Team

Expanding your team beyond you is the next step to elevating your business. It is very hard to grow your business with just you in the business—this is just a reality. I imagine that some of you are feeling some anxiety about letting other people into your business. The thought of trusting someone else to care for your business or to execute tasks with the attention to detail and excellence that you would is unimaginable. As a case in point, it was extremely hard for me to hire an assistant. The thought of letting someone into my personal email and my files was terrifying, and as a result, it took me a long time—way too long—to make my first hire, and my business was impacted by my procrastination. My business was growing, but delaying this decision meant that I was doing *everything* in the business—leading workshops, creating the slide decks, responding to all emails, scheduling appointments, running to Staples for printing—it was all too much. As a result, lots of emails fell through the cracks, and it took a long time to follow up with new clients, which meant losing business due to my slow response rate. However, once I made the decision to find additional support, I regretted that it had taken me so much time to make the hires. Expanding my team has not only helped grow my business but also significantly improved my customer service and reduced my stress.

Reflection Time

Let's take a few minutes to reflect on how you feel about hiring. Find a quiet space, and respond to the following journal prompts:

- As you think about expanding your team, what emotions come up for you?
- Are there prior experiences with hiring that are impacting how you feel about hiring now?
- What role would be your first hire?

Take Action Exercise

- List the responsibilities or tasks that you currently do that can be done by someone else?
- Identify the positions that you want to add to your team, even if you are not ready to hire yet.
- Identify a position that you would like to fill in the next 3 to 6 months. List the steps you need to take to make this hire a reality.
- List the resources you will use to create job descriptions, interview questions, and performance evaluations.
- List the resources will you use to post job positions.

Leveraging Capital for Business Growth

Obtaining capital or funding is another strategy that can truly assist a business with its growth goals. Every business needs money to operate and grow. Unfortunately, due to systemic racism, Black entrepreneurs have struggled to get adequate funding from lending sources to grow their dreams. Most have trouble getting a loan, and when they do, the loan amounts are typically less than for their White counterparts and with higher interest rates. Nevertheless, Black entrepreneurs are not deterred by this and find ways to start and grow their businesses against the odds. They often self-fund their businesses by working second and third jobs, dip into their savings, or cash out their retirement savings (Goldschein, 2021). It is important to explore the funding options that are available to you before you actually need them.

Below, I share a few common funding options—this list is not exhaustive, and additional funding resources are available as well.

- *Bootstrapping* involves entrepreneurs using their own financial resources to build their business. They may acquire capital through personal savings, retirement plans, family and friends, or revenue from the business.
- *Debt financing* involves borrowing money from a lending source such as banks or using credit cards, which is paid off with interest for specified amounts and time periods. In addition, other options such as lines of credit allow you to borrow against the equity in your business, and you only repay the money you borrow. In addition to traditional commercial banks, community development financial institutions, or CDFIs, are institutions committed to providing fair lending to individuals and businesses in underinvested communities and to businesses that would not otherwise have access to capital. The U.S. Small Business Administration (SBA) also has loan programs that can make financing easier for BIPOC entrepreneurs. Many business owners of color are also raised with messages that loans and debt are bad, so we don't explore how bank loans might help us grow our businesses. Discrimination in banking practices have inequitable outcomes for BIPOC borrowers.
- *Revenue-based financing* bases your loan payments on a percentage of the revenue you earn each month. For months when your revenue is higher, your payment would be higher, and vice versa if you have a low-revenue month. It offers flexibility in payment amounts based on the revenue the company earns, but usually has a higher repayment amount.
- *Equity financing* is a way to obtain capital by selling shares or parts of your company. Common sources for this type of funding are venture

capital and "angel" investors. According to a Fast Company article (Visram, 2023) only 1% of Black founded companies received venture capital funds in 2022 and the percentage drops to 0.34% for Black-woman owned businesses in 2022 (Alexander, 2024).

Reflection Time

Let's take some time to reflect on how raising capital may fit into your business growth goals. Find a quiet space, and respond to the following journal prompts:

- How do you feel about securing capital to grow your business?
- Are you open to borrowing money from a lender to grow your business? Why or why not?
- Are you open to selling parts of your company to raise capital? Why or why not?

PERSONAL REFLECTION: VIEWS ABOUT DEBT

Growing up, I recall my mother being proud that she was able to buy land and build her home without having a mortgage. She was proud that she did not have to take loans—you can see I learned early on that debt was bad. We have heard about others or maybe experienced ourselves being exploited by predatory lenders. All of these financial traumas can make it hard to take on debt. However, going through the Goldman Sachs Black in Business program in the fall of 2023 really helped shift my mindset about debt. One thing I learned is that securing capital is often a viable option to allow your business to grow. Without capital, your business stays stagnant.

Take Action Exercise

- What is a mindset shift that you want to make about financing and raising capital for your business?
- List three CDFIs in your community and schedule an appointment to learn more about the products they have to offer.

Remember, it's great to explore financial resources now, *before* you need them.

Partnerships

Developing partnerships with aligned organizations is another great way to increase brand awareness and grow your business. I have been fortunate to get connected to a number of organizations, even celebrity-run nonprofits. What has helped is having clear and consistent messaging about my mission and educating and advocating for the target audience. Partnerships work best when it is a win-win situation for both parties, so be sure to communicate your value and values when conducting outreach to potential partners. It is also helpful to get to know the organization leaders and even cohosting events together as a way to assess your working relationship before making partnerships official.

CHAPTER 11 MOMENTUM AND MINDSET CHECK

You are growing your Black business! You have to think about business growth even before you launch. In this chapter, we discussed how to plan for growing your business and the importance of goal setting using frameworks like the SMARTIE goals. You identified metrics and created the CEO dashboard. You planned for expanding the team, developing processes for growth, securing capital, and broadening your networks.

- What is one takeaway that you have as you finish this chapter?
- What is a mindset shift that you have made after reading this chapter?

Beyond a Traditional Private Practice

Transforming Your Wisdom Into Wealth

• •

You are a knowing being, and what you know is worthy.

RECOGNIZING THE VALUE OF YOUR WISDOM

Dear Black therapist, you have a wealth of knowledge that comes from your lived experiences, and together with your coursework, internships, and practical training, these create your wisdom and expertise. However, many graduate school training programs significantly undervalue the lived experiences that their students bring with them, especially for Black and BIPOC students, leaving them feeling disconnected from salient parts of their identities (a strategy reminiscent of colonization). By the time students leave graduate school, they often feel like novices, as the two-to-five years spent earning a degree in the mental health field is deemed unworthy. Too often I observe therapists who believe that they need more training, more supervision, more experience, more everything to practice independently, even those who are licensed. This occurs because there is an over-reliance on formal training, to the exclusion of our lived experiences. People forget how to trust their intuition or how to value their ways of knowing in graduate programs. Yes, we want to do good work and not cause harm to clients, but our lived experiences and wisdom have value too. Our clients benefit when we show up as our full, complicated selves—as people who have been through some stuff and can use all of it in the therapeutic relationship. Our clients need us to bring all our wisdom to all that we do.

You are a knowing being, and what you know is worthy. As we discussed in Chapter 5, your wisdom combined with your training offer you a unique perspective that you can leverage to create niche offerings. Most graduate school programs were not designed to support their students in generating revenue beyond earning the 9-to-5 salary through activities such as therapy, teaching, and research. However, through an ongoing process of decolonizing the mind, as we explored in Chapter 2, you realize that you have centuries of wisdom: your lived experience, plus the generational knowledge that has been passed on from your ancestors. This wisdom and expertise is what you can use to design offerings that truly meet the needs of your clients—offerings that stretch beyond traditional private practice offerings to building a speaking platform, engaging with the media, creating products and technology. Phew, you got me fired up! Now, let's get to work so you can get those coins.

Growing a Speaking Platform

Public speaking has been an unexpected but lucrative way for me to grow my business. I have been speaking for a long time, but in the past 6 years I've been intentionally building up my speaker profile so that I can command higher speaker fees. Developing a speaking platform is a way to use your expertise to share what you know and to educate others. You have learned so much, and these treasures need to be shared. I know some of you are thinking, "Nope, nah, I'm all set," because the idea of public speaking terrifies you—I know, I've been there!

If public speaking is something you have crossed off your list (or was never on your list in the first place), I invite you to rethink that decision. If you are nervous about speaking in public, that's quite alright, but it is not a reason to shut yourself out of a lucrative option. Don't let fear dictate your revenue. Public speaking is a skill, and as with any skill, you can learn it and get better with practice (growth mindset). You can get a coach, take public speaking classes, or join a speaking group. Delivering keynote speeches, serving on or moderating panels, being a podcast host or guest are all wonderful opportunities to leverage your expertise. Here is an invitation to think boldly and step aside from limiting mindsets that will hinder your growth.

Keynotes. Keynote addresses are inspirational speeches delivered by an expert on a particular topic. A keynote speech is usually delivered at the beginning of a conference to get attendees excited and engaged. Keynotes can also be delivered at fundraising events, other special occasions, or smaller events. They can be as short as 10–15 minutes and are usually no longer than an hour. Speaking fees for corporate venues usually start at a higher price point.

Panels and Moderators. Panels usually consist of two or more *panelists* who are brought together to provide a range of perspectives on a particular topic. Again, your role on a panel is to share your expertise and provide your unique perspective. In addition, panels usually have a *moderator* who poses the questions to the panelists. The moderator may also share insights and is responsible for the tone and flow of the program. Panels can be as short as 30 minutes and are usually not longer than 90 minutes.

MY JOURNEY INTO PUBLIC SPEAKING

The thought of standing in front of an audience and talking for any amount of time used to cause me great anxiety. My voice and hands would shake, I avoided eye contact with the audience, and my heart would beat so loudly I could barely hear the words I was speaking. However, I didn't let that stop me. I challenged myself to speak more in front of audiences. I took two theater classes and a public speaking class, I watched speakers I admired, and worked with a speech and performance coach. The more I spoke in front of people, the more comfortable I became. The anxiety did not fully go away, but it decreased significantly. Even now, I continue to work on being a better speaker. The highlight of my speaking journey was delivering a solid TEDx talk at TEDx Roxbury in May 2024. My scary goal is to deliver a keynote in front of an audience of 5,000 or more (as I exhale)!

Workshops and Webinars. Workshops (in-person) and webinars (virtual) are typically educational programs intended to provide a skill or to share information on a topic. They can be designed for a range of audiences, including the general public. As a trained mental health professional, you have gained and are continuing to gain a wealth of knowledge from your graduate training *and* from your lived experiences. Based on your experiences and interests, you can provide workshops to a professional audience, the general public, or both. There is an audience out there for what you know—your task is to find it (perhaps you have already?). You can be hired to lead a workshop or you can also create your own workshop content. If creating a workshop or workshop series for mental health professionals, it would be an added value to secure continuing education (CE) credits for your workshops.

Digital Courses. Pre-recorded classes are available on-demand on a wide range of topics and are a great way to earn passive income. Building your course involves designing the course curriculum and syllabus, creating engaging videos, and designing worksheets, templates, and activities that support the learning process (Harvard University Office of the Vice Provost for Advances in Learning, 2021). As you design your course, consider different learning styles and processing speeds, create opportunities for discussions among students, "spark curiosity," and provide opportunities for discovery (Harvard University Office of the Vice Provost for Advances in Learning, 2021).

You will also need to market your course. In fact, before you invest the time to build the course, you can actually start by marketing it and getting people registered. Specifically, you will need to create an engaging graphic with the name of the course, a brief description, time/time commitment; location of course, and faculty/instructors to promote the course via social media or through email marketing. When enough people sign up, you can then focus on building out your content. Your course may be 1 session or 12 sessions—it depends on the experience you want to provide for students. Be sure to include feedback surveys so that you learn how to improve the course. Plus, you can use testimonials from the surveys for future courses. Once you have your first digital courses built, continue to build your library of content, as this can generate a fair amount of passive income. Rinse and repeat . . . that's how it works.

In choosing a platform, try out a few course hosting platforms before making a long-term commitment. Some platforms will offer a free trial, a free course, or a free demo. You may also want to consider if the platform will integrate with your website, how it will affect your users' experiences, and how easily it lets you build the course. When recording your videos, record in short segments, less than 5 minutes, so that people will stay engaged. Keep the videos engaging by smiling, using good lighting, and sharing personal stories. Avoid reading note cards or teleprompter and turn on closed captions to make your videos accessible to people who need it.

EIGHT STRATEGIES TO GROW YOUR SPEAKING PLATFORM

1. *Create a signature talk(s)*, a talk on a topic that you want to be known for and that you can give with little preparation. This is a go-to talk that you can adapt for different audiences and for events of different types and lengths. Focus on your expertise and what you want to be known for. For example, I have two signature talks: *Racial Stress in the Workplace and the Impact on Emotional Well-Being* and *Reclaim Your Well-Being*, based on my TEDx talk (*Reclaiming Your Well-Being in the Workplace*).

2. *Create a one sheet*, a visual asset that provides information about you and your expertise. Unlike a resume or curriculum vitae, a one sheet typically includes expert topics, places you have spoken, testimonials, books you have written, and your contact information (see Appendix P for a sample one sheet). A one sheet is a great tool to include in emails to prospective clients as it summarizes your expertise in bite-sized sentences and engaging graphics.

3. *Submit proposals to calls for speakers* to professional associations and other organizations that host conferences. Most large conferences have a formal "call for proposals" or "call for speakers" that they send out at least 9 months before an event. Research conferences that you want to speak at and create a database with their conference dates and proposal deadlines. Then, submit proposals to their conferences, and include your one sheet. There will be a time when they reach out to you, just focus on getting visibility and making sure that the event planners know of you.

4. *Promote yourself on various social media channels* (see Chapter 6 for marketing strategies). Create graphics that show your speaking

event, with your name and photo listed. Make a BIG big splash. Additionally, you can:

   a. Add *speaker* to your LinkedIn profile and other social media platforms.

   b. Send outreach email to local and national organizations informing them of your signature talks and expertise and your availability to speak. Be sure to include your one sheet in these communications.

   c. Tell friends and family members and ask for introductions to people in their network.

   d. Share social media posts of any speaking you do, both before and after the event. Ask the organizer or a colleague to take photos and videos while you are speaking, and splash these on social media afterward.

5. *Get feedback*, especially from the attendees, using tools to provide their experience of your event or talk—a one-word survey or a longer one. Sometimes I ask one question, "How would you rate this workshop?" using a poll, or a form so that I can collect their email addresses.

6. *Stay connected to event organizers* after a speaking opportunity. Be sure to thank the organizers afterward—I even schedule a debrief session to get feedback from the organizers and to deepen the relationship. Ask for a testimonial and for referrals to people in their network.

7. *Create your own speaking opportunities.* If you are having trouble getting requests, or wish to focus on specific topics, you can create your own content. In 2017 I started a monthly in-person series for mental health professionals entitled *Social Justice and Mental Health*, and during the COVID pandemic I created a webcast called *Hope and Healing*, inviting mental health professionals to talk about their healing journeys. These speaking opportunities allowed me to get more comfortable speaking in front of an audience. Plus, it helped with my moderator skills, and I got video content, which I then reshared on my social media platforms.

8. *Create a speaker reel*, a short edited video (up to 2 minutes) of clips of you speaking. It gives event planners a sample of your talk and

your visual presentation skills. You want to create a professional video, so consider hiring a videographer. There are also computer software that can help you create speaker reels. As always, do your research to find the software that best fits your needs.

Reflection Time

Let's take a few minutes to reflect on building a speaking platform as part of your business. Find a quiet space, and respond to the journal prompts below:

- How do you feel about building a public speaking platform?
- If you are feeling hesitant, how can you apply a growth mindset to public speaking?
- What resources would you need to grow your skills as a public speaker?

Table 12.1 Sample planning sheet for talks, workshops, and digital courses

Topic	Title	Brief Description of Your Workshop/Talk	Target Audience
Mental Health Stigma	Breaking the Silence on Mental Health: How Therapy Can Help Us Heal	During this session, we will examine historical and current factors that serve as barriers to mental health care, especially for people of color. Participants will learn about various types of mental health support.	Corporations; Employee resource groups
Joy; Mindfulness; Soul-care	Cultivating Joy in Daily Life	For those seeking to infuse their daily routines with positivity and fulfillment, this workshop will include music, movement, poetry, and other creative expressions. Finding joy is not just an act of soul-care but a vital element in creating a thriving and harmonious life.	Corporations; Wellness summits

Take Action Exercise

- What is a signature talk or two that you can deliver?

Using Table 12.1 as an example, create a planning sheet that maps out your speaking, workshop, and digital course ideas.

Securing Public Speaking Deals

Here are some tips for getting the most from your speaking/workshop engagements:

- *Schedule an intake call:* Similar to an intake with therapy clients, this is a great practice to use with speaking/workshop clients as well. During the call, you want to obtain a clear understanding of the event, goals, and what success would look like to them. This will give you clarity on how to design your talk or workshop.
- *Bring your A game:* Make sure that you prepare ahead of time and deliver an excellent program. Many of my referrals come from audience members, so delivering an outstanding program is also excellent marketing.
- *Share a handout:* Provide a takeaway or tangible resource that audience members can use to keep you front of mind. People often ask for your slide deck, so have a handout ready and make sure it includes how to contact you. Typically, I give an abbreviated version of my slides, to protect my intellectual property. You want to protect your content as much as you can.
- *Offer a giveaway:* A giveaway at the end keeps people engaged and is a great way to capture their emails. Include a QR code on the giveaway slide so that they easily get to the form or website.
- *Get feedback and testimonials:* As mentioned above, take a few moments to administer a feedback survey so that you can collect information on the impact of the talk from attendees. Depending on the venue or event, you may ask attendees to provide a testimonial about your program. Also, gather feedback and testimonials from event organizers.
- *Schedule a debrief call:* Make time to circle back to the event organizer to debrief the program. As noted above, it allows you to get their

feedback, to share additional offerings that you have, and to obtain testimonials and referrals for people in their network.

* *Consider creating a workshop series*: You can offer the client this option if they want to continue working with you.

Building a Consulting Practice

Consulting is a customized approach to helping organizations navigate an issue that they are unable to address internally. Consultants provide guidance and support to organizations and clients as they execute their mission, which offers an excellent way for therapists to leverage their expertise. Your consulting engagement may look different for different clients:

* Developing or writing a new curriculum
* Reviewing and updating a current or outdated curriculum
* Providing on-call crisis or therapy support
* Supporting organizational-level culture change
* Implementing a framework that you created
* Leading a strategic plan
* Providing leadership coaching to the executive team or board on topics related to your expertise
* Working with legislators and advocates to provide testimony on your expertise

1. DISCOVERY
Data-driven, *culturally responsive* framework to examine the organization's strengths & opportunity gaps

2. STRATEGY
Create a culturally responsive **plan** to address opportunity gaps and create **metrics** & **goals** for success.

3. IMPLEMENTATION
Roll-out **culturally responsive** emotional wellbeing **initiatives** and **programming**.

4. MONITORING
Throughout the engagement, we will **track key metrics** and **provide mid- and end-of-year reports** to team leads.

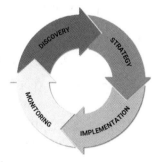

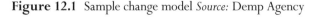

Figure 12.1 Sample change model *Source:* Demp Agency

Consultants are hired for their expertise, so make your knowledge known by promoting and marketing your business (recall Chapter 5 on communicating your brand). In addition to promoting your business, you will need to create your framework or model for change that shows customers how your system works. Create a visual of your framework (see Figure 12.1 for sample framework), and share it on your website so that clients can see it. Collect pre- and post data to enhance your program's effectiveness and to demonstrate the impact of your services.

Before beginning any consulting work, take time to fully understand the problem you've been asked to solve, the scope of work, deliverables, and time-line. You will also want to gather information about how they have addressed the issue in the past or what steps or resources have been used to date. These should also be clearly outlined in the contract. Often, as you start working with a client, the scope of work may evolve, so be sure to include how you will charge for work that is *beyond the scope*. Also, before doing any work that is outside the scope, communicate with the client and get their permission in writing to continue. Identify who your point of contact is, and establish regular meetings with that individual to provide progress updates and to solve the challenges that will inevitably arise.

Getting Paid to Write

Writing is a tried-and-true method of elevating your expertise, whether through books, blogs, or social media posts. It allows you to establish your voice and perspective on a topic, elevating your expertise on that topic. Once you are seen as an expert, this can open up additional opportunities, such as speaking engagements, partnership opportunities, and much more.

Books and Essays. There are many types of books that a mental health professional might write, including clinical guides, self-help books, and workbooks. Writing books is a popular method to establish your expertise on a topic, but it can be time-consuming, and it can be hard to get a book deal with a traditional publisher. Some authors will go the self-publishing route, which gives you creative control, but you have to invest your money upfront—the upside is that all the proceeds go to you.

E-books, or digital books, can be an easier way to get in the writing game, because they tend to be short, sometimes as short as 10 pages. Many entrepreneurs use e-books as a lead magnet to attract their target audience, to increase brand awareness, and ultimately to put potential clients in their sales funnel (see Chapter 6).

Blogs, or digital articles, are short articles that can be written to educate an audience or to share a perspective. Blogs offer another way to build up a portfolio and to establish your expertise on a particular topic through shorter articles. You can have your own blog page on your website that brings an audience to you, and you can serve as a guest blogger or contributing writer for another organization. InnoPsych has its own blog, and we have contributing writers. I have also served as contributing writer for the *PBS Teachers' Lounge*. Guest blogging may be something you do for exposure, as blogging typically does not pay very much. However, you can monetize your blog through sponsorships or advertising—you just need to invest the time to promote your blog and establish yourself as a leading voice or a voice with a unique perspective.

Social Media. Leveraging your expertise on social media is free and easy. There are many options to choose from, but I believe LinkedIn offers the best opportunity to elevate your professional presence and to open opportunities for speaking and consulting. LinkedIn enables you to expand professional connections, create articles, and host live events. Instagram allows only for short writing or snippets through captions, but it is a great way to connect with the general public and to raise visibility.

The best thing about content is that you can reuse it for so many purposes: you can use it on different platforms, and you can reshare it several times in different formats. *Content is king—repurpose it!*

TIPS FOR ELEVATING YOUR EXPERTISE

- *Clearly articulate your expertise:* Spend some time getting clarity about the expertise that you want to showcase. Think about areas where you add a fresh perspective or a topic where people crave more information. Create a model or framework that highlights how you uniquely address the problem.

- *Connect with aligned organizations or groups:* Identify your target audience and look for organizations, groups, and individuals that would want to hear your message. Make sure your outreach speaks to the pain point or problem they want to solve. For example, if you have expertise working with anxiety in school-age children, connect with schools, parent-teacher associations, pediatricians, libraries, and after-school programs. You can also create an event that will bring your target audience to you.

- *Use social media channels to establish your voice:* Create weekly posts about your expertise where you share your perspective on newsworthy ideas, teach a skill, or share a tool or resource. Remember, consistency helps to build the brand.

- *Write about the topic:* Create a blog or newsletter, write a story for a local newspaper, and share insights with journalists or reporters who cover the topic.

- *Inform your network:* Let people in your network know that you are available for speaking opportunities. You can create a one sheet (see a sample one sheet in Appendix P) to share when you conduct your outreach.

- *Join a speakers' group:* There are a number of organizations that help speakers grow their speaking platform, from speakers' associations to speakers' bureaus. Speaker's bureaus tend to be pricier as they take a percentage of the speaker fee, but they work to find you higher-paying opportunities. Do your research by talking to speakers who have used their service. Be sure to find out if they have rules about exclusivity (i.e., you pay a percentage for all your speaking contracts, even contracts that you find on your own).

Increasing Your Visibility by Talking to the Media

Building your brand visibility is another necessary component for growth. Your clients have to know you are out there and that you have amazing products and services that will solve their problems. Using media to increase your brand awareness should be part of your growth strategy, as it connects you to a wider audience. It is helpful to engage with the media even if the news outlet is not your target audience because it helps you to practice speaking to the media. I do recommend media training to ensure that you have the tools to effectively communicate with the press.

Working with the media usually requires timely responses to newsworthy stories. So if you have an opportunity to engage with the media, you want to make sure that you meet the deadlines for the story.

Op-Eds. An op-ed, short for "opposite the editorial page," from newsprint days, is an opinion piece that captures your point of view about a newsworthy issue and includes research to corroborate your perspective. Op-eds are an opportunity for you to share your perspective on a topic connected to your expertise. Op-ed pieces can be written for print or digital media outlets.

Here is the title of my first opinion piece, published on the Thomas Reuters Foundation website on June 9, 2021, about Black women and mental health (Jackman, 2021):

> "Opinion: Naomi Osaka and Meghan Markle Reveal the Racial Inequities in Mental Health Support"

Here is a second op-ed written for *Black Enterprise* that discusses Black men and mental health (Jackman, 2022):

> "S.O.S.: We Need More Black Men as Therapists Now!"

You can see a clear strategy in elevating issues of mental health affecting Black people in these two pieces.

Again, op-eds are newsworthy. If a particular news story is compelling to you and falls within your expertise, consider writing your piece and shopping it to your local newspaper or digital media outlets covering the story or topic. You have to be timely. Here is a **pro tip**: write your opinions about topics that fall within your expertise in advance. If it is not a current topic now, but is likely to become one in the near future, you will be ready to submit that op-ed piece quickly.

Media Interviews. Reporters and journalists, for both print and digital media, are always looking for experts to provide commentary on newsworthy topics. I have had the opportunity to provide expert content to a range of media outlets, including *Oprah Daily!* (No, I did not get to speak to her directly.) For media interviews, a reporter will reach out and request your thoughts on a particular topic. These are often time sensitive, but not always. They usually interview a few experts and then include experts' quotes in their article. Remember to ask for a timeline, and respect their deadline. If you do not have time to contribute, politely decline or recommend someone. Also, if the topic is not in your expertise, say no! They will respect you for that immensely.

Requests for media interviews can happen in a few ways. Reporters can reach out with a list of questions that they want you to answer in writing; they may request a phone or video conversation to discuss the topic, or they may request a virtual or in-studio interview. Sometimes the reporter is working with a tight timeline, so respond to their email or call quickly. During the initial contact they will share information about what they need, and you can inquire about what they are hoping to convey to their readers, format of the interview (e.g., written responses, audio, or video), and most important, their deadline. You will have to decide quickly, so let them know right away if you are available or not.

Once you have accepted the opportunity for *earned media*—visibility that you did not create or pay for yourself—it's time to prepare. Review the questions, if you have them, and prepare your talking points. Remember you are the expert, so offer your perspective and provide novel ideas that they may not have heard yet (see other interview tips in the box below). This will increase the chances that your quote is included in the piece.

When you submit your responses, include the hyperlink to your website. Some media outlets will include the hyperlinks in articles, and some will not. These links increase your visibility or search engine optimization (SEO) and drive more traffic to your website, so ask to include them. After the article is posted, activate your marketing by posting on social media platforms (always tag the reporter and news outlet) and in your newsletters and email campaigns.

After a few years of being interviewed, in 2023 I finally landed two interviews in a high-profile online magazine, *Oprah Daily*. In speaking with the reporters, I learned that they do research to see what you have previously contributed and review your online presence. They want to make sure that you align with their outlet and with their audience.

The first *Oprah Daily* article, "The Essential Questions You Should Be Asking Your Therapist," was written by reporter Amanda Robb (2023) and closely aligned with the InnoPsych mission as it engaged the audience in discussions of therapy. In speaking with the reporter, I was sure to add some tips that I know she was unlikely to obtain from other sources. (I think it worked, as I was the first expert named in the piece.) A bonus was that the reporter included hyperlinks to the InnoPsych website, which is a huge win. However, the second article, "Do You Have 'Good Girl' Fatigue?" (Conway, 2023), was not as closely aligned with the InnoPsych brand, but it offered an opportunity to share my perspective about the emotional costs of an experience many women face. I was able to secure these interviews because over the past 4 years I had accumulated a portfolio of media interviews with reputable outlets, which demonstrated my expertise.

Video Interviews. When providing video interviews, you want to make sure that you have a few great quotable responses or soundbites. A mistake people often make is being long-winded or rambling when responding to the reporter. Keep your responses short, clear, and succinct. The reporter will ask a follow-up question if needed. If people like what you have to stay, you might have an ongoing opportunity to make other appearances. I've also pitched stories to reporters and journalists I have worked with and they appreciate having story ideas that they can develop. Again, make sure that your idea is relevant to their audience.

For *on-camera interviews*, it is safe to avoid wearing colors that will blend into the background or clothing with busy patterns and prints. If you are going to a studio, avoid wearing black, as studios are often dark so that they can control the lighting, and avoid white if you are in a heavily lighted studio or outdoors. Do your research by watching previous episodes so that you have a sense of what would be ideal to wear. You can also ask questions of the producer/associate producer or the point of contact. They want to make sure that you look great in the interview too.

Podcasts. Another way to showcase your expertise and build your brand awareness is to appear as a guest on or to host a podcast. This usually involves a media interview with a host, who collects guest information (i.e., headshot and bio) to blast to the audience. Usually questions are sent ahead of time for guests to review, but the goal is to make the interview feel natural and conversational. Whether you create your own podcast or appear as a guest on someone else's, be sure to share it with your audience afterward. Many tools are available for recording high-level video and audio (see Appendix P). While podcasts have traditionally been audio, some hosts will simultaneously record video, so be sure to ask, so you are prepared.

TIPS FOR SHINING DURING MEDIA INTERVIEWS

- *Do your research:* Take a look at other stories the reporter or news outlet has covered. Get a sense for their style. Also, ask whether the interview is live or prerecorded and if video will be recorded. If it includes video, you will want to look polished for the camera.
- *Prepare your points:* Be prepared for your interviews by writing out the points you want to make, including any sound bites.
- *Stay in your zone:* Operate within your zone of excellence. If a topic will be far out of your expertise, please let the reporters know—they will appreciate it. If you know someone who has the expertise, offer to make an introduction.
- *Spread the word:* Media is a great marketing tool, but it only works if people know about it. So don't be shy—put yourself out there! Spread the word before and after interviews, and tag the reporter and news outlet when you post. Promote, promote, promote.
- *Create a media kit:* Create a digital file folder with a short bio (no more than 100–200 words; see Appendix F), professional headshot, company logo, and a one sheet (see Appendix P). If you have a name that might be hard to pronounce, include an audio clip with the correct pronunciation of your name. You can also include a speaker reel, testimonials, earned media features, and links to your website. For any media strategy that you use, be sure to share and repurpose your content for maximum exposure.
- *Create a press page:* Once you have a few pieces of published content, create a press page on your website to host all of your published media (for an example, see InnoPsych press page at https://www.innopsych.com/press).
- *Cultivate media relationships:* After the interview, send a follow-up email to thank the reporters. You can include any additional information you want to add or reiterate. It is a good idea to stay in touch with them, especially if they regularly report on topics that align with your expertise. You can pitch story ideas to them, which can make their job easier. If you do pitch, include any articles or supporting materials

that they can review. This is an opportunity for them to see you as a resource and may be more likely to reach out to you again.

Product Development

E-Commerce. While many therapists focus on building therapy practices, this is not the only way to leverage your expertise. I've been excited to see therapists think outside the box and create products that can be useful to clients and the general public. Additionally, creating wellness products opens up a passive income revenue stream. Once you create your products, you may have inventory at home, or you can use a company that does drop shipping (where they hold your inventory and will ship products to customers).

Card Decks. A number of mental health professionals have branded their expertise through card decks. I created a card deck game in 2019 as I was preparing to engage women of color at the Massachusetts Conference for Women. It was such a successful tool that I decided to build a product from that idea. The *My Time To Thrive* card deck provides mindfulness activities, journal prompts, and quotes that are designed to help people on their healing journey. The card deck also has a registered trademark.

Self-Help Journals and Workbooks. Self-help journals and workbooks are tools that therapists can easily create. You can adapt materials and resources that you have already created for clients and share with a wider audience.

Software Apps. Developing a software application is an involved process, but it is getting easier with technology advances. No-code app software is now available for you to use to design your apps. Jackie Vorpahl was the first psychologist I personally know who developed an app. In 2016, she created Chill Outz, a mindfulness app to address anxiety in children and to help them face and overcome fears and obstacles. Another colleague, Melissa Mueller-Douglas, a social worker I met while we were both enrolled in the Babson WIN Growth Lab, created the MYRetreat app that offers daily meditations designed to be paired with chocolate, to increase habit formation. These mental health professionals have used their experiences and expertise to create a product to address struggles their clients faced.

Wellness Retreats and Travel Experiences. There is a new emerging market for wellness retreats. According to the GlobeNewswire (2024), the wellness retreat industry was valued at $180 billion in 2022 and is expected to grow to $364 billion in 2032. Entrepreneurs curate experiences that focus on a particular wellness theme, such as yoga, mindfulness, or simply rest. Hosts often market these as luxury experiences with escapes to beautiful destinations. Other types of experiences may focus on a connection to ancestral or indigenous roots. You can partner with a travel agent to help secure accommodations and flights, practitioners for yoga and meditation, and so on.

The Merch Shop. Do you have a creative side? Even if you don't, there are many creative people out there whose services you can engage to design merchandise. Is there something that you often repeat to clients? Do you have a catchphrase that you say when you are speaking? Creating merchandise to highlight your expertise is another cool way to expand your audience and to generate passive income.

For example, we created two T-shirt lines that we thought were a little cheeky:

- Get You a Therapist
- Thriving Looks Like This

And guess what, you do not have to store large quantities of inventory in your home, as there are companies that will print, store, and ship your products for you. There are also companies that offer on-demand printing and will print per order and then ship the product to the customer. Or you can use a drop-shipping company that prints T-shirts, hoodies, mugs, and such on demand.

Reflection Time

Let's take some time to reflect on how wellness products might help you grow your business. Find a quiet space, and respond to the following journal prompts:

- What is a problem your ideal clientele have that could be solved or supported with a wellness product?
- What are innovative ways that you can share your expertise with your target audience using wellness products?

Take Action Exercise

- List five strategies (and action steps) in which you could use wellness products to elevate your expertise.
- Select one idea that you want to execute and identify the resources you would need to execute.
- Set a timeline for when you would want to execute this idea.

CHAPTER 12 MOMENTUM AND MINDSET CHECK

Your wisdom is your wealth. This chapter was geared to helping you reflect on your lived experiences and formal training so that you can develop unique offerings and expand your revenue streams—your niche. You explored what it takes to grow a speaking platform and consultation services, how to use media as a way to establish your voice in the field through different mediums, and you created some new product ideas. While you may not be ready yet to launch these services, exploring novel growth areas now will help you see opportunities and plan for the future.

- What is one takeaway that you have as you finish this chapter?
- What is a mindset shift that you have made after reading this chapter?

Protecting Your Peace: Soul-Care for the Entrepreneur

You can run a profitable business, do good, and protect your peace. It is possible!

THE ENTREPRENEURSHIP LEARNING CURVE

Congratulations! You are almost at the end of the finish line—just this last chapter to help you consolidate what you have learned so far. I imagine that you have gained a wealth of knowledge and that you are seeing entrepreneurship through a new lens. Your head might still be spinning from all the information you have packed in, but you are here: your motivation and persistence to make it to this point is clear, and these are qualities that will serve you well on the entrepreneurship journey. Yes, entrepreneurship can be intimidating, but once you have the right knowledge and skills, it is not just doable but actually enjoyable. You have started to put the pieces of your entrepreneurship puzzle together, and it is looking beautiful.

When I first started out on my entrepreneurship journey, I experienced a huge learning curve. I had the passion to start my business, but I lacked necessary business knowledge. To get up to speed, I read books written by entrepreneurs and business leaders who had been successful, and by those who had failed; I listened to podcast interviews with entrepreneurs and networked in real life with entrepreneurs who were willing to share their journey. I observed, asked questions, and launched my practice. By the time I was ready to transition to full-time entrepreneurship 15 years later, I thought I had learned all I needed to know about entrepreneurship. Wrong! I was in for a big surprise.

I had operated a private practice for 15 years, and I thought that even though the new business was a little different, what could be so hard? Apparently, quite a lot. In the 2 years prior to starting InnoPsych, I took a bootcamp seminar with the Small Business Administration. The program was general and provided broad information that was useful, but it was not specific to the type of business I was planning to launch. In talking to others and letting people know what I was planning, I learned of different educational programs (e.g., business accelerators) that I could tap into to close the gap in my knowledge base. While asking for help is often a struggle for me, I had to get past that because I needed people who had expertise with launching and operating tech companies, as my business was entering the mental health tech arena with the therapist directory.

Through the journey of starting, operating, and growing my businesses, I have learned so much about entrepreneurship *and* about myself. At every stage of my business I've had to level up my knowledge, my routines, and most of all my mindsets. There is so much more to growing a business than I could have imagined. Entrepreneurship means that you are constantly learning, and just when you figure out one thing, something new presents itself. For this special ride, you will have to level up, too. Here's the thing: what you learn at each stage will help you in your business and in your life. As your business grows, so will you, and vice versa. It's a beautiful cycle.

NAVIGATING THE ENTREPRENEURIAL JOURNEY

The entrepreneurial journey is thrilling and gut-wrenching, like a roller coaster ride. Most entrepreneurial journeys start with excitement, passion and energy. You have an idea, and you are thrilled to create a product or service that will help others, but there comes a time when it takes more time than you anticipated to execute an idea, when your clients are not as quick to buy your offerings as you predicted, or you realize your idea may not actually work. Whatever the case, disappointment, sadness, and other negative emotions can set in. Maybe you were prepared for this, but most entrepreneurs are not (and I was one of them). The emotions that you will feel along the journey will dip and peak and can change from one minute to the next—one minute you are riding high, excited by a call or potential partnership that you feel confident will transform your business, and a few hours later, you are in a downward spiral because a conversation has fallen apart. The emotional roller coaster. After going through a few cycles of my own emotional roller coaster, I came to realize that it was all part of the journey. There will be ups and there will be downs. Now that I understand the flow, I don't get pulled too far in either direction. If there is good news, I receive it, celebrate it, and keep it moving. If there is bad news, I receive it, breathe through the moment, find the lesson, and keep it moving. It's all part of the process.

Like any journey, you want to be prepared. You want to have the right equipment and tools to help you navigate the journey. But you also know that along the way something will go wrong, and you will encounter obstacles that you had not anticipated. Just remember that, in your preparation, you have gathered the tools and contacts that will help you figure out how to move forward, even if you do not have everything that you need. That's what survival is all about. Each founder will have their own unique path. Figure 13.1 reflects some of the stages that entrepreneurs will experience. Undoubtedly, the journey is marked by ebbs and flows, ups and downs, yeses and nos, which can all impact your emotional well-being. For me, entrepreneurship is like the ocean, waves come in and waves go out, sometimes there are big waves that pull you under and sometimes the waves are very calm. Your goal is to stay afloat. When you get pulled under, you find your way back to the surface. Developing the emotional stamina to navigate

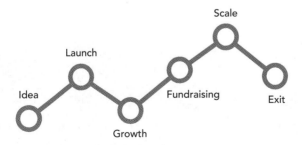

Figure 13.1 The entrepreneurial journey

the roller coaster of emotions that come with entrepreneurship will help you to thrive on your unique journey.

Let me let you in on a little secret: like therapy, entrepreneurship can be a very mysterious process. What you see from the outside does not usually tell the full story of what is going on behind the scenes. Some entrepreneurs may look successful from the outside, but you have no clue what is truly happening with their business. I also observed that when entrepreneurs talk about their businesses, they typically only report the wins and seldom speak of the challenges. Entrepreneurs have often given up quite a bit to pursue their dream, such as leaving a job with a regular paycheck, benefits, and other perks that come with full-time employment to take on entrepreneurship, where these benefits may not exist, at least not yet. Plus, when you don't work, you don't get paid, particularly in fee-for-service businesses like private practice. As a result, when people ask about your business, you may feel the need to only share the highlights, as a way to justify your good decision in leaving your 9-to-5 or not taking a "regular" job.

Talking about the hardships may feel like a betrayal to your goals, especially when talking to people who do not understand the entrepreneurship journey and may offer unsolicited advice or suggest that you give up or quit. You may feel pressure to convince family and friends that you made the right choice about becoming an entrepreneur, even on those tough days. Therefore, it is understandable that entrepreneurs avoid these sometimes awkward conversations by sharing only the good stuff.

I think it is important to share all parts of your journey. Staying silent about your struggles can cause you to feel ashamed and isolated and place you at risk for stress and mental health challenges. Sharing *all* aspects of your journey with others can also reduce the sense of isolation. Unfortunately, entrepreneur mental health is an area that does not get nearly enough attention—we will take a look at that later in this chapter.

PERSONAL REFLECTION: DEALING WITH THE STRUGGLES

There were a number of moments in my entrepreneurial journey when I thought I would have to quit because the revenue was just not coming in, but I did not share this with others—initially. It was hard to talk about the

> struggles, especially when people were congratulating me on my success. (If they only knew.) Some of these "successes" were awards, media interviews, partnerships with celebrity nonprofits that we shared with our audience, but most of them had no money attached. Honestly, these situations made me feel like a fraud. How could I talk about my struggles when people thought my business was a model of success? However, I got to a point where I realized that this was not helpful, not to me and not to others. Even though it was hard, I needed to create space to talk more openly about the business struggles, because I knew other entrepreneurs needed that space too. I was successful in creating a number of safe spaces where I can speak honestly about my journey. It has been gratifying because I don't have to pretend or show a brave face and I am committed to creating similar brave spaces for therapists too.

If you can't be fully honest with people you know or don't have their support, it might be time to find spaces with other entrepreneurs who get it and who will allow you to be vulnerable and honest with them. I've been a part of two extremely supportive groups: my vision boarding group and the Goldman Sachs growth group. These are safe and brave spaces where we can be vulnerable with each other, but we also challenge each other when we are stuck, hold each other accountable, and we share resources too. We create a community for each other and make this journey much more fun. Here are three suggestions for you to find supportive entrepreneurship communities:

1. Check InnoPsych's website for current opportunities to join InnoPsych communities.
2. Join your local chamber of commerce, an association that brings business owners together for networking and educational programming.
3. Start your group by bringing some entrepreneurs together—try to bring people together from other fields, so you can learn from each other.

Interrupting the Hustle and Grind Mentality

Let's also explore the *hustle and grind* culture and its impact on Black and Brown entrepreneurs. Due to having issues with accessing capital or funds to start a business, many BIPOC entrepreneurs will start their business while still working a full-time job. However, this means working long hours and weekends to put in the time to build businesses, while sacrificing sleep, good eating habits, health, and quality time with family and friends. According to an article in *NerdWallet* (Goldschein, 2021), only 1% of Black-owned businesses receive funding in their first year, compared to 7% of White-owned businesses. Access to working capital can be hard to come by due to systemic policies that serve as barriers to funding, and with these barriers in place, BIPOC entrepreneurs take on jobs and gigs in an effort to make their businesses viable.

PERSONAL REFLECTION: INTERRUPTING THE GRIND MENTALITY

When I started my business, my soul-care routine was nonexistent. I was so focused on growing the business that sleeping, exercise, and spending time with family and friends were annoyances that interfered with my dreams. I had seen the grind being modeled all too well by my mother when she was running her businesses. Fast forward a few years into my business, and my doctor warns me that my blood pressure is becoming an issue. I made a few short-lived changes but quickly slipped back into old habits. With more time in business, I was burning out, and I finally recognized that grinding was not so cute. It was hard on my body, and I felt disconnected from people I cared about.

I felt compelled to make significant changes, and a major decision was leaving my 9-to-5. It was one way to interrupt the grinding in my life. Old habits are still hard to break, but while my soul-care routine is not perfect, it has gotten much better. Erasing years and years of poor soul-care habits is a feat and will take time, so I'm being patient with myself.

Reflection Time

- How does the hustle and grind mentality show up for you?
- What do your soul-care practices look like now?
- How can you prioritize soul-care?

REDUCING ENTREPRENEURIAL STRESS

Entrepreneurship can be a stressful business (no pun intended). While success as an entrepreneur requires that you bring in revenue, reduce costs, and have a resilient mindset, it is equally important for you to have a healthy routine (soul-care is deep internal work that helps you feel grounded). I know firsthand how easy it is to work 24/7 in your business—the passion and drive keeps you going, but usually at a cost, especially the cost to your well-being: losing sleep, being inactive, eating poorly, and isolating from family and friends are a fast track to decline. Working long hours and not caring for yourself can also impact your business and lead to poor decision-making, which can be harmful to the entrepreneur and the business. Therefore, you have to put in boundaries that can protect you and help you attend to your well-being.

Below, I outlined six types of stress that you might encounter on your entrepreneurial journey.

1. Financial Stress

As we discussed in Chapter 11, many Black and Brown business owners have a tough time raising capital to start or grow their businesses and, as a result, take on additional jobs or drain their savings in pursuit of their entrepreneurial dreams, which This can contribute to financial stress, and being financially stressed can impact how you show up as an entrepreneur. You may be more cautious and risk averse if you are constantly worried about money, whether securing capital, bringing in revenue, or making payroll. These stressors are real and can have multiple effects on the success and growth of the company, and they can also create significant anxiety for the entrepreneur. Financial pressures and stress do not go away when a company gets funded, and it may even worsen. New worries about paying back debts or investors, bringing in a higher level of revenue, and continuing growth can weigh on the entrepreneur.

Practicing mindfulness strategies such as grounding techniques described in the MINDFUL MOMENT below can help with stress. You can also listen to Toni Jones (2019b) affirmation song "Yays Coins" on Spotify or YouTube, or even create your own affirmations.

2. Decision-Making Stress

Entrepreneurship is filled with an incessant amount of daily decision making. In a 2019 article for *Medium* Azulay (2019), estimates that entrepreneurs make over 1,000 decisions every day. Most of these are likely routine decisions, but a few will impact the trajectory of your business, your clients, and the people you lead. Can you imagine the emotional load of having to make that number of decisions every day? And guess what, failing to make a decision is also a decision—but it can leave you feeling stuck. When you don't make a decision, you spend a lot of mental energy thinking about your options and what you should do. I will confess that I am one of the most indecisive people. Maybe it's because I'm a Libra (Can I really blame my Zodiac sign?), or a perfectionist. The truth is that I can spend unnecessary time researching and thinking through my options, or I could make a decision based on what I know. The reality is that no decision is ever perfect and you will likely need to make some adjustments anyway. So, it is really a decision about how I spend my time. As the leader of the company, you will need to make decisions on *all* aspects of your business—software to subscribe to, materials to purchase, brand colors and designs, when to break for lunch, whether to schedule one more meeting or take a break. . . . As your business grows, you will have other people involved who can help, but if you don't like making decisions, you will have to get over that *fast*. Developing systems and processes as we discussed in Chapter 11 is one way to reduce decision fatigue. You can also create a process to help make decision-making easier.

FOUR-STEP DECISION-MAKING PROCESS

Use this easy four-step process to help you tackle those small and big decisions you need to make for your business (and in life).

1. *Urgency:* When does the decision need to be made? What will happen if you do not make the decision now?
2. *Information:* What do you need to know to make the decision?
3. *Support:* Who can you consult to help you make the decision?
4. *Impact:* Who or what will be impacted by the decision or by indecision?

Take Action Exercise

What is a decision you are trying to make now? Use the four-step decision process to help you decide your next step.

1. How *urgent* is making the decision?
2. What *information* do I need before making the decision?
3. Who can *support* me in making the decision?
4. What will be the *impact* of the decision or of indecision?

3. Success Stress

This might be a little surprising to you, but achieving success can also bring on stress. Think about it: you are working hard at a goal, and you finally achieve the outcomes that you want. Excellent! But then comes the pressure or internal stress to keep going. I find that many entrepreneurs like myself are perfectionists, so we are never satisfied—this can be a brutal way to live and work. While it is a key to driving success, it can also prevent us from taking time to recognize our wins and appreciate the gains we have achieved. At times we are so focused on the major goals that we forget to acknowledge the small wins that help us get to that big goal. The need to keep going while achieving success can be a double-edged sword, so make time to recognize your wins, the big ones and especially the small ones. And of course, share those wins with others. So often I see entrepreneurs keep their wins secret because they worry it will look like bragging or, worse, worry that talking about success will somehow bring misfortune. I encourage you to share those wins, as it allows others to celebrate with you. Here are three activities to practice recognizing your successes:

- *Start a success journal:* Develop a habit or a routine of writing down daily or weekly wins so you can track your record of success. Reading your success journal can serve as a great mood booster when you are feeling discouraged about your progress.
- *Create a routine for celebrating small and big wins:* Make intentional time to pause to celebrate your small wins—whether it's a happy dance, a big smile, or even a *yes!!*—and big wins. It's about recognizing that you are on a journey and honoring the hard work and effort you are investing in your business.

- *Share your wins:* Allow others to join in celebrating with you—it brings your community together and decreases the sense of isolation that entrepreneurs can often experience. Remember, your community is rooting for you.

4. Ideation Stress

I've found that the entrepreneurship process seems to unlock your creativity and opens a portal where ideas flow freely. On your entrepreneurial journey, you may find that you are bombarded by ideas for new products and services, combined with a strong desire to act on *all* of them. These ideas can pop up as a distraction when you are feeling stuck or bored with a business activity. Sometimes I feel compelled to act on an idea because I think it will go viral—until an even better idea surfaces. This can create a great deal of stress and anxiety as you try to figure out what to do with these ideas. While it is tempting to change directions to pursue a new idea, it is likely better to stay on course and focus on the current venture. You may also experience ideation stress from a lack of ideas about how to move your venture forward. It is common to experience periods where you have a lot of new information, and feel unsure about what to do next. One of my mentors called it "the spiral," when you feel like you're going around and around in circles.

5. Time Stress

For an entrepreneur, time is one of the most precious commodities. There are many, many demands for your time, such as scheduling meetings with potential clients, staff meetings, one-on-ones with team members, executing or implementing your ideas, actually sitting down and doing the work that you have been paid for, researching and envisioning new offerings, time with family and friends, laundry, eating, and of course, time for sleep—that's a lot! How you structure your time is key not only to your growth but also to your physical and emotional well-being. The more I am around entrepreneurs, the more I realize that many of us struggle with how to use time more efficiently.

When I started out, I put in tons of hours in my business. I was so energized and excited that I did not prioritize sleep or exercise. I didn't have time . . . truth is, I didn't *make* time. It was extremely hard for me to shut down in the evenings, on weekends, and even during vacations. Many days I was getting less than 4 hours of sleep, and I was constantly on the clock . . . everywhere I went, my laptop came with me: vacations, social events (even to church—OMG): "Work,

work, work, work, work, Rihanna had nothing on me" (a line from my TEDx talk [Jackman, 2024]). It was brutal. I had this scarcity mindset around time. I did not have enough of it, and I was trying to squeeze every bit of it I could find. The reality is that I was not using the time I had well—something needed to shift.

One book that I found helpful in shifting my mindset about time was *168 Hours: You Have More Time Than You Think* by Laura Vanderkam (2010), which asserts that changing your time mindset from 24 hours per day to 168 hours per week allows us to gain more time and be more productive. Well, you don't actually get *more* time (unfortunately, time does not work that way), but your perception of time and your relationship with time shift—you come to think about how you use those 168 hours differently. For example, if you think about the 24-hour day, at least 8 of those hours are spent sleeping, so you are down to 16. Maybe 3 of the 16 hours are spent commuting . . . down to 13; 2 hours spent eating meals . . . down to 11. As the time dwindles, you will likely find yourself thinking and saying "I don't have time" or "I don't have enough time." And there's the issue: you develop a scarcity mindset around time. But 168 hours—that's a lot of time! With this strategy, you can cultivate an abundance mindset around time. You can intentionally plan how to use your 168 hours to map out your ideal weekly schedule (for sample ideal weekly schedule, see Figure 13.2).

SEVEN ACTIONABLE STEPS TO MAXIMIZE YOUR WEEK

1. *Collect baseline data:* Before making any changes, spend 1 week tracking how you use your time—get as specific as possible.
2. *Create a weekly schedule:* Use the sample weekly schedule (see Figure 13.2) to capture *all* your daily activities, including travel time to in-person meetings, admin tasks (e.g., billing and writing notes), lunch, breaks, exercise, laundry, and social time. Then, stick to the schedule for one week. After the first week, review the schedule to make any adjustments. As you implement your schedule, you will need to set clear boundaries with others around it. The hardest person to set boundaries with is often *you!*
3. *Prioritize tasks:* Be clear about your priorities for each week and for each day. Every morning before you start your day (or even the night

before), identify the top three to five tasks that you need to complete, and focus on those tasks only. Do the same at the start of each week.

4. *Time blocking:* Create blocks of time for specific tasks, and you *only* do those tasks during the identified blocks. Your brain will fight you on this one—resist the temptation to jump to other tasks during this block, and cue yourself back to the task when you get distracted by saying "This is the block for [TASK] and it will be over at [TIME]." Use a timer to mark the end of the block. Email is an ideal task to time block and a great way to protect your brain from distractions. You can also block time for consulting projects, speech writing, and invoicing and billing.

5. *Delegate/outsource tasks:* Your baseline data will also highlight tasks that you are doing that you have no business doing. For example, delegate operational tasks to an assistant or research activities to an intern so that you can use your precious time on strategic and revenue-generating activities. Look to delegate or outsource at home, too. For example, it might be time to teach your children how to do their laundry or to use public transportation to get home (age dependent); delegate cooking duties to your partner, hire a personal chef, or use a meal prep service.

6. *Schedule review:* Do a weekly schedule review to reflect on how the schedule worked and make adjustments from what you've learned.

7. *Enlist an accountability partner:* Use tech or an app to help you stay committed to your time use strategy and to your weekly priorities. There are many resources designed to help people use their time more efficiently for scheduling, project management, automations, and even time tracking (see Appendix D for some productivity and project management tools available at the writing of this book).

Note: One thing I have noticed about myself is that my brain has a hard time sticking to one organization or time management strategy. I don't know, maybe it's just me. If you plan to try a new strategy for time usage (I like *using*, not *managing* my time), I suggest *fully* committing to that strategy for three weeks, and then doing a careful analysis of what worked and what did not, rather than immediately abandoning it for something new. Your strategy may work well but need some tweaking or adjustment to be a better fit for you, which is less effort than trying to learn and implement another new strategy.

Time	Monday	Tuesday	Wednesday	Thursday	Friday	Sat	Sun
6:00	Sleep	Sleep	Sleep		Sleep		
6:30				Sleep		Sleep	Sleep
7:00	School Drop-Off				School Drop-Off		
7:30		Reflection Time	Reflection Time				
8:00	Reflection Time	Marketing Call	Breakfast	Reflection Time	Reflection Time		
8:30	Breakfast		Reflection Time	Breakfast	Breakfast	Movement Time	
9:00	Partnership Call	Check Emails	Personal Growth (French Class)	Check Emails			Church
9:30							
10:00	Admin Call		Break	Admin Call	Therapy/Coaching		
10:30		Writing/Work					
11:00	Admin Tasks		Growth Group (Business)	New Business Calls			Brunch
11:30							
12:00	Movement Time	Movement Time	Movement Time	Movement Time			
12:30					Lunch		
1:00	Shower/Lunch	Shower/Lunch		Shower/Lunch			
1:30					Billing/Invoicing	Kids Activities + Family Time	
2:00	In-Person Meetings/Work Time	Writing/Work	Writing/Work	Client Meetings			
2:30					Break		
3:00							
3:30	Break	Break	Break	Break	School Pick-up/After-School Activities/Homework		Kids Activities + Family Time
4:00	School Pick-up/After-School Activities/Homework	School Pick-up/After-School Activities/Homework	School Pick-up/After-School Activities/Homework	School Pick-up/After-School Activities/Homework			
4:30					Movement Time		
5:00							
5:30							
6:00	Dinner Prep	Dinner Prep	Dinner Prep	Dinner Prep			
7:00	Dinner	Dinner	Dinner	Dinner	Family Time		
8:00							
8:30	Homework	Homework	Homework	Homework		Spontaneous	Spontaneous
9:00							
9:30							
10:00	Shower	Shower	Shower	Shower	Shower	Shower	Shower
10:30	Read	Read	Read	Read	Movie	Movie	Chill
11:00							Sleep
11:30	Sleep	Sleep	Sleep	Sleep	Sleep	Sleep	

Figure 13.2 My weekly schedule

Relationship Stress

With all the demands that are required of business owners, it can be very easy for entrepreneurs to neglect their most precious resources: family and friends. Knowing that they will be around, you can easily take them for granted. As you work on different aspects of the business, you can lose track of time. There are so many times where I think, *I just need 10 minutes to finish a task*, an hour or two goes by, and I'm still at it. My children often call me out for losing track of time. In a 2024 *Fortune Well* article, results from a survey of 1,000 entrepreneurs showed that nearly half reported having a "poor romantic life" and were "64% more likely to prioritize their business successes over their romantic partners" (Mikhail, 2024). Unfortunately, these patterns and choices can lead to higher rates of divorce in this group (Business Woman Media, 2021). Some of the reasons for these higher rates of divorce include financial stress and insecurity, long working hours, poor communication, and overall high levels of stress (Holmstrom, 2022; *The Times*, n.d.; Business Woman Media, 2021). To support these relationships, prioritize spending quality time with your loved ones, engage in healthy communication, and talk openly about finances.

MINDFUL MOMENT

Tuning in is a grounding technique that engages your five senses to help you connect back to the environment. Take three deep breaths, and then scan your environment to find:

- Five things that you can see
- Four things you can touch or feel
- Three things you can hear
- Two things you can smell
- One thing you can taste
- Bonus: One good thing about you

Reflection Time

Let's take some time to reflect on your own habits and needs for soul-care. Find a quiet space, and respond to the following journal prompts:

- What situations trigger your stress about finances?
- What helps you to reduce stress about finances?
- How do you feel about all the decisions you have to make as a business owner?
- How do you feel about celebrating your wins?
- How do you manage distractions? What helps you to stay on task?
- When you have felt stuck, what are some strategies you use to get unstuck?
- What are some challenges that you are experiencing with organizing your time?
- What changes do you want to make in your schedule to better use your time?
- How do you spend time with your family and friends?

Breaking the Silence on Entrepreneur Mental Health

You may not know it, but entrepreneurs experience high rates of mental health conditions. Unfortunately, it's an aspect of entrepreneurship that does not get enough attention, and as a result, many entrepreneurs suffer in silence. Data from a survey of 242 entrepreneurs (Freeman, Staudenmaier, Zisser, et al., 2018), revealed that 72% of the entrepreneurs disclosed a self-reported history of mental health concerns, with depression (30%), ADHD (29%), substance use (12%), and bipolar disorder (11%) being the leading concerns topping the list. Another study led by Silver Lining (n.d.) found that 56% of entrepreneurs are diagnosed with anxiety, depression, or other stress-related disorders. It is also clear that most entrepreneurs (75%) are worried about their mental health, according to Haden (2023).

What was most alarming from these findings is that entrepreneurs do not seek treatment due to cost (73%) and time (52%) (Silver Lining, n.d.). With the competitive nature of entrepreneurship, attending to one's emotional health may be a second or third thought, if at all. Health insurance is a costly expense, and if the entrepreneur is not taking a salary (which, as you may recall from Chapter 9, is something I do not advise) they may not have access to health care benefits or they may have a no-frills benefits plan with a high deductible or high co-pays. As a business owner, you may find yourself assessing whether you or a family member really needs to see a doctor or go to the emergency room (I know all too well how this feels). Taking care of your health versus having to pay a huge medical bill is a tough decision that many entrepreneurs in the United States face each day. Additionally, taking time off for a doctor's appointment may seem like a major inconvenience. While all these factors may ring true, it is equally important to take the steps to take care of yourself. What good is the business if you are not around?

The Upside to Entrepreneurship

If entrepreneurship is so stressful, why do so many people still pursue it? Great question. While entrepreneurship comes with its unique set of stressors, research shows that entrepreneurs actually tend to be *less* stressed than people who are not entrepreneurs. And for good reason. Entrepreneurship offers noneconomic benefits that Obschonka, Pavez, Kautonen, et al. (2023) refer to as *psychological utility*. These noneconomic benefits include a sense of freedom and autonomy to engage in meaningful work—your passion work. Plus, while entrepreneurs tend to work long hours, they need less recovery time than others and have fewer workplace stressors (Kibler, 2023).

In my opinion, entrepreneurship comes with less emotional labor. For example, you understand how every task of the business is connected to your mission and vision, and you are not assigned meaningless tasks by a supervisor who may or may not respect you. The truth is, every job has some level of stress, but the purpose, meaning, and freedom that entrepreneurship offers far outweighs the stress involved.

WHAT DO I NEED? CARING FOR YOU AS YOU CARE FOR YOUR BUSINESS

Soul-care is the intentional practice of asking, "What do I need?" and engaging in self-nurturing rituals to bring harmony to mind, body, and spirit.

Dear Black therapist, you know all about soul-care, but knowing and doing are very different things—so, let's be real. If you want to launch and grow a thriving business, you have to be in a thriving place too.

Some of you reading this book may have great soul-care practices, but many of you probably do not. Without a doubt, there will be stress along the entrepreneurial journey, so finding ways to destress is critical. My personal experiences as a therapist and entrepreneur have taught me the importance of caring for my health, particularly as I want to experience longevity in business and in life. However, making time for soul-care can be tricky, especially if your perception of time gets warped by your passion or if your burned-out brain is in control. Engaging in regular soul-care practices—caring for your mind, body, and spirit—helps you maintain a balanced life.

If an entrepreneur is stressed out, it will show up in their business practices, interactions, and decisions. It will show up in how they communicate with customers, vendors, and their team. It will impact how they make decisions and resolve problems and how they show up for themselves. Developing practices to stay grounded during tough times and to manage the emotional roller coaster, mindset challenges, and physical toll of entrepreneurship is a must.

The Soul-Care Well-Being Wheel

Emotional well-being needs to be a metric on every CEO's dashboard.

The Soul-Care Well-Being Wheel is a model that I developed to capture the essential aspects of well-being that entrepreneurs and leaders must prioritize in order to grow profitable businesses. While the practices captured in the wheel are likely not new to you, I want to emphasize the importance of integrating these practices into your life in service of your business. While many entrepreneurs put the business at the center, I believe that it should be the other way around. The business owner or entrepreneur needs to be at the center—without you, there is no business. By making space and time to ask yourself the question *What do I need?* and then engaging in self-nurturing practices to bring mind, body, and spirit into alignment is a gift to your business and your personal life.

The graphic in Figure 13.3 captures the areas of the soul-care wheel that have

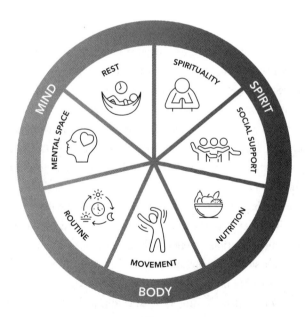

Figure 13.3 The soul-care well-being wheel *Source:* Charmain F. Jackman and Demp Agency

been significant for my entrepreneurship journey, and I imagine that they will resonate with you as well.

Below I describe how nurturing each of the seven facets of this soul-care wheel continues to contribute to my personal and business growth.

Movement

As described earlier, the entrepreneurship journey can be stressful—and our bodies hold onto that stress. Cortisol, a stress hormone, is released naturally when we are stressed, and chronic stress, associated with high levels of cortisol, is also associated with a number of health concerns, such as issues with cardiovascular, metabolic, and mental health (LeWine, 2024; Mariotti, 2015). Engaging in regular activities to decrease stress can help reduce its toxic effects on our body. One way to release stress and cortisol from the body is through movement. As your body allows, build a daily routine for movement with activities such as stretching, chair yoga, yoga, walking, jogging, biking, rowing, and weight-lifting. Whether it's for 5, 15, or 30 minutes or more, incorporating some form of movement into your daily life will do wonders. Consult your doctor or other health professional before starting new physical activity. Other body-based activities include:

- *Body scan:* This practice helps you tune in to your body and assess what it needs by pausing to pay attention to the different sensations in the body. Starting at your head and moving all the way down to your toes, notice sensations in your body, such as tightness, tension, tingling, and temperature. Once you have noticed what is happening in your body, you can engage in movements to offer relief and release. Many apps offer body scans and other wellness practices (for resources, see Appendix D).
- *Energy healing:* This holistic practice fosters healing and well-being by restoring balance to the body's energy systems that are experiencing blocks or disruptions in energy flow. These disruptions can cause emotional, physical, and spiritual imbalances. Many mental health practitioners are obtaining additional training in these energy healing practices as a way to expand healing beyond traditional talk therapy, such as Emotional Freedom Technique (EFT)/tapping, Reiki, sound healing, qigong

and tai chi, reflexology (acupressure points on the feet), meditation, chakra healing, crystal healing, massage, and shamanic healing.

PERSONAL REFLECTION: SOMATIC OR BODY-BASED HEALING

In 2023, I became very interested in incorporating more body-based strategies into my practice as a therapist, but it was actually more for myself. I had transitioned from a very crisis-driven job, and I did not have practices that allowed me to release built-up negative energy in my body. I was desperate to engage in body-based strategies and ended up in a yoga and qigong class. It was amazing! I fell in love with the practice and ended up taking an online course to learn more. I wish this had been part of my clinical practice much earlier in life.

How do you plan to integrate movement into your daily life?

Rest

Making time for rest will help you recharge and feel more focused and grounded. In post-pandemic work life, people are spending long hours on screens, often with few screen breaks. Taking breaks and resting may feel like a distraction or interruption of your flow, but these breaks from work can actually foster better creativity and problem solving.

In addition to taking breaks, getting adequate sleep is key to your success in business. Sleep deprivation impacts your memory, focus, and energy levels. If you are lacking sleep, you may be easily distracted, have trouble with focus or concentration, and struggle with decision making and problem solving. Additionally, poor sleep can make you feel angry and irritable and cause trouble with emotional regulation. As an entrepreneur, it can be hard to have a shut off time, but taking time to rest and reset helps you to come back to work with a clear mind. Prolonged sleep issues like insomnia can impact your mental health (e.g., depression, anxiety, thought disorders) and cause disruptions in your cardio-vascular and endocrine systems, which can lead to chronic health issues such as

heart problems, high blood pressure, and diabetes (issues that already dispropor-
tionately impact Black people).

Please Note. If you have more concerning sleep issues, such as insomnia, I recommend that you consult with your primary care physician, a sleep specialist or
therapist who has expertise in providing interventions for sleep conditions.

I have always been a night owl. I have the ability to push the limit on sleep, but
it shows up the next day—I am grumpy and tired. In this season of my life, my
goal is to get into bed by 11:30 p.m. and wake up at 6:30 a.m. five days per week.
Some nights it works well, other times, not so much. I will continue to work on
this goal because I know that it benefits me and my business.

What is one change that you intend to make to foster better sleep? Why is
this important? or How will you add intentional rest to your weekly schedule?

Nutrition

Again, nothing new here, but remember that food nourishes your brain, and
your business needs your brain running at full capacity. So eat nutritious meals,
drink lots of water, and consult with your doctor and a registered dietitian to
ensure that you are feeding your body what it needs.

I come from a line of amazing home chefs, so healthy nutrition is a big part of
my life. I also love to cook and prepare delicious meals for my family. As a full-
time entrepreneur, I get to have a predictable lunch schedule, something that did
not often happen when I worked a 9-to-5. In my calendar, 12:00 to 1:00 p.m. is
blocked off Mondays to Fridays. This guarantees that I do not schedule clients
during that time and forces me to step away from my desk so that I can replenish.

What do you want to add and/or remove from your current nutrition plan?

Pro Tip: If you really want to up your game regarding your nutrition, prepping
your meals the night before and sharing your goals with an accountability partner can help you stay on track (see Appendix D for nutrition resources available
at the writing of this book).

Social Support

Community care is an essential part of soul-care.

You are not alone. Many entrepreneurs are working in their businesses alone, or
they are solo when it comes to the vision of their business. As I shared earlier, some

entrepreneurs are so passionate about their business and driven to success that they neglect the people around them. It can be very easy to tip into workaholic mode, spending all your time in the business. However, as an entrepreneur, it is crucial that you cultivate a support system that will help you thrive. Connecting with people and asking for help are vital skills that entrepreneurs need to hone.

Make time to engage with family and friends. If you are so focused on your business that you exclude your community, you could end up achieving success but with no one to share it with. Not cool, right? Rethink how you prioritize work and family time. Be sure to schedule family time and friendship time in your calendar. The journey is not meant to be done alone.

PERSONAL REFLECTION: REDESIGNING MY SOCIAL LIFE

As I was starting InnoPsych, I was putting in many hours. I was working full-time and would use my evenings (after the kids went to sleep) and weekends to work on the business. I was literally working around the clock. My conversations with my husband were mostly about logistics, such as children's school pickup schedule and household chores. I was also skipping gatherings with friends. When I did attend non-work-related events, I would usually arrive late, as I would work as long as I possibly could and I would always bring my laptop with me, in case I had time to work. I would not give myself permission to take a break. It was draining, and I was often jealous of the fun my friends were having. My friends would joke that I was a workaholic, and I would deny it and laugh it off. But when I took a critical look at how I was living my life, I had to admit that they were right.

It finally dawned on me one day that I had a choice—that I was in control and I could do things differently. I wanted to have more meaningful time with family and friends. I didn't want to be someone who was so successful, but then looked around and found that there was no one to share those moments with. I have made significant changes in this area. I schedule dates with my husband and have more quality time with friends. I still walk around with my laptop or iPad, but sometimes I leave it at home!

In addition to maintaining your connections with family and friends, connect with other entrepreneurs—they understand the journey and may be able to share how they have navigated different parts. As I mentioned above, you can create your own personal network of entrepreneurs, who can offer advice when you need it.

I have also found it helpful to have mentors, coaches, and mentees/interns in my network. Coaches help me to strategize, mentors make introductions, and mentees/interns keep me up to date with trends happening in the field. It is a great exchange of information.

Who in your life do you want to spend more quality time with?

Routine

Time is one of the most precious commodities you have as an entrepreneur, and the success of your business will reflect how you use or spend your time. *Routines* help you carefully plan out and manage your time—without routines, you are operating on a whim, which can lead to inefficient use of your time. Creating a daily routine with your revenue-generating and most important tasks will help you stay focused on the goals. Working in or on your business does not mean working 24/7. When you pair affirmations or actions with your routine, you get rituals.

What is a routine you want to add (or adjust) to your schedule?

Mental Space

Creating space that is just for you provides a desired and needed resource for many entrepreneurs to reflect and reset. When I've talked to entrepreneurs about their soul-care needs, time and time again they express a desire for quiet time—time away from the noise of daily life, to turn inward, to gain more awareness about patterns and triggers, and to reflect on their vision and goals. This intentional mental space is especially important for entrepreneurs who are parents and caregivers, as alone time can be hard to find. This mental space is an important way to unplug and can include such activities as attending retreats, solo travel, 10 minutes sitting in the car before entering your home, uninterrupted bathroom time (parents of young children, you know what I mean), but maybe as simple as taking time to read or do puzzles.

In addition to taking time away, attending to your physical space contributes to having a healthy mental space. Your physical environment, including your work and living space, can actually impact how you work. Having a clear, organized space can do wonders for your mood and thinking and can help you be more productive, focused, and creative. When your space is cluttered and messy, that can be symbolic of how you are approaching your business. Some people can work in chaos (I've been there many times), but I bet most do better when their spaces are clean and clear. What is a mental space activity you want to build into your life?

Spirituality

Tapping into your spiritual beliefs can be extremely grounding and offer a source of strength along the entrepreneurial journey, whether it is through faith practices, reading a holy text, praying, listening to faith-based music, reflecting on scriptures, meditating, connecting with nature, or finding peaceful moments to listen to the divine. My spiritual practices include daily prayer, attending church, giving back to my faith communities, and using my calling as a mental health professional as my ministry. These help ground me, deepen my faith, and connect to my higher power. There were times that I would get disappointed because I did not get an opportunity that I really wanted, but then something would happen that would boldly show me why it was not right thing for me or something better would unfold. After a few times of this, I finally listened—it has actually been a comfort to feel watched over and protected.

What are some spiritual practices that help ground you?

Take Action Exercise

Turning your attention inward to explore what you need to feel fulfilled is a necessary step for soul-care, follow the instructions below:

1. Use the Soul-Care Well-Being Wheel above to rate how fulfilled you feel in each area from 1 (Totally Unfulfilled) to 10 (Very Fulfilled).
2. Write that number in the appropriate area of the circle.
3. If you had to make a significant change, which two areas would you focus on in the next month?
4. Indicate which area is causing you the most pain.

While working in your business is critical to growth, how you define work will set the tone and culture for all you execute on your business goals and how you

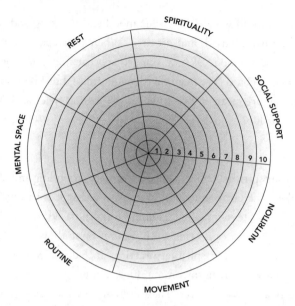

Figure 13.4 What do I need?

balance business and life. Working in your business can include breaks for lunch, time for exercise, screen-free activities like reading magazines or listening to podcasts, creative activities like making art or listening to music, and hands-on activities like gardening, cooking, or baking. These activities help stimulate your mind and foster creative problem-solving. Many of us have this idea that to grow a business you have to be constantly working in the business, and that cannot be further from the truth—trust me, I know all too well. Being busy *in* your business does not mean that you are working on your business. Instead, it can just be a "busymess" (Jones, 2019a). Take time to step away so that you can get a wider perspective on what your business needs., As Uncle Denzel Washington wisely shares, "Just because you are doing a lot more, doesn't mean you are getting a lot more done . . . You can run in place . . . . and never get anywhere." (Washington, 2015).

EXITING YOUR BUSINESS

The final stage of the entrepreneurial journey is exiting your business. Can you imagine a time when you are ready to retire from your business, sell it to someone else, or close it? Maybe your business has done so well and you are able to live that soft life you dreamed of, or maybe you have hit the age when you planned to retire (whatever age that is for you) and you are ready to pass the baton to someone else. What would that look like to you in 10, 15, or 20 years?

"What is your exit plan?" This was a question that I would often have to answer when I thought about exploring the venture capital route with my business. I had definitely not considered that question. InnoPsych was my baby, and you don't sell your baby. In the venture capital world of investing, the expectation is that you will exit your business.

While thinking about your exit plan might feel overwhelming to answer, especially if you are just starting your business, there is value in reflecting on this question. First, it allows you to truly consider where you want to go with your business. Is it a legacy business that you hope to pass on to family? Is it a business you want to retire from? Or would you consider selling your business and, if so, at what stage? Only you can answer these questions, and while they may be hard to answer, it is worthwhile to explore them. As you launch and grow your business, your answers might evolve, so it's alright to be uncertain too.

Reflection Time

Take some time to reflect on how you might exit your business. Find a quiet space, and respond to the following journal prompts:

- As you think about exiting your business, what feelings come up?
- When would you ideally want to exit your business?
- How will you plan to exit your business (sell, close, pass to family)?
- Who in your network can you contact for support in this (e.g., mentor or financial planner)?

CHAPTER 13 MOMENTUM AND MINDSET CHECK

You are a thriving therapreneur—you have explored the entire entrepreneur journey, from idea to exit and all the places in between. Now it's time to execute. There will be stress and there will be joy along this journey—how you care for yourself will make the difference. As therapists, you understand more than most, the importance of prioritizing your well-being on this journey, something often overlooked by entrepreneurs. It can be very easy to let your passion be your sole driver, but building routines and habits will help you stay in balance with your business, health, wealth, and life.

Pursuing passion work can serve as a protective factor for entrepreneurs. You will gain agency in selecting the types of client concerns that allow you to operate in your zone of genius, in deciding your schedule, and in setting your rates. Entrepreneurship is a journey with twists and turns, and putting in markers and intentional spaces to rest and recover is necessary. Remember, *you* are your business's most valuable asset—nothing else comes first.

- What is one takeaway that you have as you finish this chapter?
- What is a mindset shift that you have made after reading this chapter?

NOW . . . IT'S TIME TO LAUNCH!

Congratulations . . . you did it! You have made it to the end of the book. What a journey it has been. It probably feels like your journey is just beginning—and it is. It has been amazing to be on this ride with you and I am excited to learn about your business launch and your entrepreneurial journey. You have done all the visioning, reflecting, and planning to get you started. There is nothing more rewarding than setting a goal and watching it come to life. I hope you are excited to see how your vision will unfold as you take the action steps to launch. You got this!

Stay connected with me through social media and I look forward to seeing you in the Therapists Thriving Together community.

Sample Net Worth Worksheet

Assets	Amount ($)	Liabilities	Amount ($)
Cash and cash equivalents		*Short-term liabilities*	
Checking account		Credit card debt	
Savings account		Medical bills	
Money market/CDs			
Cash		*Long-term liabilities*	
Investments		Mortgage	
Stocks		Home equity loan	
Bonds		Car loans	
Mutual funds		Student loans	
Real estate		Personal loans	
Primary residence		Professional liability insurance	
Other real estate (investment properties, vacation homes, etc.)		Business loans	
Personal property		Other	
Vehicles		Other	

Jewelry		Other	
Art/collectibles		**Total Liabilities**	
Office equipment (e.g., computers, furniture)			
Other assets			
Life insurance (cash value)			
Business interests			
Retirement accounts (401(k), IRA, etc.)			
Intellectual property (e.g., books, courses)			
Other			
Other			
Other			
Total Assets			
	Net Worth Calculation		
	Total Assets		
	minus Total Liabilities		
	Net Worth		

Net Worth Calculation	
Total Assets	
minus Total Liabilities	
Net Worth	

APPENDIX B

Sample Budget Calculator

Note: The numbers included here are just for illustration and there may be additional income and expense categories for your practice that need to be taken into account when you calculate your own budget. You should tailor this sample to include the income and expense categories that fit your own practice and, of course, your own projected and actual budget numbers.

(Year 1)			(Year 1)		
Income	**Projection**	**Actual**	**Expenses**	**Projection**	**Actual**
Referral streams			Accounting	$2,000.00	
Insurance	$33,000.00		CEs/professional dues	$2,000.00	
Self-pay	$5,000.00		Office rent/lease	$12,000.00	
Evaluations	$35,000.00		Office furnishings	$2,000.00	
Other			Utilities (internet/heat/phone/fax)	$2,000.00	
Other			Insurance (health, disability, general liability)	$20,000.00	
Consulting	$45,000.00		Malpractice insurance	$500.00	

Public speaking	$15,000.00		Legal advice	$200.00	
Workshops	$30,000.00		Marketing (website, SEO, directory listings)	$700.00	
Writing	$2,000.00		Meals and entertainment	$500.00	
Grant	$0.00		Subscriptions: magazines	$200.00	
Online course	$0.00		Subscriptions: software (electronic health records, accounting)	$1,200.00	
Royalties	$0.00		Postage (PO box, mailings)	$200.00	
Pitch competition	$0.00		Office supplies		
Products	$0.00		Taxes/tax preparation	$5,000.00	
Other			Testing materials	$1,500.00	
Other			Payroll	$100,000.00	
Gross Income Total	$155,000.00		**Expenses Total**	$150,000.00	

Net Profit/Loss Calculation	
Gross Income	$155,000.00
Total Expenses	−$150,000.00
Net Profit/Loss	**$5,000.00**

APPENDIX C

Instructions for Creating Memorable Visuals of Your Vision

VISION BOARDS

Creating a vision board requires first reflecting on your goals and vision, and then finding images that speak to these goals and vision, and costly creating a visual product by hand or using a digital platform. You do not need to be an artist, and there is no right or wrong way to create a vision board

Steps

1. *Reflect:* Reflect on your short-term and long-term goals, such as your personal aspirations, family life, professional development, business goals, self-care, and other areas that are important to you.
2. *Research:* Spend time looking through magazines or searching online to select images and words that speak to you. You can also type words or quotes that you want. And, I definitely recommend a trip to an arts and crafts store for inspiration.

3. *Create:* Arrange the items you've collected on a poster board or, for a digital vision board, in your graphic design software, in any order that makes sense for you.

SYNERGY MAPS

You can create a synergy map by hand or use a mind map creator or graphic design software:

1. On a piece of paper, napkin, or blank document, put the name of your umbrella company in the center.
2. Consider the different products, services, and businesses that you plan to create, and arrange them around the umbrella company based on how they connect to each other and/or the umbrella company.
3. Draw arrows to show how the different products/services connect back to the umbrella company and to each other.
4. Name each arrow to describe the relationships among the different products, services, and businesses.

Sample Business Resources

The following is not an exhaustive list and the features, functionality, and availability of these resources may change over time. These are some resources that I have come across in my own entrepreneurship journey and are offered not as an endorsement but as a starting place for you to find tailored resources to meet your own specific needs. Be mindful of your own budget when selecting services and products, as costs can add up quickly.

ACCOUNTING SOFTWARE

- QuickBooks
- Mint (personal finances organizer)
- Melio Payment

CALENDAR SCHEDULING

- Calendly
- Acuity
- Google Calendar
- Doodle
- Meet With Me

CUSTOMER MANAGEMENT RELATIONSHIP SOFTWARE

- HubSpot
- Click Up
- HoneyBook
- Dubsado

DIGITAL COURSES PLATFORMS

- Thinkific
- Teachable
- Canvas
- Google Classroom

FOOD AND NUTRITION

- DASH (Dietary Approaches to Stop Hypertension) Plan: https://www .nhlbi.nih.gov/education/dash-eating-plan
- Cultured Health: to find registered dietitians: https://www.iamcultured health.com

GOVERNMENT RESOURCES

- Business structure categories: https://www.irs.gov/businesses
- U.S. Copyright Office: https://www.copyright.gov
- Internal Revenue Service: https://www.irs.gov
- Patents and trademarks: https://www.uspto.gov
- Small Business Administration: https://www.sba.gov
- Social Security Administration: https://www.ssa.gov/prepare/get-benefits-estimate

GRAPHIC DESIGN SOFTWARE

- Canva: Canva.com.
- VistaCreate: Create.vista.com
- Adobe: Adobe.com

ELECTRONIC HEALTH RECORDS AND PRACTICE MANAGEMENT SOFTWARE

- Simple Practice
- TherapyNotes
- Valant

LEGAL RESOURCES

To find an attorney:
- Check with your state bar association
- Local chamber of commerce
- Local law school
- Check out local nonprofit legal organizations offering free or reduced fee for legal services

MANIFESTING AND AFFIRMATIONS

- Toni Jones, *Affirmations for the Grown Ass Woman* (2019 album)
- Oprah's Super Soul Sunday interview with Dr. Michael Beckwith: https://youtu .be/oEGZNtv0lOA?si=hSGWQBoFRPcfPCh8
- Scriptures shared by Steve Harvey James 4:2 (NIV) "You do not have because you do not ask God." or "You have not because you ask not"
- Habbakah 2:2–3 "Write down the revelation and make it plain . . . though it may linger, it will surely come."

PROJECT MANAGEMENT

- Asana
- Trillo
- Monday
- HoneyBook

SOCIAL MEDIA SCHEDULING

- Buffer: https://buffer.com. As of this writing, offers 50% discount for Black entrepreneurs: https://buffer.com/blacklivesmatter
- Zapier
- HootSuite

VIDEO AND AUDIO PODCAST RECORDING

- YouTube
- Zoom
- Riverside FM
- StreamYard
- Vimeo

WESBITE HOSTING

- Wix
- Squarespace
- GoDaddy

WELLNESS APPS

- ChillOutz: https://www.chilloutz.com
- MyRetreat app
- Libbie Health app
- Exhale app
- Shine app
- How We Feel app

Sample Brand Story: InnoPsych

INNOPSYCH'S ORIGIN STORY

InnoPsych was birthed from Dr. Charmain's own experiences and challenges during her search for a therapist. She knew she wanted a therapist who was a woman of color but the process proved itself to be a challenge. As she searched through website after website there were either too few therapists listed to choose from and/or there was no way to filter lists by ethnicity. The process then became lengthy and cumbersome. Whenever she did find someone that she liked who fit the criteria, they were either "not taking new clients" or they did not take her insurance.

Dr. Charmain knew that there needed to be a simpler and faster way for people of color to find therapists of color and she was going to create it! Not only did she want to create a directory of therapists of color, but she also wanted to facilitate the process for therapists of color to launch their own private practice in order to increase the pool of therapists of color in the field.

THE STORY OF SANKOFA

Our logo is inspired by the Sankofa, a mythical bird with origins in Ghanaian folklore, which in Twi means "go back and get it." Sankofa is commonly associated with the Akan proverb, "Se wo were fi na wosan kofa a yenki" (It is not taboo to go back and fetch what you forgot or left behind).

The Sankofa bird is typically depicted with its feet facing forward and its head turned backward, picking up an egg from its back. The idea of looking back or reflecting on the past to inform the future is the cornerstone of the therapeutic process, which is why the Sankofa bird is a fitting image for InnoPsych, Inc. As therapists, we use clients' reflections to help them build new narratives for the future and avoid repeating past mistakes.

In our rendition, the Sankofa bird is holding a lavender plant in its mouth, instead of an egg, because of lavender's relaxing and calming properties and its symbolic representation of healing. Communities of color have experienced significant traumas, and we must engage in strategies that will bring about healing for future generations. As the Sankofa bird looks back on the past, it will bring healing to the future.

AFRICAN FOLKTALE OF SANKOFA

The story begins with a bird named Sankofa. She grows up in her community being confident in herself and loving life. One day, she decides to sneak away from her village. When she does, she meets a bird who insults her and causes her to doubt herself. Sankofa has to return to her village in order to find herself again and confront this "voice" of the big bird. She is supported by all of her friends and ancestors. When she returns to the bird with her own sense of self-knowledge, the other bird disappears. When she goes back home, her image is carved so that other youth in the village can remember her and her story. Because she had forgotten where she came from, Sankofa was carved with her neck turned backward.

Instructions for Writing a Bio

TEMPLATE FOR WRITING A BIO

Here is list of items to consider including as you write your compelling bios, and as you update them as your business progresses:

- Expertise you want to highlight
  - XX of years as a therapist working with [TYPES OF CLIENTS]
  - Leadership experience
  - Institutions where you trained (optional)
- Impact
  - Helped [XX/%] people with [IDENTIFIED PROBLEM], and [RESULTS OR OUTCOMES, IF YOU HAVE THEM]
  - Created/wrote [TITLE OF WORK], which reached [XX] visitors/readers, with [REVIEWS].
  - Brought in over $XXXX in grant funding
- Thought leadership
  - Awards
  - Media features

- Personal touch
  - Relevant hobby
  - Civic engagement
  - Personal struggle you overcame

The sample bios below, from shorter to longer, will give you a sense of their different contents.

SAMPLE BIOS

Short (48 words)
Dr. Charmain Jackman is an award-winning psychologist, TEDx speaker, author, and founder of InnoPsych. She is an expert on workplace well-being, burnout, racial stress, entrepreneur's mental health. She has also been featured in prominent national media outlets, including the *New York Times*, *NPR*, *Black Enterprise*, and *Oprah Daily*.

Short (102 words)
Dr. Charmain Jackman, an award-winning psychologist, author, TEDx speaker, leadership coach, and CEO/founder of InnoPsych, is a champion for inclusive mental health and psychologically safe workplaces. She leverages her experiences with burnout and racial stress to elevate conversations about healthy self-care practices and to inspire others to take daily actions to prioritize their mental health through joy and mindfulness. She has received several awards for her impactful work including City of Boston's 2021 Black History Month's Innovator of the Year, and has been featured in prominent media outlets, including the *New York Times*, *NPR*, *PBS*, *Oprah Daily*, *Essence*, and the *Boston Globe*.

Education (135 words)
Dr. Charmain "Dr. Charmain" Jackman (she/her) is a licensed psychologist, author, and TEDx speaker with 25+ years in the mental health field. She is the founder and CEO of InnoPsych, a platform providing inclusive mental health solutions to people, communities. and organizations. Prior to starting InnoPsych, Dr. Charmain worked as a forensic psychologist in the Boston juvenile courts and as a school-based clinician for 17 years. She also served as the dean of health and wellness at Boston Arts Academy for 10 years, where she supported

school leaders in cultivating emotionally safe work cultures for students and staff. Dr. Charmain authored a chapter on family engagement in *The Parent's Guide to Psychological First Aid* (revised edition) and is a regular contributor to the PBS Teachers' Lounge column. She is a mom to two wonderfully creative children.

Entrepreneurship (203 words)

Dr. Charmain Jackman is an acclaimed psychologist with over 25 years of experience in the mental health field. Transitioning from a traditional 9-to-5 role in education, Dr. Jackman embraced the entrepreneurial path in 2021 by founding InnoPsych, Inc., a pioneering mental health tech company. InnoPsych is dedicated to disrupting racial inequities in mental health and fostering healing and thriving in communities of color. The InnoPsych platform connects people of color with therapists of color and offers programming on critical topics such as racial trauma, burnout, mental health stigma, and employee emotional well-being. Dr. Jackman is a trailblazer in cultivating psychologically safe work cultures that enable both organizations and individuals to thrive. She is the creator of the *My Time to Thrive* card deck, an innovative tool designed to reduce stress and promote healthy coping mechanisms. Her impactful work has earned her numerous accolades, including the *Boston Business Journal*'s 2022 Power 50 Movement Makers, the American Psychological Association's 2021 Citizen Psychologist Award, and the City of Boston's 2021 Innovator of the Year award. As a sought-after thought leader, Dr. Jackman has been featured in prominent national media outlets such as *New York Times, NPR, PBS, Oprah Daily, Essence, Black Enterprise*, and the *Boston Globe*.

Sample Opening Announcement for a Private Practice

Dear [RECIPIENT'S NAME],

I hope this letter finds you well. I am thrilled to announce the opening of my new private practice, [YOUR PRACTICE NAME], dedicated to providing specialized care for [GROUP, e.g., children and adolescents] facing [CONDITIONS, e.g., anxiety, depression, and ADHD] in the [CITY/AREA] community.

With [XX] years of experience in [child and adolescent therapy], I have had the privilege of working with many [young] clients and their families to help them navigate and overcome their mental health challenges. My style combines evidence-based therapeutic techniques with a compassionate, [child]-centered approach, ensuring that each client receives personalized and effective care.

At [YOUR PRACTICE NAME], we offer a range of services designed to meet the unique needs of each [child], including:

- Individual therapy: We use culturally affirming and trauma-informed approaches that focus on the specific issues each [child] is facing, including practical strategies and tools to help manage symptoms and improve functioning.

- Family therapy: Collaborative sessions that involve family members to improve communication and support systems.
- Group therapy: Peer support groups that provide a safe space for [children] to share their experiences and learn from others.

Our goal is to create a supportive and nurturing environment where [children] can feel safe to express themselves and work through their challenges. We believe that early intervention and a collaborative approach involving [parents, teachers, and health-care providers] are key to the successful treatment of these conditions.

I am reaching out to you because I know that [ROLE, e.g., school counselors and pediatricians] play a critical role in identifying and supporting [children] who may benefit from mental health services. I would greatly appreciate it if you could consider referring clients to [YOUR PRACTICE NAME] when you encounter [children] who might benefit from specialized therapeutic support for [anxiety, depression, or ADHD].

For your convenience, I have included my contact information below. Please feel free to reach out to me directly if you have any questions or would like to discuss how we can collaborate to support the [children] you serve. In addition, I am available to provide informational sessions or workshops for your staff on recognizing and addressing mental health issues in [children].

Thank you for your time and consideration. I look forward to the opportunity to work together to enhance the well-being of the [children] and their families in our community.

Warmly,

[YOUR NAME AND PRACTICE NAME]

Sample Private Practice Launch Checklist

This checklist is meant as a starting place. You should check for any additional or different requirements where you do business and follow the guidance you receive from the lawyers, accountants, and other professionals you consult with.

BUSINESS STRUCTURE/LEGAL

- Design business plan/Lean Canvas
- Decide business structure
- Obtain federal Employer Identification Number (EIN)
- Register business with the state
- Register business with the city/town
- Consult with a tax accountant
- Create your business name
- Open a bank account
- Consult with an attorney

LEGAL PROTECTION

- Consult with an attorney
  - Business structure

- Contracts
- Intellectual property
- Terms of service
- Disclaimers

INSURANCE

- Health
- Malpractice
- Property (slip and fall)
- Commercial property
- General liability
- Renter's
- Income replacement
- Cybersecurity insurance
- Workers' compensation

FINANCES

- Business bank account
- Financial worksheet
- Income sources
- Expenses
- Assess billing process
- Accounting software

OPERATIONS

- Office space
  - Credentialing
  - Practice management software
  - Project management software
- Billing

MARKETING STRATEGY

- Attend networking events
- Define brand as therapist
- Review online profile
- Send thank-you notes to referral sources
- Send outreach communications
- Explore speaking opportunities
- Add three to five new referral sources
- Identify ideal clientele
- Create online profile

EIN Application Form

The following list are the items that, as of this writing, you will need to complete the EIN Application Form. As the form is revised from time to time, this list is subject to change.

- Legal name of Entity or Name (if individual)
- Trade Name (if applicable)
- Address
- Name of Responsible Party and Social Security number
- Type of Entity (business structure)
- Why you are applying for EIN
- Number of employees (it is acceptable to enter 0 if no employees)
- Date of first wages or annuities
- Main business activity and type of products sold (if applicable)

Sample Consulting Contract

This is a sample Consulting contract. If you consider using this for your own practice, you should consult with an attorney qualified to practice where you do business to ensure that it is tailored to meet your specific state and other requirements.

[ADD LOGO/LETTERHEAD]

CONTRACT FOR SERVICES

This Contract for Services is made effective as of [DATE], by and between [NAME OF CLIENT] (the "Organization") with an address of [ADDRESS] and [YOUR COMPANY NAME] (the "Consultant") with an address of [ADDRESS].

1. Description of Services.
   The Consultant will provide to the Organization the following services (collectively, the "Services"):
   [LIST SERVICES]
   The Organization will
   [LIST EXPECTATIONS]
   Compensation

- SERVICE A: Daily rate: $XXXX.
- SERVICE B: hourly rate: $XXX per hour (billed in 15-minute increments).

2. Payment.

The Organization agrees to pay an initial retainer of $XXX.XX, which will be due upon signing of the agreement. Additionally payments will be billed on [DATE/TIME FRAME]. An itemization of services will be provided when the retainer is exhausted.

Payment shall be made by checks payable to [NAME, ADDRESS] or by submission of electronic payment (bank information will be provided on invoice).

If the Organization fails to pay for the Services when due, the Consultant has the option to treat such failure to pay as a material breach of this Contract, and may cancel this Contract and/or seek legal remedies.

3. Terms and Termination.

This Contract will terminate automatically upon completion of the Services required by the Contract. This Contract is an at-will agreement that may be terminated by the Organization or the Consultant at any time, with 15 days' written notice. The Organization will be responsible for any fees associated with work completed prior to notice to terminate this contract.

[ADD ANY ADDITIONAL TERMS OR CONDITIONS]

4. Work Product Ownership.

Any intellectual property created in connection with the contract is the property of [COPYRIGHT NAME] and is being licensed to the Organization on a nonexclusive basis. The Organization may use materials generated over the course of this contract for the productions listed in the *"Description of Services"* only and may not offer these materials for sale. The organization may not create derivatives without permission.

5. Modifications to Contract.

Both parties agree to act in good faith under the terms of this contract. At any time, this contract may be modified with the agreement of both parties.

CONSULTANT NAME: ORGANIZATION:

_____   _____

Representative's Signature   Representative's Signature

_____   _____

Printed Name   Printed Name

_____   _____

Date   Date

_____   _____

Sample Contract for Speaking Services

This is a sample contract for speaking services. If you consider using this for your own practice, you should consult with an attorney qualified to practice where you do business to ensure that it is tailored to meet your specific state and other requirements.

[ADD YOUR LOGO]

CONTRACT FOR SERVICES: [SPEAKING ENGAGEMENT TYPE]

Submitted To: Date:
[CONTACT NAME, ROLE]   [MM/DD/YYYY]
Organization Name:
[ORGANIZATION CONTACT INFO]
Need:
To provide [TYPE OF SPEAKING ENGAGEMENT] to [address/support/ transform IDENTIFIED NEED/CONCERN] for [SPECIFIC GROUP] to [OUTCOME]

Services To Be Provided:
Type of speaking engagement

Length of event/engagement

Date

Time/time zone

Duration

Location (include building and room numbers if available)

Title Of Talk:

Description:

* [3- TO 5-SENTENCE OVERVIEW OF TOPIC TO BE COVERED]

Objectives:

* [2 OR 3 OBJECTIVES]

Investment:

The total cost for the work described above is $XXX.XX and is due upon signing. [Once the contract is signed, we will work with the planning team to schedule meetings and workshop dates] OR [in order to hold your event dates in our calendar].

Requests for date changes must be made at least 14 days prior to the event. Calendar change requests made outside this time frame will forfeit the payment. Your primary contact will be [NAME, EMAIL]. Please contact [NAME] if you need to reschedule your event or have any questions.

ADDITIONAL TERMS:

The workshop will be conducted [virtually/in-person]. The Organization will be responsible for providing video conferencing logistics at least 1 week prior to the event. [There is no recording allowed./Recording is not reflected in the current pricing for this event.]

[PARKING REQUIREMENTS, IF NEEDED]

[TECH CHECK OR OTHER PLANNING MEETINGS, IF NEEDED]

If you accept these terms, please sign below:

[YOUR COMPANY]	[ORGANIZATION]
Representative's Signature	Representative's Signature
_____	_____
Printed Name	Printed Name
_____	_____
Date	Date
_____	_____

APPENDIX L

Strategies for Building a Decolonized Business

Decolonization is the resistance to colonial norms and active shifting of power toward Indigenous people. It's a nuanced and positive process that occurs through recognizing and reforming political, economic, and cultural structures. The questions below offer a starting place for building a decolonized business, but it is not a comprehensive list. The reflection questions can guide you in creating a workplace culture that prioritizes people, treats them with dignity, and values people over profits:

- What are the core values of your business and how do you center people's humanity?
- Is your mission inclusive?
- How is power shared in your company?
- How are newer members engaged in the organization?
- Do all team members feel empowered to speak up?
- Do team members feel free to share ideas and to present contrary information?
- How do you invite disagreement?
- Does your team represent different social identities and experiences?
- Are voices from your target audience represented in your hiring, and service delivery decisions?

Do you purchase products and services from certified underrepresented
businesses?

How do you engage with the community in design, implementation, and
feedback?

Is there profit sharing for employees?

How do think about feedback, transparency, and communication?

Sample Script for Discovery Sale/Call

Hello [CLIENT'S NAME], I'm [NAME, CEO of ORGANIZATION] and I'm thrilled to connect with you today. I've been really impressed with the work [ORGANIZATION] is doing, especially in [SPECIFIC DETAIL].

. To start, I'd love to learn more about you and the impactful work you're leading at [ORGANIZATION]. Could you share a bit about your role and your team's goals?

. . .

DISCOVERY

Thank you for sharing. I'm particularly interested in understanding your top concerns regarding the [emotional well-being and mental health of your employees], particularly your employees [of color]. What specific challenges are you facing in this area?

. . .

Those are concerns that other leaders like yourself have shared with us as well. What initiatives or resources have you implemented to make your workplace well-being programming [more inclusive]? What is your overall strategy regarding well-being, and who have you collaborated with so far?

. . .

I appreciate your insights. At [InnoPsych], we've recently launched our workplace well-being services designed to address the very concerns you mentioned. Our approach is unique because [UNIQUE VALUE PROPOSITION]. Would you be open to hearing more about how our solutions can support your efforts?

. . .

Excellent. Our service is tailored to support leaders in creating psychologically safe cultures and develop an emotional well-being strategy that benefits all employees. To give you an idea, we've helped organizations like [BRIEF TESTIMONIAL OR CASE STUDY]. They saw significant improvements in [SPECIFIC RESULTS, e.g., employee engagement, reduced turnover]. Our signature offer is [YOUR SOLUTION] for an investment of [LIST COST]. We can get a contract sent over to you later today.

. . .

SALES

[IF YES]: My team is excited to work with you and your team on this programming. Our next steps will be to send out our contract and then schedule a call with your project lead. Let's take a few minutes to review your needs so that we have a clear scope.

. . .

[IF NO/NOT NOW]: I understand that you need time to consult with other team members. I believe our partnership could make a significant positive impact at [ORGANIZATION]. Could you tell me more about your company's decision-making process for such investments? . . . Let's schedule a call with [DECISION MAKER].

OR When would be a good time to set up a follow-up meeting with other team members?

. . .

Again, it was great to connect with you today. I'll send over a summary of our conversation along with some additional information about InnoPsych. I am looking forward to our next conversation!

[Make sure to follow up with the action steps and scheduling calls within 24 hours.]

Sample Service Offerings and Pricing Template

Specific Service Offerings	Billing	Pricing
On-Demand Courses		
Thriving Therapreneur course	Per student subscription	
Healing from Racial Stress course	Per student subscription	
Forensic Services		
Evaluation services	Evaluations (hourly rate)	
Private	Evaluations (hourly rate)	
Speaking Engagements		
Keynote address live	Flat rate: includes content creation/prep, tech/sound check, debrief	
Keynote address webinar	Flat rate: includes content creation/prep, tech/sound check, debrief	
Media/podcasts	Free/rate offered	
Panelist	Flat rate: includes prep, tech/sound check	
Moderator	Flat rate: includes prep, tech/sound check	
Therapy Services		
Group (coping, grief, crisis response)	Hourly rate	
Individual	Hourly rate	
Short-term therapy	Hourly rate	

Workshops and Webinars		
Topics: Diversity, equity, inclusion, belonging (DEI); entrepreneurship/innovation; family engagement/parents/caregivers; adolescent development	Flat rate: includes prep, tech/sound check	
Nonprofit versus corporate rate	90 minutes to 2 hours	
	2–3 hours	
	Half-day rate	
	Full-day rate	
Writing Services		
Blogs/reviews	Starts at (flat rate)	
Book chapters	% royalty; flat rate; free books	
Audience support resources	Hourly consulting rate	
Coaching and Consultations		
General consultation services	Hourly rate + indirect costs	
DEI/antiracism consultation	Hourly rate + indirect costs	
Forensic consultations	Hourly rate + indirect costs	
Creative arts wellness consults	Hourly rate + indirect costs	
Professional coaching services	Package	
Leadership coaching and consulting	Package	
Clinical supervision	Hourly consulting rate	
Advocacy/policy	Pro bono	
Community crisis response	Nonprofit rate	

APPENDIX O

Sample Discounted Rate Policy

Use a policy such as this to determine if you will honor a request for a discounted rate:

- I will consult with my team (even if it is only me) before agreeing to a discounted rate.
- Requests for discounts must come in writing using the [FORM: create a form that collects the information that you want to have, such as in-kind offerings they could provide].
- Requests must be made at least XX weeks before the event date.
- Responses to requests will be given after XX weeks.
- I will discount for [ORGANIZATION TYPE] that will focus on [ISSUES ALIGNED WITH YOUR VALUES/VISION].
- I will discount the rate by $XX amount or XX%.
  - In exchange for a discount, organization will agree to [LIST REQUIREMENTS, e.g., attendee list, testimonial, sponsorship-level equivalent for their annual event, tickets to their annual gala]

Sample One Sheet

Source: Demp Agency. Photo by Alexandria Pierre-Etienne

Diversity Business Certifications Checklist

The following list are the documents that, as of writing this, you will need as proof of your identity and ownership of the business.

Proof of Ownership:
- Canceled checks (both sides) with original bank deposits
- Loan agreement

Proof of Business Formation:
- Corporations: articles of incorporation; bylaws
- Partnerships: Partnership agreements
- List of board of directors

Proof of Business Activity:
- Tax returns for the past 3 years or for the duration of the business if the business is younger than 3 years
- If you have not filed taxes:
  - Income statements
  - Balance sheets
  - Cash flow statements

Proof of Expertise:
- Resume or curriculum vitae

Proof of Identity:
- Government-issued identification
- Proof of U.S. citizenship (for federal certifications)

References

Alexander, A. (2024, August 16). Black founders still struggle for their share of venture capital funding. *Forbes.* https://www.forbes.com/sites/asia alexander/2024/06/24/black-founders-still-struggle-for-their-share-of -venture-capital-funding/

American Psychiatric Association (2021, January 18). APA's apology to Black, Indigenous and People of Color for its support of structural racism in psychiatry. Retrieved September 17, 2024. https://www.psychiatry.org/news -room/apa-apology-for-its-support-of-structural-racism

American Psychological Association. (2003, February). Professional will: A responsible thing to do. *Monitor on Psychology, 34*(2), 34. https://www.apa .org/monitor/feb03/will

American Psychological Association. (2004). Are you prepared for the unexpected? Retrieved September 17, 2024. https://www.apaservices.org/practice/business /legal/professional/will

American Psychological Association. (2014a). Further instructions and considerations in preparing a professional will. https://www.apaservices.org/practice /business/management/professional-will-instructions

American Psychological Association. (2014b, Spring-Summer). Your professional will: Why and how to create. *Good Practice.* https://www.apaservices.org /practice/good-practice/professional-will-instructions.pdf

American Psychological Association. (2017). Ethical principles of psychologists and code of conduct. https://www.apa.org/ethics/code/ethics-code-2017.pdf

American Psychological Association. (2018). Standards of accreditation for health service psychology and accreditation operating procedures. https://irp.cdn-website.com/a14f9462/files/uploaded/standards-of-accreditation.pdf

American Psychological Association. (2021a, October). Apology to people of color for APA's role in promoting, perpetuating, and failing to challenge racism, racial discrimination, and human hierarchy in the U.S. Retrieved September 17, 2024. https://www.apa.org/about/policy/racism-apology

American Psychological Association. (2021b, October). Historical chronology: Examining psychology's contributions to the belief in racial hierarchy and perpetuation of inequality for people of color in U.S. Retrieved September 17, 2024. https://www.apa.org/about/apa/addressing-racism/historical-chronology

American Psychological Association. (2022a). 2021 survey of health service psychologists: Technical report. https://www.apa.org/workforce/publications/health-service-psychologists-survey/full-technical-report.pdf

American Psychological Association. (2022b). Health service psychologists across work settings [Interactive Data Tool]. Retrieved September 17, 2024. https://www.apa.org/workforce/publications/health-service-psychologists-survey/work-settings

American Psychological Association. (2023). Report on an offer of apology, on behalf of the American Psychological Association, to First Peoples in the United States. https://www.apa.org/pubs/reports/indigenous-apology.pdf

Azulay, Y. (2019, March 27). Entrepreneurs make more than 1,000 decisions a day! What's the key for successful decisions? *Medium.* https://medium.com/@yossi.azulay/entrepreneurs-make-more-than-1-000-decisions-a-day-whats-the-key-for-successful-decisions-6d9a4e6c1beb#:~:text=Entrepreneurs%20Make%20More%20than%201%2C000,by%20Yossi%20Azulay%20%7C%20Medium

Beltis, A. (2022, November 7). Everything you need to know about value-based pricing. *HubSpot.* https://blog.hubspot.com/sales/value-based-pricing

Britt, S. L., Klontz, B., Tibbetts, R., & Leitz, L. (2015). The financial health of mental health professionals. *Journal of Financial Therapy, 6*(1), 3. http://dx.doi.org/10.4148/1944-9771.1076

Brown, C. (2015, May). Know your worth, and then ask for it [Video]. TEDx
Talks. https://www.ted.com/talks/casey_brown_know_your_worth_and
_then_ask_for_it?language=e

Business Woman Media (2021, December 18). Divorce rate is higher for business owners: Here's why. https://www.thebusinesswomanmedia.com/
divorce-rate-is-higher-for-business-owners-heres-why/https://www
.thebusinesswomanmedia.com/divorce-rate-is-higher-for-business-owners
-heres-wh

Centers for Medicare and Medicaid Services. (n.d.). No surprises: What's a
good faith estimate? [Fact sheet]. https://www.cms.gov/files/document/no
surpriseactfactsheet-whats-good-faith-estimate508c.pdf

Coelho, P. (1993). *The alchemist: A fable about following your dream.* HarperCollins.

Comas-Díaz, L., & Torres R. E. (Eds.). (2020). *Liberation psychology: Theory,
method, practice, and social justice.* American Psychological Association.

Commission on Accreditation for Marriage and Family Therapy. (2017). Accreditation standards: Graduate and post-graduate marriage and family therapy training programs. https://www.coamfte.org/documents/COAMFTE
/Accreditation%20Resources/2018%20COAMFTE%20Accreditation
%20Standards%20Version%2012%20May.pdf

Common Future. (2021, July 26). Why credit scores are racist. *Medium.* https://
medium.com/commonfuture/why-credit-scores-are-racist-da109fcfb300

Conway, A. (2023, March 29). Do you have "good girl" fatigue? *Oprah Daily.*
https://www.oprahdaily.com/life/relationships-love/a43337971/good-girl
-fatigue/

Council on Social Work Education. (2022). Educational policy and accreditation
standards for baccalaureate and master's social work programs. https://www
.cswe.org/getmedia/bb5d8afe-7680-42dc-a332-a6e6103f4998/2022-EPAS
.pdf

DeBaun, M. (Host). (2021–2023). *The Worksmart Podcast. [Audio podcast].* https://
podcasts.apple.com/us/podcast/the-worksmart-podcast-with-morgan
-debaun/id1547363866

Delaney, S. (2016, Fall). Why is it hard to talk about money? *Good Practice.* https://
www.apaservices.org/practice/good-practice/talk-money.pdf

Dweck, C. (2006). *Mindset: A new psychology of success.* Random House.

Ecko, M. (2013). *Unlabel: Selling you without selling out.* Atria Books.

Economic Times. (2022, July 6). Rihanna becomes America's youngest female self-made billionaire, says Forbes 2022 list. https://economictimes.indiatimes.com/news/international/us/rihanna-becomes-americas-youngest-female-self-made-billionaire-forbes-2022/articleshow/92680338.cms?from=mdr

Egede, L. E., Walker, R. J., Campbell, J. A., Linde, S., Hawks, L. C., & Burgess, K. M. (2023). Modern day consequences of historic redlining: Finding a path forward. *Journal of General Internal Medicine, 38*(6), 1534–1537. https://doi.org/10.1007/s11606-023-08051-4

Finer, N. (n.d.). Perfect pricing tips for female entrepreneurs. *Bluchic.* https://www.bluchic.com/perfect-pricing-tips-little-voice-big-business/

Forbes Coaches Council. (2020, September 9). Fourteen pricing tips to help new entrepreneurs set realistic rates. *Forbes.* https://www.forbes.com/sites/forbescoachescouncil/2020/09/09/14-pricing-tips-to-help-new-entrepreneurs-set-realistic-rates/?sh=3f72e9726aca

Forsey, C. (2024, April 1). Marketing budget: How much should your team spend in 2024? [By industry]. *HubSpot.* https://blog.hubspot.com/marketing/marketing-budget-percentage

Fortune Business Insights. (2023, October 25). US behavioral health market size to surpass USD 115.21 billion by 2030, at a CAGR of 4.7%. Yahoo Finance. https://finance.yahoo.com/news/us-behavioral-health-market-size-112900436.html

Freeman, M. A., Staudenmaier, P. J., Zisser, M. R., & Abdilova Andresen, L. (2018). The prevalence and co-occurrence of psychiatric conditions among entrepreneurs and their families. *Small Business Economics, 53*, 323–342. https://doi.org/10.1007/s11187-018-0059-8

GlobeNewswire. (2022, December 6). Digital mental health market size worth USD 69.44 billion by 2030 at 20.3% CAGR—Report by market research future (MRFR). Retrieved September 17, 2024, https://www.globenewswire.com/en/news-release/2022/12/06/2568512/0/en/Digital-Mental-Health-Market-Size-Worth-USD-69-44-Billion-by-2030-at-20-3-CAGR-Report-by-Market-Research-Future-MRFR.html

GlobeNewswire. (2024, April 15). Wellness Retreat Market to Reach $363.9 Billion, Globally, by 2032 at 7.4% CAGR: Allied Market Research. https://www.globenewswire.com/en/news-release/2024/04/15/2862793/0/en/Wellness-Retreat-Market-to-Reach-363-9-Billion-Globally-by-2032-at-7-4-CAGR-Allied-Market-Research.html

Goldman Sachs. (2024, February 6). New survey data shows black small business

owners less likely to secure loans. 10,000 Small Businesses. https://www
.goldmansachs.com/citizenship/10000-small-businesses/US/voices/news/
feb-6-2024-press-release.html#:~:text=Access%20to%20Capital%3A%20
Black%20small,77%25%20of%20small%20business%20owners

Goldschein, E. (2021, January 8). Racial funding gap shows black business owners are shut out from accessing capital. *NerdWallet*. https://www.nerdwallet
.com/article/small-business/racial-funding-gap

Goode-Cross, D. T., & Grim, K. A. (2016). "An unspoken level of comfort": Black
therapists' experiences working with black clients. *Journal of Black Psychology,
42*(1), 29–53. https://doi.org/10.1177/0095798414552103

Govindarajan, V. (2016). *The three box solution: A strategy for leading innovation.*
Harvard Business Review Press. https://www.hbs.edu/faculty/Pages/item
.aspx?num=50752

Haden, J. (2023, May 18). A new study says 75 percent of entrepreneurs are
concerned about their mental health. *Inc.* https://www.inc.com/jeff-haden/a
-new-study-says-75-percent-of-entrepreneurs-are-concerned-about-their
-mental-health.html

Harris, R. (2024, March 19). *Don't mess up your pricing strategy—Here's how to
do it right.* The .360 Blog. https://www.salesforce.com/blog/pricing-strategy
-examples/#h-5-different-types-of-pricing-strategies

Hart, S. A. (Host). (2016–2023). *Trailblazers.FM* podcast. [Audio podcast]. https://
stephenahart.com/project/episode0/

Harvard University's Office of the Vice Provost for Advances in Learning. (2021,
August 5). Designing Your Course for Online Instruction: Principles and
Tips. https://teachremotely.harvard.edu/files/teachremotely/files/designing
_your_course_for_the_fall.pdf

Harvey, S. (2019, September 15). *Write your vision* [Video]. YouTube. https://
youtu.be/DlMAIYd7-J4?si=_ypnORd_kL-sH7_0

Hodgkinson, S. (2005). *The leader's edge: Using personal branding to drive performance and profit.* iUniverse.

Hodgkinson, S. (2009, March). Personal Branding. [Keynote]. The Partnership,
Inc. Boston, MA.

Hollingshead, T. (2023, June 16). Banks offer Black entrepreneurs inferior loans
even when they are better qualified than peers. *BYU News.* https://news.byu
.edu/banks-offer-black-entrepreneurs-inferior-loans-even-when-they-are
-better-qualified-than-peers

Holmstrom, J. (2022, September 14). Is it worth sacrificing your marriage for your startup? Sifted. https://sifted.eu/articles/worth-sacrificing-your -marriage-for-your-startup

Holt, D. (2024, July 29). Understanding Insurance Clawbacks: What health-care providers need to know. [Blog]. Retrieved September 17, 2024. https://djholtlaw.com/understanding-insurance-clawbacks-what-healthcare -providers-need-to-know/

Hudder, J. (2023, June 1). Shifting from doubts to dollars: Overcoming pricing struggles for women entrepreneurs. Honeyflow Coaching. https://www .honeyflowcoaching.com/post/overcoming-pricing-struggles-for-women -entrepreneurs-1

InnoPsych [@innopsych]. (2024, March 24). We're thrilled to revisit a groundbreaking project we worked on at the end of last year. The conversation around mental [Photo]. Instagram. https://www.instagram.com/p/C4yuPlwO1Gx/?igsh =MWt1aDF1YmRmM215bg==

Jackman, C. F. (2002). A comparison of male juvenile offenders and non-offenders of color with respect to their perceptions of self, peers, and police officers. Dissertation Abstracts International: Section B: The Sciences and Engineering, 63, 509.

Jackman, C. (2021, June 9). OPINION: Naomi Osaka and Meghan Markle reveal the racial inequities in mental health support. Thomas Reuters Foundation News. https://news.trust.org/item/20210609122836-oki0f/

Jackman, C. (2022, December 25). S.O.S: We need more Black men as therapists now! Black Enterprise. https://www.blackenterprise.com/s-o-s-we-need-more -black-men-as-therapists-now/

Jackman, C. (2023, November 6). The New "Silent Killer": Racial Trauma in the Workplace and Impact on Mental Health & Emotional Well-being. [Keynote Address]. DEIB Wellness Day. Worcester Polytechnic Institute. https://www .wpi.edu/sites/default/files/2023-10/DEIB-Wellness-Day-Program-231009 -FINAL.pdf

Jackman, C. (2024, May 4). Reclaiming wellbeing in the workplace [Video]. TEDx Talks. https://www.youtube.com/watch?v=Twtz8OafnBE

Johnson, D. A., Jackson, C. L., Williams, N. J., & Alcántara, C. (2019). Are sleep patterns influenced by race/ethnicity—a marker of relative advantage or disadvantage? Evidence to date. Nature and Science of Sleep, 11, 79–95. https://doi .org/10.2147/NSS.S169312

Jones, T. (2019a). Worth ethic [Song]. On *Affirmations for the grown ass woman*. Sheart Works.

Jones, T. (2019b). Yays coins [Song]. On *Affirmations for the grown ass woman*. Sheart Works.

Keisler-Starkey, K., Bunch, L. N., & Lindstrom, R. A. (2023). Health insurance coverage in the United States: 2022 (Current Population Reports, P60-281). U.S. Government Publishing Office.

Kibler, E. (2023, April 24). Does entrepreneurship cause stress and burnout? True or false: Five claims about entrepreneurs' wellbeing. Aalto University. https://www.aalto.fi/en/news/does-entrepreneurship-cause-stress-and-burnout-true-or-false-five-claims-about-entrepreneurs#:~:text=On%20average%20entrepreneurial%20work%20produces,admin%20tasks)%20than%20employed%20work

Kirk, D. (2013, July 25). Embrace the controversial: Why you should publish pricing on your website. *HubSpot*. https://blog.hubspot.com/marketing/why-publish-pricing-on-website-var

Klontz, B. T., & Britt, S. L. (2012). How clients' money scripts predict their financial behaviors. *Journal of Financial Planning, 25*, 33–43.

Klontz, B., Britt, S. L., Mentzer, J., & Klontz, T. (2011). Money beliefs and financial behaviors: Development of the Klontz Money Script Inventory. *Journal of Financial Therapy, 2*(1), 1–22. https://www.researchgate.net/publication/265907828_Money_Beliefs_and_Financial_Behaviors_Development_of_the_Klontz_Money_Script_Inventory

Kohatsu, K. (2018, February 6). Female entrepreneurs: Know (and charge for) your worth. *Forbes*. https://www.forbes.com/sites/forbeslacouncil/2018/02/06/female-entrepreneurs-know-and-charge-for-your-worth/?sh=26e7df1e2e91

Kunthara, S. (2021, July 16). Black women still receive just a tiny fraction of VC funding despite 5-year high. *Crunchbase*. https://news.crunchbase.com/diversity/something-ventured-black-women-founders/

Lake, R. (n.d.). FICO score vs. other credit scores. Investopedia. Retrieved September 17, 2024. https://www.investopedia.com/fico-score-vs-credit-score-5214435

LEANFoundry, LLC. (n.d.). Lean Canvas: Deconstruct your big idea on one-page. Retrieved September 17, 2024. https://leanstack.com/leancanvas

Leppert, R. (2024, February 16). A look at Black-owned businesses in the U.S. Pew Research. https://www.pewresearch.org/short-reads/2024/02/16/a-look-at-black-owned-businesses-in-the-us/

LeWine, H. (2024, April 3). Understanding the stress response: Chronic activation of this survival mechanism impairs health. Harvard Health. https://www.health.harvard.edu/staying-healthy/understanding-the-stress-response

Mariotti, A. (2015). The effects of chronic stress on health: New insights into the molecular mechanisms of brain-body communication. *Future Science OA, 1*(3), FSO23. https://doi.org/10.4155/fso.15.21

Martinez, D. B., & Fleck-Henderson, A. (2014). *Social justice in clinical practice: A liberation health framework for social work.* Routledge.

McIntyre, G. (2020, November 20). What percentage of small businesses fail? (And other need-to-know stats). *Fundera.* https://www.fundera.com/blog/what-percentage-of-small-businesses-fail#:~:text=20%25%20of%20small%20businesses%20fail,their%2010th%20year%20in%20business

McKenzie, C. (n.d.). Fact sheet: Black women's financial trauma. Georgetown Law Center on Poverty and Inequality. https://genderjusticeandopportunity.georgetown.edu/wp-content/uploads/2021/04/Black-Womens-Financial-Trauma.pdf

Merriam-Webster. (n.d.). Thriving. In Merriam-Webster.com dictionary. Retrieved December 6, 2024, from https://www.merriam-webster.com/dictionary/thriving

Mikhail, A. (2024, February 8). One in 20 business owners have shut their doors due to the financial strain of divorce. Why their relationships fail, and how you can beat the odds. *Fortune Well.* https://fortune.com/well/2024/02/08/business-owners-divorce-financial-strain/

Mohr, T. S. (2014, August 25). Why women don't apply for jobs unless they're 100% qualified. *Harvard Business Review.* https://hbr.org/2014/08/why-women-dont-apply-for-jobs-unless-theyre-100-qualified

Moshary, S., Tuchman, A., & Bhatia, N. (2021, October 29). *Investigating the pink tax: Evidence against a systematic price premium for women in CPG.* University of Chicago Booth School of Business and Northwestern University Kellogg School of Management. https://www.ftc.gov/system/files/documents/public_events/1588356/mosharybhatiatuchman_updated2.pdf

Mullan, J. (2023). *Decolonizing therapy: Oppression, historical trauma, and politicizing your practice.* Norton.

Mulvaney-Day, N., Dean, D., Jr., Miller, K., & Camacho-Cook, J. (2022). Trends in use of telehealth for behavioral health care during the COVID-19 pandemic: Considerations for payers and employers. *American Journal of Health Promotion, 36*(7), 1237–1241. https://doi.org/10.1177/08901171221112488e

Muñoz, A. P., Kim, M., Chang, M., Jackson, R. O., Hamilton, D., & Darity, W. A., Jr. (2015). *The color of wealth in Boston*. Duke University, The New School, and the Federal Reserve Bank of Boston. https://www.bostonfed.org /publications/one-time-pubs/color-of-wealth.aspx

National Association of Social Workers. (2021). Undoing Racism Through Social Work: NASW Report to the Profession on Racial Justice Priorities and Action. https://www.socialworkers.org/LinkClick.aspx?fileticket=29AYH9q AdXc%3D&portalid=0

National Board for Certified Counselors. (2020, July). National certified counselor (NCC) required coursework. [Fact Sheet]. https://www.nbcc.org/ assets/NCCRequiredCourseworkDescriptions.pdf

Noll, M. (2021, December 14). Four signs of financial trauma and steps for resolving it. *Yahoo! Life*. https://www.yahoo.com/lifestyle/4-signs-financial -trauma-steps-224921975.html

Obschonka, M., Pavez, I., Kautonen, T., Kibler, E., Salmela-Aro, K., & Wincent, J. (2023). Job burnout and work engagement in entrepreneurs: How the psychological utility of entrepreneurship drives healthy engagement. *Journal of Business Venturing, 38*(2). https://doi.org/10.1016/j.jbusvent.2022.106272

Office of the U.S. Surgeon General. (2021). *Protecting youth mental health: The U.S. surgeon general's advisory*. U.S. Department of Health and Human Services. https:// www.hhs.gov/surgeongeneral/priorities/youth-mental-health/index.html

Office of the U.S. Surgeon General. (2022). The U.S. Surgeon General's framework for workplace mental health and well-being. U.S. Department of Health and Human Services. https://www.hhs.gov/surgeongeneral/priorities/ workplace-well-being/index.html

Office of the U.S. Surgeon General. (2023a). Our epidemic of loneliness and isolation: The U.S. surgeon general's advisory on the healing effects of social connection and community. U.S. Department of Health and Human Services. https://www.hhs.gov/sites/default/files/surgeon-general-social-connection -advisory.pdf

Office of the U.S. Surgeon General. (2023b). Social media and youth mental health: The U.S. surgeon general's advisory. U.S. Department of Health and Human

Services. https://www.hhs.gov/sites/default/files/sg-youth-mental-health-social
-media-advisory.pdf

Office of the U.S. Surgeon General. (2024). *Parents under pressure: The U.S. Surgeon General's advisory on the mental health and well-being of parents.* U.S. Department of Health and Human Services. https://www.hhs.gov/sites/default/files/parents-under-pressure.pdf

Patel, N. (2015, January 16). 90% Of Startups Fail: Here's What You Need To Know About The 10%. *Forbes.* https://www.forbes.com/sites/neilpatel/2015/01/16/90-of-startups-will-fail-heres-what-you-need-to-know-about-the-10/

PR Newswire. (2000, June 16). Boston Children's Hospital ranked #1 in the nation by U.S. News & World Report for seventh year in a row. https://www.prnewswire.com/news-releases/boston-childrens-hospital-ranked-1-in-the-nation-by-us-news--world-report-for-seventh-year-in-a-row-301077691.html

Ramirez, M. (2024, January 30). Americans don't sleep enough. The long-term effects are dire, especially for Black people. *USA Today.* https://www.usatoday.com/story/news/nation/2024/01/29/poor-sleep-black-people-health-issues-racism/71480690007/

Robb, A. (2023, January 31). The essential questions you should be asking your therapist. *Oprah Daily.* https://www.oprahdaily.com/life/relationships-love/a42437235/best-questions-for-therapists/

Salsberg, E., Quigley, L., Richwine, C., Sliwa, S., Acquaviva, K., & Wyche, K. (2020). The social work profession: Findings from three years of surveys of new social workers. George Washington University Fitzhugh Mullan Health Workforce Institute. https://www.cswe.org/CSWE/media/Workforce-Study/The-Social-Work-Profession-Findings-from-Three-Years-of-Surveys-of-New-Social-Workers-Dec-2020.pdf

Sauer, M. (2022, July 4). Rihanna is now worth $1.4 billion—making her America's youngest self-made billionaire woman. CNBC. https://www.cnbc.com/2022/07/04/rihanna-is-now-americas-youngest-self-made-billionaire-woman.html

Silver Lining. (n.d.). The SMB De-stress guide: A practical and actionable guide to help Small Business Owners build a strong mindset and optimize their mental health. Retrieved September 17, 2024. https://online.fliphtml5.com/mhxlt/pzzm/#p=1

Sinek, S. (2009). *Start with why: How great leaders inspire everyone to take action.* Portfolio.

Stobierski, T. (2022, November 10). A beginner's guide to value-based strategy. Harvard Business School Online. https://online.hbs.edu/blog/post/value-based-strategy

Tamashiro, T. (2018, September 8). *How to ikigai* [Video]. TEDx Talks. https://www.ted.com/talks/tim_tamashiro_how_to_ikigai

Taylor, R. & Jackman, C. F. (2022). Healing from Financial Trauma and Cultivating Generational Wealth. [YouTube]. Webinar hosted by InnoPsych. https://youtu.be/6s0WJAamY40

The Times (n.d.). 5 reasons why start-up owners are more likely to get divorced. https://thetimes.com.au/business-news/32484-5-reasons-why-start-up-owners-are-more-likely-to-get-divorced.

Thimble. (2021, March 12). Ten daily habits of successful entrepreneurs. https://www.thimble.com/blog/10-daily-habits-of-successful-entrepreneurs

Trapital. (2020, April 2023). How Issa Rae became the modern mogul. https://www.trapital.co/memos/how-issa-rae-became-the-modern-mogul

U.S. Department of Health and Human Services (n.d.). Fiscal Year 2024: Budget in Brief. https://www.hhs.gov/sites/default/files/fy-2024-budget-in-brief.pdf

Vanderkam, L. (2010). *168 Hours: You have more time than you think.* New York: Portfolio.

Visram, T. (2023, October 20). 1% of venture capital goes to Black founders. California's new bill hopes to shame VCs into change. Fast Company. https://www.fastcompany.com/90969457/1-of-venture-capital-goes-to-black-founders-californias-new-bill-hopes-to-shame-vcs-into-change

Walker, A. (2024, January 21). Studies on negative impacts of sleep deprivation continue to sleep on Blacks. *Defender.* https://defendernetwork.com/culture/health/black-sleep-disparities-racism/

Walter, R. (2016, September 6). How to price your therapy services to achieve your number one business goal. *Family Therapy Basics.* https://familytherapybasics.com/blog/2016/9/5/how-to-price-your-therapy-services-to-achieve-your-1-business-goal

Washington, D. (2015, May 9). Commencement Speech Address [Video]. Dillard University. https://www.youtube.com/watch?v=ROiNPUwg9bQ

Washington, D. (2019, June 6). Lecture to fellows on a Career in Film for the

Harold Lloyd Master Seminar [video]. American Film Institute Conservatory. https://www.youtube.com/watch?v=wyxVKwebuFg

Williams, W. (2023). *Black women at work: On refusal and recovery*. Praeger.

Xiong, D. (2024, February 29). "Forced to price down": B.C.'s Black entrepreneurs feeling squeezed for sales. *Business Intelligence for BC*. https://www.biv.com/news/forced-to-price-down-bcs-black-entrepreneurs-feeling-squeezed-for-sales-8373560

Zippia. (2024a). Mental health counselor demographics and statistics in the U.S. Retrieved June 8, 2024. https://www.zippia.com/mental-health-counselor-jobs/demographics/

Zippia. (2024b. Marriage and family therapist demographics and statistics in the U.S. Retrieved June 8, 2024. https://www.zippia.com/marriage-and-family-therapist-jobs/demographics/

Index

Note: Italicized page locators refer to figures;
tables are noted with a *t*.

wisdom, 83, 84, 85, 225–26
Witter, J., 67
Wix, 280
W-9 forms, 129, 199
Woman Business Enterprise (WBE), 130
Woman-Owned Small Business (WOSB), 130
women, diversity certification status and, 129
word of mouth, 106
workbooks, self-help, 241
workers' compensation insurance, 147
workforce issues in mental health, HRSA grants and, 14
work for hire, 153
work-life harmony, 20
workshops, 161, 227–28, 231t
workshop series, creating, 233

Worksmart podcast (DeBaun), 26
WOSB. *see* Woman-Owned Small Business (WOSB)
writing, 161, 234–35
  blogs or digital articles, 235
  books and essays, 234
  e-books, 235
written processes, developing, 218–20
W-2 form, 163

"Yays Coins" (Jones), 251
yoga, 263
youth mental health, critical challenges related to, 13
YouTube, 76, 107, 280

Zapier, 280
Zoom, 280

About the Author

Charmain Jackman, PhD, is an award-winning psychologist, TEDx speaker, author, and leadership coach with over two decades of experience in mental health. She is a visionary entrepreneur, storyteller, and a global mental health advocate. As the founder of InnoPsych, she empowers lives by connecting individuals with therapists of color, transforming the narrative around therapy, and championing emotional well-being in the workplace. Dr. Charmain's impactful work has garnered numerous accolades including the 2024 *Boston Business Journal's* Innovators in Healthcare award and the 2021 American Psychological Association's (APA) Citizen Psychologist Award. As a media contributor, Dr. Charmain has been featured on national media outlets including *Oprah Daily*, *CNN*, *The New York Times*, *NPR*, *Forbes*, *Essence*, *Shondaland*, and *The Boston Globe*. She graduated from the University of Southern Mississippi, trained as a pediatric forensic psychologist at Harvard Medical School, and is a proud alum of Goldman Sachs's Black in Business program.